History of Bourgeois Perception

History of Bourgeois Perception
Donald M. Lowe

The University of Chicago Press

for

Lisa

and

Lydia

Donald M. Lowe is professor of history at
San Francisco State University.

The University of Chicago Press, Chicago 60637
The Harvester Press Limited, Brighton, Sussex

Library of Congress Cataloging in Publication Data
Lowe, Donald M.
   History of bourgeois perception

   Includes bibliographical references and index.
   1. Social perception.   2. Middle classes—
Psychological aspects.   3. Social Sciences—
Methodology.   4. History—Methodology.   I. Title.
HM132.L68   302   81–7529
ISBN 0–226–49428–4 (cloth)   AACR2
ISBN 0–226–49429–2 (paper)

To perceive is to render oneself present to something through the body. All the while the thing keeps its place within the horizon of the world, and the structurization consists in putting each detail in the perceptual horizons which belong to it. But such formulas are just so many enigmas unless we relate them to the concrete developments which they summarize.

Maurice Merleau-Ponty
The Primacy of Perception

Contents

Contents

Preface

In concentrating on specialized monographs, most historians have neglected the study of the whole for its parts. This omission is due in part to a crisis in methodology. How do we make connections in historical knowledge, when neither chronological narrative nor objective social science seems to suffice? About thirteen years ago, I came across the quote by Merleau-Ponty that I have chosen for my epigraph, and thought that it was possible to apply what he said to history. The present work is the attempt to think through the different aspects of the history of bourgeois perception. It has been a long and necessary journey in self-education, during which I learned a great deal from both phenomenology and Marxism. Therefore, I hope this work will be considered as a contribution to the dialogue between these two leading schools of thought.

My good friends Peter Carroll, Rochelle Gatlin, and Sally Scully read and criticized an earlier version of the book. In addition, my partner, Tani Barlow, not only criticized that version, but went over it with me sentence by sentence, so that my thoughts could become more explicit and connected. This work has benefited from their generosity.

At one stage of my writing, I enjoyed extensive conversation with Ronald Levaco concerning semiology and film. That helped me greatly. Over the years, Hayden White continued to encourage my project, though it differs from his. And my students at San Francisco State University challenged and stimulated me with their forthright questions.

History of Perception

What I am proposing here, the history of perception, is neither intellectual history nor structuralist analysis. The former is concerned with the content of thought, namely, ideas, and organizes them as clusters or traces them to individual thinkers. Intellectual history is therefore idealist. On the other hand, structuralism posits a synchronic system to determine the content of thought. It is from my point of view too formalist, not able to account for changes in the content of thought. My history of perception is a study of the dynamic interaction between the content of thought and the institutionalization of the world. In other words, the phenomenology of perception is that connecting link which on the one hand is able to provide an immediate context for thought, and on the other is determined by the institutionalization of the world. Instead of thought (or consciousness) and society, I am proposing *the history of perception as the intermediary link between the content of thought and the structure of society.*

By "perception" I do not mean the neurophysiology of perception, or the behavioral psychology of perception, but an immanent description of perception as human experience.[1] As Merleau-Ponty emphasized in his seminal work, *Phenomenology of Perception,* the human being is connected to the world via perception.[2] Perception as the crucial connection includes the subject as the perceiver, the act of perceiving, and the content of the perceived. The perceiving subject, from an embodied location, approaches the world as a lived, horizonal field. The act of perceiving unites the subject with the perceived. And the content of the perceived, which results from that act, affects the subject's bearing in the world. Perception is therefore a reflexive, integral whole, involving the perceiver, the act of perceiving, and the content of the perceived. The immanent description of perception must approach it from these three aspects.

I propose that perception as a reflexive, integral whole is the immanent, hermeneutic context in which to locate any content of thought. This perception is bounded by three factors, namely: (i) the communications media which frame and facilitate the act of perceiving; (ii) the hierarchy of sensing, i.e., hearing, touching, smelling, tasting, and seeing, which structures the subject as an embodied perceiver; and

(iii) the epistemic presuppositions which order the content of the perceived. The three are related, interacting with each other. Together they constitute a field of perception, within which specific knowledge becomes possible.

Not only are they related. Recent scholarship reveals that communications media, hierarchy of sensing, and epistemic order change in time. Hence the perceptual field constituted by them differs from period to period. There is a history of perception, to delimit the changing content of the known.

Communications Media

In the present century, media of communications proliferate, each succeeding, and superimposing itself upon, the previous ones. Thus, film has dynamized photography; and television has transformed radio broadcasting. We are increasingly aware that these media not only transmit information, but package and filter it, thus changing its meaning. Take, as a specific example, the depiction of a scene in the novel and in film. Fictional narrative, using a system of linguistic signs, cumulatively describes a scene by adding one item of information onto another. There is no other way to do it, in print. But cinematography, using discontinuous "moving" images, can either introduce a mise-en-scène or zoom from a close-up to the entire scene. The medium may not be the message, but it determines the message for the addressee. Thus, we need to study communications media as a determining factor in perception.

Currently, we have a number of theories of communication to account for the state of the media, ranging from the mathematical model of Shannon-Weaver, to the semiotics of Umberto Eco and Thomas Sebeok. Among them all, I am disposed to favor that summarized in Walter Ong's *The Presence of the Word*. Ong's theory is not an entirely original one, but a succinct summary of the works of many people, including his own on Ramean logic. Although the theme of Catholicism informs his account (Ong is a Jesuit), nevertheless, his theory is the most comprehensive; and I shall base my discussion of communications media on it.[3]

Culture can be conceived of as oral, chirographic, typographic, or electronic, in accordance with the communications media which sustain it. Each of these four types of culture organizes and frames knowledge qualitatively in an entirely different manner than the other three. And they are historically successive, in that each subsequent type is superimposed on the previous one, though residues from the earlier type persist to affect the later one.

An oral culture has no written language, and therefore no record, no text. Speech in that society fulfills a combination of functions which typographic culture tends to compartmentalize. In a typographic culture, speech is communication, whereas knowledge is preserved not by speech, but in print. And we all know how oral communication can unwittingly change the content of knowledge. However, in an oral culture without the benefit of any written record, speech has to fulfill both functions of preserving knowledge as well as of communication, for only in the act of speaking can its knowledge be preserved.

Though without the support of print, speech in oral culture is assisted by the art of memory.[4] Rhythmic words are organized into formulas and commonplaces, then set to metric patterns. In this way, they can be recalled and recited with great facility. That which can be recited and repeated will be preserved. The metric recitation of rhythmic formulas and commonplaces provides a communicational grid to determine knowledge in oral culture. Only those phenomena which fit existing formulas and commonplaces can be preserved as knowledge. The new and the distinctly different will soon be forgotten. Knowledge in oral culture therefore tends to be preservative and unspecialized, its content nonanalytical, but formulaic.

The introduction of a written language, whether ideographic or alphabetic, and its preservation in some type of manuscript constituted a chirographic culture. Although it took a long time to accomplish, writing eventually detached knowledge from speech and memory. A written language preserved knowledge after the act of speech and beyond the lapse of memory. One could go over a piece of writing at will, learn it, and criticize it; whereas formerly, in an oral culture, knowledge depended upon the performance of the speaker.

The separation of knowledge from speech is an extraordinarily difficult accomplishment, which each literate society must struggle to achieve, over a prolonged span of time, with a different outcome. The chirographic culture of classical antiquity introduced a new ideal, namely, an abstract, formal logic.[5] Nevertheless, the oral tradition in the organization of knowledge, e.g., rhetoric and disputation, persisted from classical antiquity through the Middle Ages into the Renaissance. As long as knowledge of writing was the monopoly of a scribal elite, apart from the nonliterate masses, chirographic culture could never entirely displace oral culture. Instead, the former was superimposed over the latter, and only slowly filtered downward. A recent monograph has documented the gradual penetration of chirographic culture in medieval England.[6] Throughout that period, to "read" was to read aloud; and people still trusted oral tradition much more than the written record. However, the production and retention of written records cumulatively transformed England into a "literate" society by the early fourteenth century.

The typographic revolution of the mid-fifteenth century introduced an entirely new, and much more dynamic, culture of print media, with consequences as momentous as those of the transition from oral to chirographic culture. In fact, the impact of the typographic revolution on chirographic culture was speedier than that of writing on oral culture. Elizabeth Eisenstein, in *The Printing Press as an Agent of Change,* has enumerated the main features of this transformation.[7] Print disseminated texts from different periods and countries, to provoke the awareness of differences and the need for critical comparison. It standardized not only texts, but also calendars, dictionaries, maps, charts, diagrams, and other visual aids, so that the value of the "exact repeatable pictorial statement" was enhanced. Familiarity with the use of alphabetical order, Arabic numerals, punctuation marks, sectional divisions, indexes, etc., all helped to systematize thinking. And print put an end to the problem of corruption through memory or manuscript. Instead, the new typographic fixity of information was a basic prerequisite in the rapid and cumulative advancement of knowledge.

Chirographic culture made possible the discovery of a formal abstract logic, apart from speech and memory; but, it remained for typographic culture to introduce a new ideal of objective knowledge, i.e., seventeenth-century science. Somehow, chirography never succeeded in overcoming the oral connection between the speaker and the content of knowledge. And pretypographic knowledge was still organized as rhetoric, polemic, or disputation. Print finally standardized the communication of knowledge, regardless of a particular speaker or manuscript. Typographic standardization shifted the knowable entirely to the "content." This meant a formalization of the known as content, detached from the knower. Previously, it was very difficult to separate the two, and certain bodies of knowledge depended on personal transmission by a master. But now formalized, i.e., depersonalized, content in print could be accessible to any competent, qualified reader. Thus typographic standardization made possible the new ideal of objective knowledge. (By arguing for "possibility," I do not mean print caused objective knowledge; rather, print was one of the necessary conditions for the discovery of objective knowledge.)

We in the twentieth century are entering into an electronic culture. By that I mean a culture of communication based upon such electrical and electronic media as telegraph, telephone, phonograph, radio, film, television, audio-video tape and disc, computer, plus others yet to come. The new electronic culture is being superimposed over the old typographic culture, without entirely displacing it. This is truly a transitional era, comparable to the sixteenth-century transition from chirographic to typographic culture. Because we are entering into a new culture of communications media, we have become more aware of the contour of the old typographic culture. But the perceptual implications of the new electronic culture, coming at us subliminally, are much more difficult to figure out.

Here, I believe, J. R. Pierce's *Symbols, Signals and Noise,* a nontechnical presentation of the information theory of Claude Shannon, is very helpful.[8] Information theory is the statistical, mathematical basis for the communication of messages across electrical media. According to it, any message at a source, whether in language or in picture, can be encoded into the binary digits of 1 and 0. The bit (a contraction of the term "binary digit"), which is simply a choice between the positive and the negative, is the basic unit of information to be transmitted across an electrical medium, then decoded at the receiving end. This is the way language can be delivered across a cable, or picture via the television. In the process of encoding, transmission, and decoding, the number of bits of information that can be sent across a certain channel capacity within a limited time span, allowing for a tolerable amount of interference and delay, can be statistically calculated. Information theory is therefore concerned with what kind of message can be most efficiently communicated across what type of channel.

The transition from typographic to electronic culture is fundamentally a switch from communication by means of the type to that by means of the bit. If the type has made chirographic knowledge more formalized and objective, then the problem for us is how has the bit transformed typographic knowledge? Whereas the type has fixity, the bit is merely a statistical unit, already a mathematical translation of an existing language or picture. It espouses an elemental logic of binary oppositions, i.e., all phenomena can be broken down into codes based on a positive and a negative, 1 and 0. Hence, the logic of objective science is being displaced by the binary-digital logic of computer science. Binary oppositions cut across all levels of any structure. The old fixity in print is being subverted by a new knowledge of statistics and probabilistics.

The Hierarchy of Sensing

Those studying the history of communications media, including Ong, have emphasized how certain media are related to specific organizations of the human senses. This aspect of their study has been reinforced by the works of the *Annales* historians,[9] and by the phenomenology of sense perception.[10] On the basis of these, I shall, in this section, explain what is the hierarchy of sensing, then propose how different cultures of communications media imply specific hierarchical organizations of sensing.

The five human senses, i.e., hearing, touching, smelling, tasting and seeing, connect the subject to the world. Each sensing is already qualitatively a different connection between the subject and the environing world. But none of the senses is entirely autonomous. For instance, tasting is reinforced by seeing and smelling; without the correlation of the latter two senses, food will not taste the same. Together, the five senses provide for the experience of reality.

Of the five senses, hearing is most pervasive and penetrating. I say this, although many, from Aristotle in *Metaphysics* to Hans Jonas in *The Phenomenon of Life* (1966), have said sight is most noble. But sight is always directed to what is straight ahead, not too far and not too close, for otherwise one can no longer see clearly. And sight cannot turn a corner, at least without the aid of a mirror. On the other hand, sound comes to one, surrounds one for the time being with an acoustic space, full of timbre and nuances. It is more proximate and suggestive than sight. Sight is always the perception of a surface, from a particular angle. But sound is that perception able to penetrate beneath the surface. For example, sound can test the solidity of matter; and speech is a communication connecting one person with another. Therefore, the quality of sound is fundamentally more vital and moving than that of sight.

Touching is the most realistic and assuring of the five senses. What we see or hear, we always want to verify by the tactile sense of touch. Touching is tangible and substantive. It is the ultimate perceptual connection between a subject and an other, so that we can be assured of what we saw or heard. Only when I touch it do I know how hard or resistant an object is, qualities which sight and sound cannot reveal. Again, when I touch and then feel another person, I have made contact with another life. Touching is fundamental bodily contact. It characterizes each of us as sensual, sexual being, seeking physical union with another being.

Seeing, in contrast to hearing, touching, smelling, and tasting, is preeminently a distancing, judgmental act. The data of the other four senses come to us, so that perceptually we connect our selves to what is proximate. But sight is extension in space, presupposing a distance. We see by frontally opening before us a horizontal field, within which we locate the objects of our attention—frontal, in the sense that we see only what is presented before our eyes. And we assume an upright posture in relation to the data of sight. We can hear, touch, smell, and taste in any position we like, without affecting that particular sensing. But seeing is most certain when we assume an upright posture, because from that accustomed perspective we then can compare and contrast the objects of our attention, against a broad, diffused background. Within this frontal, upright, horizonal extension, seeing is judgmental. The other four senses can be very refined and discriminating; but only sight can analyze and measure. Seeing is a comparative perception of things before our selves, the beginning of objectivity. That is why sight has been closely related to the intellect.

We perceive not by sight alone, but through a combination of the five senses, which verify and reinforce one another. Otherwise, our experience of reality would be quite impaired. Furthermore, each person has a slightly different combination of sensing ability. A musician would have better hearing than most other people; and a good chef has better taste buds. Therefore, each of us has a somewhat different experience of reality, owing to the differing combination of the five senses.

The argument in the history of perception does not concern individual variations. Instead, it proposes that the communications media in each period, whether oral, chirographic, typographic, or electronic, emphasize different senses or combinations of them, to support a different hierarchical organization of sensing. And change in the culture of communications media ultimately leads to change in the hierarchy of sensing.

In an oral culture, hearing surpasses seeing as the most important of the five senses. In such a culture, oral communication is aural communication. In the absence of written language in manuscript or in type, knowledge is communicated exclusively by speech. And speech has to be heard proximately and instantly, since there is no telephone, phonograph, radio, or audiotape and disc to relay a spoken message across space or time. Speech is assimilated directly by the ear, without the mediation of the eye. And we are moved more by sound than by sight, since the former surrounds us, whereas the latter distances. The rhythmic, metrical speech thus constitutes the oral/aural communication of knowledge as a public event, making it more intense and real than chirographic, typographic, or even electronic communication. In an oral culture, hearing and not seeing, is believing.

The transition from an oral to a chirographic culture was not so much a displacement as a superimposition of one culture of communications media over another. And chirographic culture did not alter the primacy of hearing in the hierarchy of sensing. The chirographic culture of the Middle Ages, as the *Annales* historians maintain, continued to emphasize the priority of hearing and touching over seeing. People attached more credence to what they could hear and touch than to what they saw. Throughout this period, writing was the monopoly of a small clerical elite, and reading was always accomplished with a great deal of difficulty. In fact, reading was still reading aloud, so that the ear could assimilate the message. Before the invention of typography, visuality never succeeded in overthrowing the aural and tactile emphasis of the human senses.

Typographic culture finally broke the aural-tactile constraint imposed by oral and chirographic cultures, and in its stead introduced the primacy of sight in the hierarchy of sensing. The printed page, with its standardized type, punctuation, and sectional divisions, gradually accustomed the eye to the presentation of messages in a formal, visual space. That standardization of visual space was not yet available in chirography, whereas acoustic space-time was the perceptual framework for oral culture. With this shift in the hierarchy of sensing, "reading" gradually became silent assimilation of the message by the eye. In addition, as William Ivins, Jr., so convincingly argued in *Prints and Visual Communication,* the standardization of prints made visual information for the first time more reliable than aural and tactile information.[11] Previously, manuscript copying inevitably corrupted the illustration after a few hands. But now pictorial prints were identical for all copies of the same edition. In fact, prints were more useful than words in transmitting technical, scientific information. Seventeenth-century science came after, and therefore presupposed, both the typographic revolution in communications media and the primacy of sight in the hierarchy of sensing.

Only now, after we have entered into an electronic culture, has the sensing hierarchy in typographic culture become recognizable. While we are within the framework of a culture of communications media, its perceptual dynamics are much more difficult to discern. Walter Ong claims that the electronic culture has extended and heightened our senses, to promote a new orality, with greater prospect for verbal communication.[12] I agree that electronic media extend our senses, but anticipate quite different consequences for the hierarchical organization of the senses.

My position is that the electronic media have extended and extrapolated sight and sound, to alter our everyday reality. The photographic revolution of the mid-nineteenth century made the object of sight, the visual image, much more exact in all its details than the print illustration. The graphic image has become photographic. However, as Susan Sontag pointed out in *On Photography,* although photography is able to perpetuate an exact visual image, the original context for that image is lost. Nor is the image related in any other way to the real-life experience of the subsequent viewer. Thus, photographic seeing is sight out of context.[13] Nevertheless, the photographic image is accepted by the twentieth century as being "realistic." And this "realism" has been enhanced by the motion picture of the silent film. Correlatively, telephone, phonograph, radio, hi-fi stereo, and audio tape and disc have amplified and extended sound across space and/or time. This amplification of sound is analogous to the photographic extension of sight. Each overloads a single channel of information, at the expense of the rest. Now film and television here created a "reality" out of the extended sight and sound, without reference to the other three senses. At present, in our everyday life, we are bombarded by these new visual and audio images. The "reality" communicated by electronic media is superimposed over the older reality sustained by typographic media. Therefore, quite literally, the former is a surreality. The electronic surreality is multi-perspectival and environmental, whereas the typographic reality is uni-perspectival and objective. This surreality is obtained by the extension and extrapolation of seeing and hearing, at the expense of touching, smelling, and tasting.

Epistemic Order

Michel Foucault, in his brilliant work *The Order of Things* proposed that discourse is governed by unconscious epistemic rules or presuppositions, and that these rules as a whole change from one period to another.■ There is no universal logic of discourse; and knowledge resulting from discourse is discontinuous. In fact, each set of epistemic rules defines a different order, with each order staking out a different terrain of knowledge.[14] Foucault, in that work, was concerned to show how epistemic orders were transformed from the Renaissance to the nineteenth century. Following his suggestion, I shall, in this section, review very briefly the transformation of epistemic orders from the Middle Ages to the present.

The oral-chirographic culture of the Middle Ages was ordered by the epistemic rules of anagogy. Communications media do not dictate epistemic order, though the former necessarily delimit the possibility of the latter. Medieval anagogy presupposed the absolute being of God, with all else, including the knower and knowledge, dependent upon him. Instead of immanent knowing, anagogy descended from being to becoming. Transcendent being created and sustained immanent be-

---

■   Though I have borrowed from Foucault the concepts of epistemic order and of historical discontinuity, my intent is quite different from his. Foucault is studying the changing historical rules of *discourse*, whereas I am concerned with the history of *perception*.

9

coming. Therefore, one could know only in reference to God. And this knowledge was an intellectual assent based on faith. The medieval intellect perceived the world as a manifestation of signs. But the intellect by itself could discover no inherent connection among the disparate signs. Instead, from the standpoint of an intellect based on faith, all the signs pointed to the Grand Design of God and derived their meanings accordingly. Hence, anagogy was that set of epistemic rules which ordered the intellectual knowledge of becoming in terms of faith in God's absolute being. Knowing the immanent from the standpoint of the transcendent, the medieval intellect delighted in the play of signs as figure, metaphor, analogy, symbol, and vision.[15]

The epistemic order of the Renaissance, as Foucault discussed it, was founded upon the rules of similitude or resemblance. Instead of the medieval anagogic subordination of immanent becoming to transcendent being, which did not approach the world as a self-contained whole, Renaissance similitude proposed a converging, centripetal world of order. The order of macrocosm resembled that of microcosm; that of the universe corresponded to that of the human being. The four principal figures of resemblance employed in the Renaissance were *convenientia* (a resemblance based upon a graduated scale of spatial proximity); *aemulatio* (a sort of *convenientia* without spatial restriction, thus able to connect from a distance without actual motion); analogy (now reinforced by *convenientia* and *aemulatio,* so that the entire universe could be drawn together, with the human microcosm at its center); and sympathy (which excited things to movement and drew even the most distant ones together). As Foucault characterized the epistemic order of the Renaissance: "To search for a meaning is to bring to light a resemblance. To search for the law governing signs is to discover things that are alike. . . . The nature of things, their coexistence, the way in which they are linked together and communicate is nothing other than their resemblance."[16]

In the seventeenth and eighteenth centuries, continued Foucault, the order of similitude was displaced by one of representation-in-space. "The circular world of converging signs is replaced by an infinite progression."[17] Instead of the centripetal cosmos of the Renaissance, modern science opened forth an empirical space of infinite extension. And the knowledge within this vast spatial expanse was not a similitude of the signs, but a representation based upon the comparison of identity and difference, as well as upon the measurement of the new mathematics. The new analytical reason of comparison and measurement destroyed the Renaissance hierarchical world of resemblance and correspondence. It aspired to know comprehensively and scientifically, since all phenomena could be compared and measured with certainty.

Nevertheless, this was not yet a world wherein the experience of time was a sui generis consciousness. The seventeenth and eighteenth centuries (at least up to the industrial revolution of the last third of the eighteenth) conceived of time as simply another dimension, identical to space. Hence the epistemic order of representation-in-space was fundamentally nontemporal and classificatory, i.e., a static taxonomy. But what about the self, as well as knowledge of others in the past? These were the two anomalies in the taxonomic space of representation.

The epistemic order of bourgeois society, from the last third of the eighteenth to the first decade of the twentieth century, was founded on the rules of development-in-time. No longer comparable to space, time since the economic and political revolutions of the late eighteenth century was experienced as a new, qualitatively different dimension. What spatial reason could not comprehend within one expanse, time, that hitherto unrealized dimension, could incorporate. The logic of identity and difference was enhanced by one of analogy and succession. Development-in-time was to cover the gaps that had recently been discovered among the various disparate taxonomic orders of representation-in-space. With time, one order in space could be connected to another order in another space. Yet development was a new connection which posited dynamics (as opposed to stasis); transformation (as opposed to unrelated, specific change); structure (as opposed to taxonomy); and totality (as a spatio-temporal whole). Anything and everything in bourgeois society had to be comprehended and explained as an order of development-in-time. And that development was necessarily dynamic, transformative, structural, and whole. The new spatio-temporal order defined, as well as validated, new knowledges of history, society, language, philosophy, and even the human psyche.

However, in the twentieth century, the superimposition of electronic culture over typographic culture, with the accompanying extrapolation of sight and sound, has rocked the belief that analytical reason could develop connections within objective space and time. Instead, space and time are no longer the absolute framework of perception, but themselves have become mere functions within a system. In place of development-in-time, the new epistemic order is founded upon the synchronic system of binary oppositions and of differences without identity. Neither spatial nor temporal, but systematic and synchronic, the new order has dispensed with the problem of relation between a concept (the signified) and the intended object, as well as the explanation of change across time. Thus, knowledge is reduced to the synchronic system of the *langue* (as opposed to speech). And that system is composed of units, possessing only differential values in relation to each other. As Saussure pointed out in his *Course in General*

Linguistics (1915), the sign is composed of the signified and the signifier, and the relation between the two is purely arbitrary. Such was the epistemic foundation for structuralism and semiology, the new disciplines which have revealed the void and determination surrounding the old order of development-in-time. Yet the new synchronic order of binary oppositions and of differences without identity is itself a constricted positivity.

The Field of Perception

The subject, from an embodied location here and now, approaches the world as a horizonal field. And aspects of that world open forth as being there and then. The spatial dimension between here and there, the temporal dimension between now and then are the perceptual coordinates which define the framework of living for the subject. It is a horizonal field, because the subject approaches it prospectively, from the intimate and familiar to the distant and typified, for the sake of living.

This horizonal field is constituted by the perceiver, the act of perceiving, and the content of the perceived. In each period, the culture of communications media frames the act of perceiving; the subject is delimited by a different hierarchical organization of sensing; and the content of the perceived is ordered by a different set of epistemic rules. Therefore, the perceptual field constituted by them is a historical formation, which differs from one period to the next.

The field of perception in the Middle Ages was constituted by an oral-chirographic culture, a hierarchy of sensing which emphasized hearing and touching, and the epistemic order of anagogy. Perceptually, the medieval world was not centered upon itself, but open-ended. And life was led under the aegis of the unbounded forces from beyond. Hence the interpenetration of transcendence and immanence, the heterogeneity of space and time. The reality within that field was more intense and fluid, less exact and discriminating than ours. For example, Emmanuel Le Roy Ladurie, in his study of village life at Montaillou in the late Middle Ages, showed that, beyond specific, personal experience, concepts of space and time were very vague and inexact among its inhabitants.[18] And, D. W. Robertson, Jr., has pointed out that "medieval men thought of one another . . . not as personalities with deep inner drives and tensions, but as moral characters whose virtues and vices were apparent in their speech and actions."[19]

The perceptual field of the Renaissance was reconstituted by a culture of communications media in transition from chirography to typography, though with the persistence of an underlying orality at the popular level; by a gradual shift in the hierarchy of sensing from the emphasis on hearing and touching to the primacy of sight; as well as by the epistemic order of similitude. In contrast to medieval Christendom, the Renaissance cosmos was much more centripetal and immanently preoccupied. A self-contained world of portents and signs emerged, to be interpreted by the order of resemblance and correspondence which bond together divinity and nature, sphere and center, universe and mind, heavenly stars and the human face. Pictorial perspective from Brunelleschi and Alberti onward, with its emphasis on the dynamic distance between the viewer and the viewed,[20] as well as humanist historiography since Leonardo Bruni, with its sense of the dynamic distance betrween the historian and the historical event,[21] attested to the new reflexivity of space and time in this perceptual field. All elements in the cosmos cohered; each could be the starting point leading to the whole; but the human microcosm was the crucial link, comprehending the macrocosm from within. However, by the sixteenth century, with the increasing shift to typography and visuality, the human being became more aloof and self-conscious in the world, concerned with "outward bodily propriety"[22]—how one should present oneself to, and be seen by, others.

In the estate society of the seventeenth and eighteenth centuries (that is up to the industrial revolution in Britain and the French Revolution of 1789), a new perceptual field, constituted by typographic culture, the primacy of sight, and the order of representation-in-space, was superimposed over the previous ones. No longer a concentric cosmos, the world became a spatial extension; and nature was no longer animate, but a machine whose regular workings could be disclosed by the new reason. As Alexandre Koyré so aptly phrased it, with "the destruction of the cosmos and the geometrization of space,"[23] the closed world of Hermes Trismegistus was displaced by the infinite universe of Galileo and Newton. Knowing was no longer an intimation of the world based upon similitude, but a self-contained, universal system of signs, whose function was to represent forms, magnitudes, quantities, and relations of objects, in a homogeneous, detemporalized space discovered by the mechanical sciences. Representation-in-space was a one-level system of identities and differences, which could not comprehend the reflexive connection between being and the world. And the perspective underlying this objective order was Archimedean, i.e., a perspective which claimed to be perspectiveless! From a null point, hypothetically outside of space and time, Archimedean perspective could then convert the connections in the world into quantities and extensions.[24] The perceptual field thus constituted was fundamentally nonreflexive, visual, and quantitative.

The field of perception in bourgeois society, from the last third of the eighteenth to the first decade of the twentieth century, was constituted by a typographic culture which was supplemented by the photographic revolution, and thus by an extended visuality, as well as by the epistemic order of development-in-time. No longer a spatial extension, the field of perception opened forth by the dynamics of bourgeois society had new depths which temporality alone could connect. Hence the taxonomic knowledge of the previous period was displaced by a different knowledge of dynamic process. "Development" was a new word, indicating a new consciousness of time as process. For example, Foucault showed that the new "philology, biology, and political economy were established, not in the places formerly occupied by general grammar, natural history, and the analysis of wealth, but in an area where those forms of knowledge did not exist."[25] And within this dynamic field, the subject began to realize new depth, new reflexivity. "Personality" by the beginning of this period acquired its modern meaning, i.e., an individual person.[26] And by the end of this period, Freud proposed the subconscious as the causality for this new personality.

Finally, the emergent perceptual field of the present century, I hazard, is constituted by the electronic culture; the extrapolation of sight and sound; and the synchronic systematization of binary oppositions and of differences without identity. Unlike the objective reality of bourgeois society which was defined from a single perspective, the surreality within the new perceptual field is multi-perspectival and environmental. The disorientation occurs when we try to judge the new in terms of the objective, uni-perspectival standard of the old. It is my argument that the perceptual revolution of 1905–15 has destroyed the framework of objective space and time. And within the new field, the ideal of an individual personality as well as the Freudian causality of the subconscious is no longer viable, for the contemporary person has much less of an integrated personality, much less of an inside. If nothing else, the future is unlike the past, not even the immediate past. Nor can it be projected within a time series.

Two additional qualifications are necessary to what I have been discussing in this chapter, concerning the history of perception. First, the successive perceptual fields do not simply displace one another. Rather, a new one is superimposed over the old, so that within a period we find sedimentation of perceptual fields; but the dominant field exercises a Gramscian hegemony over the others. Second, the field of perception determines the content of knowledge; but that field is itself determined by society as totality. For knowledge within totality is much more than simply ideology or superstructure. It is the intentional

The History of Perception

Communications Media	Sensing Hierarchy	Epistemic Order

The Middle Ages

Chirography over Orality	Hearing/Touching over Seeing	Anagogy

The Renaissance

from Chirography to Typography	from Hearing/Touching to Primacy of Sight	Similitude

Estate Society

Typography over Chirography and Orality	Seeing over Hearing/Touching	Representation in Space

Bourgeois Society

Typography Supplemented by Photography	The Extension of Sight	Development in Time

Twentieth Century

Electronics over Typography	The Extrapolation of Sight/Sound	Synchronic System

consciousness within a perceptual field. But the communications media, the hierarchy of sensing, and the epistemic order which constitute that field are determined by the structure of totality. The dialectical concept of determination within totality is much more complex and realistic than the linear, positivist concept of cause and effect. With these two caveats, let us proceed to the history of bourgeois perception.

Bourgeois Society

By bourgeois society I mean the society of Western Europe, especially Britain and France, from the last third of the eighteenth to the first decade of the twentieth century. At the start of the period, the industrial revolution began to pick up speed in Britain; a bit later, the political revolution occurred in France. Together they comprised what E. J. Hobsbawm has called the dual revolution, which marked the opening of the modern age. First in Britain, then in France, the economic, demographic take-offs and their accompanying social transformation altered the very world in which the British and the French had lived.[1] The period came to an end in the decade just prior to the first world war. What I call the perceptual revolution of 1905–15, as well as the impact of the world war and the structure of corporate capitalism, brought that period to an end. Since then, it has been a bureaucratic society of controlled consumption, as Henri Lefebvre so aptly termed our world.[2] The relations between production and consumption, between economic structure and ideology, between state and society are at present so different from those in bourgeois society that I will insist these are two separate periods in history.

We can undertake the study of society from two methodological standpoints, namely, Marxism and phenomenology. Marxism conceives of society as a structured totality:

> The totality of these relations of production constitutes the economic structure of society, the real foundation on which arises a legal and political superstructure and to which correspond forms of social consciousness. . . . The changes in the economic foundation lead sooner or later to the transformation of the whole immense superstructure.[3]

The Marxist concept of a multi-level structure in transformation is still the best general framework we have for the critical study of society. On the other hand, phenomenology describes society as an intentional field, with its embodied location here and now extending into the spatio-temporal horizons there and then.[4] We get from this latter methodology a knowledge of how the inhabitants of a world approach it from the inside as an ongoing reality, with its future not yet disclosed. As Merleau-Ponty pointed out, "the world is not an object . . . , it is the natural setting of, and field for, all my thoughts and all my explicit perceptions."[5] Marxism and phenomenology each locate the content of perception, i.e., thought, or consciousness, differently. That content is, for Marxism, an ideology, to be explained by the substructure. But phenomenology locates that content at the center of a lived, intentional field.

We thus have (1) the content of perception, i.e., thought, or consciousness; (2) the field of perception, which is constituted by communications media, hierarchy of sensing, and epistemic order; and (3) the multi-level structure in transformation. Each has its own conceptual logic or causality. But thought or consciousness is immediately framed, i.e., determined, by the field of perception, which in turn is framed by the social structure. It is in this sense that the content of perception is ultimately determined by social structure. Nevertheless, the human being approaches the world from the inside, using the available content of perception to comprehend and master the world, often with minimal awareness of the determination by the perceptual field. Therefore, thought is not a mere passive reflection of social structure, but is the reflexive consciousness by means of which the social structure is lived as intentional, ongoing relations. In other words, consciousness infiltrates and activates all levels of the social structure as intersubjectivity.

Much has been written about bourgeois society from the standpoint of its social structure, but almost nil concerning bourgeois perception. In this work, I shall describe bourgeois perception.

The Bourgeois Field of Perception

The new dominant field of perception in bourgeois society was constituted by the predominance of typographic media, the hierarchy of sensing which emphasized the primacy of sight, and the epistemic order of development-in-time. Typography promoted the ideal that knowledge could be detached from the knower to become impartial and explicit. The primacy of sight made possible scientific verification of that knowledge. And the order of development-in-time provided a temporal connection for observable phenomena beyond their representability in space. In other words, knowledge within the new, dominant field of perception had to be objective, visual, and spatio-temporal. Objectivity and visuality were norms already established in the estate society of the seventeenth and eighteenth centuries; but development-in-time was a new epistemic order. Together they constituted a new field for bourgeois perception.

I call this perceptual field bourgeois for three related reasons. First, the new field of perception reflected the secular experience generated by the industrial revolution and the French Revolution. Second, the objective, visual, spatio-temporal knowledge within the field promoted the class interests of the triumphant bourgeoisie. And, third, because of this affinity between the knowledge within the field and their own class interests, members of the bourgeoisie were predisposed to accept the validity and underlying presuppositions of this knowledge, without much questioning. This does not mean that all bourgeois automatically accepted this knowledge, or that some from other classes could not subscribe to it. But, fundamentally, it can be characterized as a bourgeois field of perception.

Within the new bourgeois field of perception, there emerged different, new experiences of time, space, and bodily life. These I shall describe in the next three chapters. But here I would like to characterize bourgeois perception by singling out the new concepts of "labor," "development," and the "subconscious."■ They reflected new, dynamic experiences in the bourgeois field of perception.

Labor, so argued Hannah Arendt in *The Human Condition,* was different from work; however, in premodern times, one was unable to distinguish labor from work.[6] I would argue that this inability accurately reflected the premodern experience of work. Work had connected the toiler to the product. Economic action based upon this connection of toiler, work, and product was embedded in a host of noneconomic considerations, such as the mutual obligation between craft master and apprentice, the traditional organization and routinization of work, the skill and pride in the quality of one's handicraft. Hence there was a limit to the autonomy of work as rational economic action. However, with the establishment of the factory system in the last third of the eighteenth century, culminating in the assembly line production of Henry Ford in the early twentieth century,[7] industrial production was rationalized as a linear, accountable system of input/output, cost and profit calculation. Assisted by the machine, work became standardized. The status or quality of a person was of little value, so long as he or she could attend the machine for ten to twelve hours or more per day.

■ Throughout this work, I assume that new or changing meanings of certain words testify to conceptualization of new or changing experiences, and therefore can be used as evidence for the study of change in the history of perception. People mean exactly what they say; and if they have no words for certain experiences, they cannot conceptualize them.

The anonymous worker alienated a quantity of labor to industrial production. That quantity could be purchased in a free market and was useful in producing a certain amount of commodities. Labor, unlike work, was a discrete, quantifiable entity within an accountable system of production. Thus, quantifiable labor freed economic action from the noneconomic considerations surrounding work, so that the rationality of economic action could prevail across space and time. In bourgeois society, the ascendancy of rational economic action founded upon quantitative labor put pressure on all other types of action founded upon loyalties to person, family, group, or stratum. Social relations increasingly came under the pressure of economic rationality and had to be justified in terms of economic function. By the late eighteenth and early nineteenth centuries, contemporaries perceived social distinctions not merely as orders and ranks, but as economic classes which they increasingly experienced as being determined by the social relations of production.[8] I would characterize the social structure of bourgeois society as an institutionalization founded on labor, because quantifiable labor increased the rationality of economic action, transforming the previous structure of social relations.

Labor was the new dynamic in a demythicized, secular world. It reduced the human being to the status of an "economic man" and organized production into an accountable system. It opened the world to new prospects for action, and transformed time into a process of cumulative changes. The bourgeoisie as the entrepreneur of labor was in command, at the center of this universe. The bourgeois experienced the world spatially as the rational exploitation of nature and temporally as the conscious postponement of desire. Within this lived spatio-temporality, emerged a new "bourgeois" personality. The proletariat which provided the labor was, on the other hand, dragged into the process by the necessity for subsistence. The other classes in bourgeois society, such as the landed aristocracy, gentry, and peasantry, as well as the clerics, were precapitalist in experience and outlook, and therefore occupied peripheral positions in the process. Yet they all sooner or later came under the pressure of the new economic action. It was a perceptual stratification.

Quite appropriately, contemporary perception reflected and tried to order the new experience of labor. In 1763, at the very start of this period, Adam Smith singled out the division of labor as the new economic phenomenon.[9] Then, in *The Wealth of Nations* published in 1776, he detached economic action from the considerations of moral philosophy and explained its workings by the labor theory of value. An autonomous discipline of political economy emerged to account for the new economic action founded on quantifiable labor. Subsequently,

David Ricardo and John Stuart Mill refined this "dismal science." By the middle of the nineteenth century, Marx derived his theory of surplus value from the labor theory of value and displaced political economy by historical materialism.

Development was a new word in bourgeois society, meaning "evolution or bringing out from a latent or elementary condition," or "the growth and unfolding of what is in the germ."[10] It reflected the new experience of time as cumulative change. The concept was absent before this period. Previously, temporal changes were experienced as seasonal, cyclical, or restorative. They could be ritualized as mythic imitation of some cosmic archetype. Or, as in the seventeenth and eighteenth centuries, time was compared with and likened to space. However, the dynamics of the economic and political revolutions which ushered in bourgeois society broke the bounds of the traditional experience and conceptualization of time. In their stead or overlaying them, new forces were at work to promote the secular sense of time as cumulative change, leading to the unexpected, the new. This experience of time was a drastically different, new dimension which could no longer be contained by the epistemic order of representation-in-space. Within the new perceptual field, the succession of new, different, noncomparable phenomena was ordered by the logic of analogy and succession as a development-in-time.

The new order was assumed to be an objective process, i.e., really out there, not the projection of the human mind. Furthermore, it was assumed that Archimedean reason could comprehend the process as stages in a linear, mechanical series. The prime example was the Darwinian theory of evolution. Development was an extension of the seventeenth- and eighteenth-century representation from space to time. And in bourgeois society two basic methodological problems resulted from the order of development-in-time. One was the gap between the human being and that objective process. In other words, what was the place of the subject in the objective process? Marx, in *The Economic and Philosophic Manuscripts of 1844*, saw the gap objectively as alienation (*Entäusserung*) and subjectively as estrangement (*Entfremdung*). The second problem was the connection between functional/organic/structural order in space and dynamic change across time. How could the same Archimedean reason which accounted for order in space also explain change across time as necessarily stemming from that order? This was the problem of social static versus social dynamic, as confronted by Auguste Comte and Herbert Spencer. The dialectic of a multi-level structure in transformation, as proposed by Marx in the 1859 Preface to *A Contribution to the Critique of Political Economy*, was one eminent solution.

21

On the one hand, development reflected the new dynamics of bourgeois society. It enabled the bourgeois to exploit the world and believe in progress. On the other hand, the Archimedean perspective underlying that concept objectified both time and space, and located the bourgeois in a centerless world. It could not comprehend the lived temporal experience between now and then, the lived spatial experience between here and there. In bourgeois society, there was an unspeakable gulf between the subjectivity of the self and the objectivity of the world. Reality itself became the end product of a linear, genetic causation, so that what-it-is was explained away by the knowledge of how-it-came-about. Nor could Archimedean perspective comprehend the prospective reality of another place, another time. What in other realities could not be objectified and explained, it would stereotype as primitive or exotic. In fact, "primitivism" and "exoticism" were two new interests in bourgeois society,[11] to compensate for the estranged experience of the bourgeois self.

The concept of the subconscious as a specific form of the unconscious lying under or below consciousness[12] came into use in bourgeois society, testifying to a new dichotomy between consciousness and the unconscious. The subject lives in and engages the world. The consciousness which reflects that being-engaged-in-the-world is perspectival and partial. There is always more to the subject, to the world, and to being-engaged-in-the-world than consciousness of them. Therefore, the unconscious as the opposite of consciousness is not an unreal void.[13] Potentially, it includes everything other than consciousness, whether within or beyond the person. However, in bourgeois society, as Archimedean perspective succeeded in enveloping the world within an objective spatio-temporality, everything out there became objectifiable and quantifiable. Thus what could not be known, the unconscious, came increasingly to be located within the subject, as the subconscious.

In 1775, quite appropriately at the start of the period of bourgeois society, the physician Franz Mesmer triumphed over the exorcist Father Johann Joseph Gessner with a scientific explanation for the unconscious. The unconscious could no longer be comprehended by religious explanation. As the spatio-temporal objectification of the world proceeded in the nineteenth century, there was a corresponding proliferation of compensatory interests in animal magnetism, somnambulism, hypnotism, spiritism, and parapsychology. However, as the world became objective, having in it a few traces of the scientifically unknowable, concern for the unconscious shifted from phenomena beyond the subject to phenomena within. During the second half of the nineteenth century, there was the study of hysteria, which culminated in the psychoanalytic concept of neurosis.[14] It was not Freud but the French psychologist Pierre Janet who first formulated the theoretical concept of the subconscious, and then tried to distinguish the therapeutic concept of the subconscious from the philosophical concept of the unconscious.[15] But Freud insisted there was no unconscious except the id within the person. This was no mere terminological quibble, but one based upon clinical observation and the perceived reality in bourgeois society. With the world becoming scientifically known, there could be no unconscious beyond. Hence, contemporaries accepted Freud's concept of the unconscious within, and soon forgot Janet's distinction between the subconscious and the unconscious.

The shift from the unconscious beyond to the subconscious within implied that there was little mystery left in the objectified world of bourgeois society. But objective knowledge could not account for the reflexivity of conscious, embodied life. The subject experienced being moved by one-knew-not-what. Instead, the reflexive, dialectical connection between the subject and the world, between consciousness and the unconscious, was explained by the concept of the linear development of the psyche, where conscious life was caused by the subconscious. Objective knowledge did not free the human being, but rather enhanced his or her sense of being determined. And the unconscious within must assume the burden of accounting for that determinism. The concept of the linear development of the human psyche was the appropriate symbolization of the new bourgeois fate.

There was no "labor," "development," or "subconscious" before this period. And if they had no words for them, people could not conceive and talk of such experience. Labor as distinct from work; development-in-time; and the subconscious reflected, within the bourgeois perceptual field, the new dynamics of bourgeois society. Within the field emerged fundamentally different, new experiences of time, space, and bodily life. They will be the concerns, respectively, of the next three chapters. However, before embarking on them, I shall in the next two sections of this chapter discuss first the sedimentation and transformation of bourgeois perception before this period, and then the stratification of other perceptual fields by the dominant bourgeois field in the period of bourgeois society.

Bourgeois Perception in Former Times

The new perceptual field reflected and confirmed the hopes and expectations of the triumphant bourgeoisie, while submerging those of the other classes. However, prior to this period, bourgeois hopes and expectations were themselves constricted in other fields of perception.

The "bourgeois" was not a static ideal-type, as envisaged by Max Weber, with a single career which we can follow across time. The bourgeoisie was a changing social formation in different social structures, never an identity. It occupied a different place within a different perceptual field in each period. There is no continuity from one period to the next. And I shall survey the relation between the changing bourgeoisie and different perceptual fields since the Middle Ages, not to show how-it-came-about, but to expose their differences.

Medieval Christendom was a disparate world of irreconcilable institutions and values.[16] It did not possess any synthesis. For the inhabitants of that world, institutionalization was based upon the particular, personal experience of *socius*.[17] There were innumerable, as yet unstratified *socii*, but no sense of a society at large, except maybe participation in the ideal of Christendom. Within that world, the dominant perceptual field was constituted by a culture of **oral-chirographic** media, by a hierarchy of sensing which emphasized hearing and touching, and by an epistemic order of anagogy. The perception in that world was at once more intense and outwardly directed, and less exact than ours.

The burghers of the Middle Ages did not overstep the bounds of this perceptual field; their outlook was contained by it. From the late tenth century onward, towns grew up as centers of trade. But these were mostly small, isolated organizations in a predominantly rural economy. The burghers themselves had little knowledge of trade practices, beyond that derived from personal information and custom. They lacked the economic rationality of a later age. In fact, most of them could not use figures to make calculation, and viewed money as an incomprehensible phenomenon.[18] The medieval town itself was not a bastion of secular reason in a world of anagogy. Even in the towns, Christianity provided for the hierarchical values of life, delimited business activities, regulated the guilds, and **molded** the very outlook of the burghers. For the modern bourgeois, religion was a Sunday affair; but for the medieval burgher, business was not yet a totally absorbing calling. The latter possessed neither the outlook nor the personality of his modern descendant. Too often, in retrospect, we exaggerate the origins of modern economy, and reduce the prospective reality of Christian belief in the medieval towns. In fact, during the thirteenth century, when credit, exchange, and banking enhanced business activities, Christianity maintained its vital hold on the urban population by the counteroffensive of the orders of Franciscans and Dominicans. Furthermore, the church took advantage of the new wealth to organize itself and extend its control into the countryside.

24

Bourgeois Society

The fourteenth-century economic and demographic crises were interpreted by contemporaries as the vicissitudes of Fortune in human affairs. Somehow, the crises jarred the medieval field of perception. In that century, the new psychological awareness in the thought of Master Eckhart and William of Ockham,[19] the pictured space in the paintings of Duccio and Giotto,[20] the humanist ideal in the literature of Petrarch, Boccaccio, and Salutati all attested to a shift of perception to focus upon the world. The initiative for this shift came from northern Italy, where the tradition of urban economy and oligarchic wealth was strong.[21]

In contrast to medieval Christendom, the world of the Renaissance was more self-contained and self-conscious. Contemporaries were concerned with tangible human institutions, such as the family, the guild, and the constitution of the corporate community, in order to guard against uncertainties. The family was the focus of a new conjugal affection; the guild was a protection against economic ups and downs; and the constitution of the corporate community was emphasized to ensure against the danger of possible decay.[22] Modern class society is a social structure girded by horizontal stratification and perpendicular mobility (more by the former and much less by the latter). But the Renaissance lacked a commonly perceived ground upon which all the diverse social experiences could be subsumed. Nevertheless, Renaissance society had advanced beyond the medieval institutionalization of *socius*. It was an institutionalization based on the hierarchy of estate orders, with each estate itself further divided into graded ranks and degrees. Each social unit was a self-contained microcosmic reflection of the universe; together, they constituted a body politic.

The Renaissance field of perception was constituted by a culture in transformation from chirographic to typographic media, though with the persistence of an underlying orality; by a gradual shift from the emphasis on hearing and touching to visuality; and by the epistemic order of similitude. Within that centripetal field, what we now know as the demographic, economic growth of the late fifteenth and sixteenth centuries was not perceived as such by contemporaries. Instead, they approached money and price as correlated signs in a stable universe.[23] And scholasticism provided a system of moral theology and law with which to judge economic phenomena as public weal, rather than wealth per se.[24] The burghers of the Renaissance were distinguished from the aristocracy and the peasantry by their commercial capitalist activities;[25] but the Renaissance field of perception limited their economic rationality. For the burghers, the search for security was more pressing than any "spirit of capitalism." Having recently recovered from the crises of the fourteenth century, they were consolidating the guild order.

Most of them were content within that order; few ventured beyond it to tackle the new, unknown forces. Most continued to base their calculation on personal and practical considerations, unable to recognize the impact of the new economic forces, although by the sixteenth century they began to use number and measurement with greater ease and frequency.[26] The Renaissance burghers, except for those in late-sixteenth-century Netherlands and England, were not yet a conscious economic stratum.

Seventeenth- and eighteenth-century society was still a hierarchy of estates and orders. However, the perceived ties of personal allegiance, corporate body, and regional loyalty were weakened by the new forces of commercial capitalism. There was need for a rational, visible principle to comprehend the diverse social experiences. For lack of such a principle, institutionalization in this period was a formalization and consolidation of the hierarchy of estates. The estates and orders were less self-contained than in the Renaissance, as is illustrated by the emergence of the nobility of the robe in France. Hence the need to emphasize and formalize the hierarchy of ranks, titles, and privileges in this period.[27] The forms of that hierarchy had to go on display, for all to witness.

The perceptual field in that estate society of formalized hierarchy was consitutted by a typographic culture superimposing itself over an oral-chirographic culture; by the primacy of sight; and by the epistemic order of representation-in-space. Within the new field, perception was visual, nonreflexive, and quantitative. The new perceptual field was centered in the towns, from which it radiated outward, pressing down on the folk culture and magico-religion of the lower strata.[28] It affected most members of the bourgeoisie as well as of the aristocracy, enabling them to consolidate their own intersts. In addition, its impact was evident in the town planning, road construction, and landscape gardening of the period. Even madness was spatially institutionalized.[29]

The estate society of the seventeenth and eighteenth centuries was still predominantly rural. But the demographic growth of the sixteenth century had greatly stimulated capitalist economy. Thanks to the importance of the overseas commerce, the economic center of gravity for Europe shifted from the Mediterranean basin to the Atlantic seaboard. This expansion of commercial capitalism gradually subverted the tradition of status and rank. Nevertheless, within the perceptual field of estate society, economics was restricted to the analysis of wealth.[30] Money was the universal means to represent wealth. But wealth was determined by its usefulness, pleasurability, availability, or rarity. Since the amount of money in circulation at any given time was ascertainable and the sum of represented wealth was constant, the

26

analysis of wealth was for contemporaries the regulation of its exchanges. And the theory of mercantilism claimed for the new monarchy the central role in that regulation.

In that estate society, the bourgeoisie was less than an estate, but not yet a class. As a business and professional stratum, it was a part of the third estate. Nor did it possess class solidarity, since the upper bourgeois usually dissipated his wealth by purchasing office, land, or marriage for his offsprings, rather than further investing in capitalist undertakings. Lacking the *esprit* of the nobility, the bourgeoisie was that new, functional stratum catering to the commercial economy. The new visual, nonreflexive, quantitative rationality enabled the bourgeoisie to enlarge its calculation. But reason was no substitute for social solidarity. Nevertheless, the bourgeoisie felt superior to the other members of the third estate. Inherently traditional and security minded, it was propped up by a web of corporate regulations and "liberties." The very success of the bourgeoisie in this period made it incongruous within the formalized hierarchy of estates.

The bourgeoisies of France, England, and the Netherlands in the seventeenth and eighteenth centuries were variations of the above characterization. In France, the increasingly prosperous bourgeoisie was straightjacketed by both the centralizing monarchy and the declining aristocracy. Yet both monarchy and aristocracy depended on bourgeois wealth to maintain its respective claim to glory and honor. Monarchy, aristocracy, and bourgeoisie, each with rival yet related interests, therefore formed a triangular interplay.[31] In England, on the other hand, Parliament had succeeded in restraining the power of the Crown. And relations between landed gentry and urban wealth were more open in England than those between aristocracy and bourgeoisie in France. With the English economy more commercialized than the French, the English Crown and gentry were more accommodating to business and professional interests.[32] Finally, the Netherlands was a confederation of oligarchical towns, without a monarch or landed aristocracy to speak of.[33] From France to England to the Netherlands, the power of monarchy and aristocracy decreased, while that of the bourgeoisie increased. Nevertheless, in all three countries, the bourgeoisie remained oligarchic and corporative, prone to imitate aristocratic forms and manners. Not only was the bourgeoisie confined to the formalized hierarchy of estate society, but its outlook was restrained within that field of perception. Two revolutions were necessary in order to destroy that formalized hierarchy and displace its perceptual field.

There was no continuous development of the bourgeoisie across time. Instead, we have a discontinuous history of a bourgeoisie that was a different social formation in each period, and in each was contained by a different perceptual field. Bourgeois class-consciousness was under the cultural hegemony of different precapitalist social formations. Only in the period of bourgeois society proper were its hopes and expectations fully reflected and confirmed in a perceptual field constituted by typographic culture, visuality, and the order of development-in-time.

Perceptual Stratification in Bourgeois Society

Bourgeois society was a class society, in the sense that economic action triumphed over social status to redefine social structure. For the first time, class structure was a perceived stratification for its inhabitants. In estate society, in spite of increasing economic activities, social stratification was still perceived as orders of rank and degree, separating the privileged and the *roturiers*. In England, the concept of class gradually came into use during the late eighteenth century. But only by the second quarter of the nineteenth century did the vertical antagonism and horizontal solidarity of class interests become a perceived reality.[34] In France, against the background of a somewhat more rigidly stratified society and despite a slower pace of capitalist development, the political discontinuity of the Revolution and the Restoration promoted class consciousness.[35] We have ample evidence of this in the fiction, journalism, and political and historical literature of the period. The emergence of class consciousness confirmed the transformation from an estate to a class society, since class was no longer an aggregative term but a perceived collectivty.

The class stratification of bourgeois society was also a perceptual stratification dominated by the triumphant bourgeois field of perception. The bourgeoisie was contained by other perceptual fields in former times, but in bourgeois society the bourgeois field of perception exercised a hegemony over the perceived realities of the other classes and strata. Gentry-aristocracy, organized religion, the peasantry, the proletariat, and even the occult—each possessed its own reality, a self-contained world of internal coherence and validation. Nevertheless, under pressure from the bourgeois perceptual field, each of these realities or worlds had to retreat and make internal adjustments.

The World of the Gentry-Aristocracy

The gentry-aristocracy lived in a personalized hierarchy which comprehended all the different levels of a community. Within a locale, members of the gentry-aristocracy had intimate dealings with those above themselves, as well as those below. Everything here was governed by customs, precedence, and genealogy. That world was characterized by its sensitivity to the particular or specific, rather than to any abstract principle or belief. This sensitivity thwarted any rational calculation of change. And landownership, the economic foundation of that world, was perceived as the basis of social status and political power.

However, captialism had successfully invaded the English rural economy by the eighteenth century, to make farming more scientific and businesslike. In fact, by the mid-nineteenth century, there was a profession of land management to take care of the business of agriculture.[36] In France, capitalist agriculture was not as advanced. However, the different land policies of the Revolution and the Restoration had so thoroughly mixed bourgeois with aristocratic ownership[37] that Marx could say, "Large landed property despite its feudal coquetry and pride of race, has been rendered thoroughly bourgeois by the development of the modern society."[38]

Notwithstanding, this incursion of capitalism did not completely alter the reality of the world of the gentry-aristocracy. In economic action the gentry-aristocracy had to learn rational calculation. But in status and power it continued to rely on its own tradition, although by now it had become more conscious of ranking within its own hierarchy.[39] And as Karl Mannheim maintained, the combination of aristocratic particularism with bourgeois reason led to a post-Jacobin ideology of conservatism.[40] Conservative consciousness of tradition, unlike preconservative tradition, promoted a romantic sense of the past. But familiarity with bourgeois reason also led the gentry-aristocracy to make other adjustments. Under the pressure of rational values, the forms of aristocratic life became more visualized and the person more inhibited than before. Yet ultimately the gentry-aristocracy's sense of the particularity and tradition of its own world enabled its members to ward off, in varying degrees, the bourgeois objectification and estrangement of the subject.

The World of Christian Religion

Christianity possessed an outlook which transcended bourgeois society. Economic calculation in bourgeois society was immanent, within an objective spatio-temporality. But Christianity believed space and time were finite, beyond which was the transcendent, absolute God. The believer located in space and time could obtain by faith an intimation of God and his design. In the Middle Ages, the order of anagogy constricted the rationality of the burghers. Now, in bourgeois society, Christianity had to readjust to a world objectified by bourgeois reason.

Pressures on Christianity always led to a liturgical response, because liturgy rather than theology has been the fundamental Christian form of expression combining belief with worship, directing the outlook of the entire person to the beyond. Thus, when religious reality was threatened by alien values, the true believer had to answer at the fundamental, liturgical level. In bourgeois society, both Protestantism and Catholicism responded to the new pressures in this way. The Oxford Movement's Anglo-Catholicism was a return to the traditional form of worship. But the Church of England was so obviously a product of historical transformation, lacking the mysterious, sacerdotal claim of the Catholic Church, that the conversion of someone like John Henry Newman to Catholicism was only one further step in this return. Nineteenth-century Catholicism began to pay greater attention to the sacrament of the Eucharist. And there was the start of a Catholic liturgical movement. In additon, a most significant Catholic liturgical response in this period was the proclamation of the dogma of Immaculate Conception, in 1854. For the true believer, the reaffirmation of the veneration of the Virgin Mary was a necessary, meaningful response to the cold, mechanical world of bourgeois society.

Liturgical response was more crucial than such religiously peripheral activities as the Salvation Army, Y.M.C.A., Christian Socialism, or even the social teachings of Leo XIII. These activities were peripheral in that they tried to ignore the inevitable conflict between the transcendent outlook of Christian religion and the immanent rational preoccupation of bourgeois society. In attempting to hold onto both, they exuded an air of hypocrisy. Yet neither liturgical response nor social religion could smother that inevitable conflict. In the meantime, English Methodism was the best compromise to bridge the two worlds of Christian religion and bourgeois economy.

The World of the Peasants

The peasantry was spatially organized around the land. Not land per se, but how it was held, used, divided, and passed on from one generation to another would define the organization of the peasant community. The peasant household, the farming strips, and the common all reconfirmed the traditional peasant dependency on the land. Temporally, the peasant world was molded by the cycles of nature and of life. The annual season from spring to winter dictated the range of human activites on the land, from sowing to harvest. The life cycle of birth, marriage, natality and death paced the continuity from one generation to another. Within this enfolding, cyclical spatio-temporality, peasant culture was primarily oral rather than literate, emphasizing hearing and touching over seeing. Even in the late nineteenth century, one-third of all French peasants were still illiterate,[41] and the percentage of those who relied on word of mouth for their primary source of knowledge was undoubtedly much higher. In this world of oral culture, with its emphasis on the formulaic transmission of techniques and wisdom, the perception of the peasant correspondingly emphasized the specific, the perennial.

For centuries the peasant world had been infiltrated by the forces of technology and the market economy. But the agricultural revolution in the eighteenth century finally transformed the countryside. That, together with the enclosure movement and the demographic migration to the cities, challenged the integrity of the world of the English peasantry much more than that of the French peasantry.[42] Rural custom and tradition had to retreat, under the onslaught of technological innovation and the market economy. Yet only the upper stratum of the peasantry succeeded in learning new ways and abandoning some of the old; as for the other strata, the reality of their world contracted. At the core, peasants held tenaciously to those customs and practices which still survived the challenge of the new. From within this contracted reality came a heightened distrust of everything unknown, all marked by a tremendous gulf separating "us" from "them," between the familiar and the new.

The urban laboring poor were even more vulnerable than the peasantry. Uprooted from the land and crowded into slums, they were quite defenseless against the threats of unemployment and hunger. The city concentrated poverty, and accentuated the chasm between the wealthy and the poor. The urban poor were caught in a twilight zone of demoralization, because for them the traditional values of land were no longer binding, yet the ideology of the bourgeoisie still made no sense. Not only did the bourgeois perceive the urban poor as a mixture of criminal and laboring elements, but the poor themselves accepted this deprecatory self-image.[43]

The World of the Proletariat

Against this background, the world of the proletariat was a new social formation in the early nineteenth century. Leadership in the social construction of a proletarian reality fell on the artisan, handicraft elite, for they possessed the skills, the sense of community of work, and the tradition of mutual aid, all of which enabled them to respond positively to the new pressures of industrial capitalism. In their response, they discovered two instruments, economic strike and political agitation. By the thirties and forties, their protest movements coalesced into trade union organizations with a proletarian class con-. sciousness.[44]

Unlike the gentry-aristocracy and the peasantry, the proletariat was a new class, resulting from the pressures of industrial capitalism upon the urban working population. As opposed to the individualism and utilitarianism of the triumphant bourgeoisie, proletarian reality emphasized mutual aid and collectivity. The rationality it learned from the bourgeoisie was secondary. The world of the proletariat occupied the alienating space of the factory and slum dwelling. And its sense of time was externally imposed, being the necessary pace of factory machines. Thus the spatio-temporality of the proletariat was an artificial one, dictated by industrial capitalism. The workers felt determined, pulled along without being in control. However, the proletarian ideal of collectivity and mutual aid was a positive response to that deterministic world. Alienation of labor was the common fate which united the factory workers. That fate provided for proletarian solidarity. But their solidarity was directed toward only economic improvements of working conditions, wages, hours, etc. Revolutionary politics was not a part of the expectation of the proletarian world; instead it had to be imposed from without. There was no continuity from proletarian spontaneity to revolutionary consciousness.

The World of the Occult

The occult—magic, astrology, witchcraft and sorcery—was furthest removed from the bourgeois perceptual field. Yet it too was affected by that field. In the estate society of the seventeenth and eighteenth centuries, the upper strata of urban population gradually became more secular, rational, and tolerant in their outlooks. The occult retreated to the lower, rural strata of society.[45] The Renaissance tradition of Hermes Trismegistus and the Cabala went underground, to reappear sporadically in conjunction with the Rosicrucian and the Masonic secret societies.[46] We still have little knowledge concerning occult practices in the outlying rural regions during the period of bourgeois society,[47] although we can assume that they persisted from earlier times. But the new occult in bourgeois society seems to have originated in the upper, urban strata, rather than in the lower, rural strata of society. In the early nineteenth century, the upper classes in the cities, estranged by an increasingly objectified world, took up illuminism and spiritism.[48] By the second half of the century, interest in the occult proliferated. In the fifties and sixties, Alphonse Louis Constant revived the Hermetic-Cabala tradition with a series of works on ritual magic.[49] In the following decade, Helena Blavatsky taught an eclectic theosophy of Eastern mysticism and Western magic. She was one of the founders of the Theosophical Society in 1875, which proclaimed the aim of an occult wisdom in opposition to mechanistic, scientific knowledge.[50] The ritual magic of Constant was taken up in England subsequently, with the founding of the Hermetic Order of the Golden Dawn in 1888; and Aleister Crowley, the self-proclaimed magus, joined it briefly in the late nineties.[51] The height of upper-class interest in the occult came in the nineties, when practices of astrology were revived.[52]

The world of the occult was the direct opposite of bourgeois society.[53] The occult aspired to a knowledge of the beyond. It harked back to the centripetal, animate cosmos of the Renaissance, with its perceived connections between being and the world, between microcosm and macrocosm. In direct contrast to the occult, the bourgeois field of perception promoted an objective, nonreflexive, quantitative knowledge unrelated to the self. However, without the support of a Renaissance cosmos, the nineteenth-century occult of Constant and Crowley contracted into itself. On the other hand, the theosophical eclecticism of Blavatsky dangerously compromised the integrity of the occult. In bourgeois society, the occult could find no perceptual support beyond itself. And the self-styled magus without a macrocosm became in effect a false prophet.

Temporality

The experience of lived time is different from and more fundamental than the mechanical measurement of clock time. The latter is impersonal and objective, whereas lived time is personal, as well as dependent on the environing world within which the subject lives. It is a *Gestalt* between the rhythm of the person and the symbolized, institutionalized paces of that world. Each person has a physiological rhythm; and different periods have different symbols and institutions to pace duration. There are in effect different kinds of social time, whether liturgical or secular, archetypal or historical, seasonal or mechanical, cyclical or linear, intersubjective or objective. After the two revolutions of the late eighteenth century, representation-in-space could no longer contain the dynamics of bourgeois society. Within the new perceptual field constituted by typographic culture, the primacy of sight, and the order of development-in-time, time was objectified as a different dimension from space. This objectification of time led to other related, compensatory developments. In this chapter, I shall discuss new experiences of time, distances from the past, visions of the future, temporal process, and immanent dynamics in bourgeois society.

New Experiences of Time

Clocks and watches were used before this period. The mechanical clock was invented in the second half of the thirteenth, and the pendulum clock in the mid-seventeenth century. In the seventeenth and eighteenth centuries, improved escapements and temperature and barometric compensations made timepieces more precise and accurate. By the following century, watches were mass produced with interchangeable parts. Before then, watches were partly ornamental, partly utilitarian. However, in early-nineteenth-century England, they became a necessity. The prevalence of clocks and watches testified to the new importance of objective time. But that was only a symptom of the changing paces of life in bourgeois society.[1]

Three

Urbanization and Time

The crucial, determining factor in this period was the tempo of urban transformation. Urbanization occurred later and somewhat more slowly in France than in England, owing in part to the relatively stationary demographic trends in France, and in part to the fact that industrialization in France came half a century later than in England. Nevertheless, the metropolises in both countries, i.e., London and Paris, experienced remarkable expansion, as did some of the new manufacturing towns. During the first half of the nineteenth century, London's population trebled, whereas Paris's doubled. By 1891, more than four million people lived in the former, and two and one-half million in the latter. Not only did urban population grow in absolute figures, but the ratio of people living in urban areas also increased. At the beginning of this period, approximately one-sixth of the English and Welsh population lived in towns with populations of 20,000 or more. By the end of this period, it was three-quarters. In France, at the beginning of the period, somewhat less than one-seventh of the population lived in towns of 5,000 or above. By the end of the period, nearly two-fifths.[2]

In other words, more and more people were living in an urban environment. The increasingly more specialized and diversified activities in the towns and cities could not depend on the natural cycle of day and night, of dawn and dusk. Instead, they had to be more exactly coordinated by clock time. Thus, the heightened pace of urbanization exposed an ever larger number of people to mechanical time.

Mechanization and Time

Of course, urbanization had been proceeding long before the period of bourgeois society, and the reliance on clocks and watches was cumulative. But the mechanization of work in the factory introduced an experience of time which was unique to this period.

Within the factory, work was routinized, standardized, and divided into a series of simplified motions-in-time. Labor and technology became mutually convertible, depending on which was more easily available and cost less. Mechanization integrated labor into an increasingly efficient process of industrial production. Previously, the tempo of work had depended on the organic rhythm of the human being. Now, however, in the factory, the physiological rhythm of the worker was sacrificed for the sake of the artificial tempo of the machine. The factory worker, recently uprooted from manual or agricultural work, was not accustomed to the new mechanical pace. He or she had to be coerced to serve the new tempo. Time, therefore, became more external and repressive for the worker, and labor discipline emerged as a new problem. This process began earlier in England; but as industrialization spread, whether in France or subsequently elsewhere, the mechanical tempo prevailed.[3]

Rationalization and Time

By the middle of the nineteenth century, a new profession of industrial managers and engineers emerged to meet the demand for work mechanization. It was the task of these new experts to systematize production and get the most efficient use out of labor and technology. Even more than that of the bourgeoisie, the very outlook of these proto-technocrats was identified with the principle of efficiency.

Take for example, the time-and-motion approach to scientific management of Frederick W. Taylor, which was the culmination to the earlier works of Charles Babbage, Andrew Ure, J. Slater Lewis, and Charles Dupin. Taylor's system, also known as Taylorism, dissected the work process into its simplest mechanical motions. It completely ignored the human, subjective aspect of work: the more efficient, the better. Scientific management enhanced the schism between the mechanical tempo of industrial work and the physiological rhythm of the human being. In order to succeed, industry had to repress human subjectivity. Taylor, himself plagued by symptoms of repressed tension, was so engrossed in the cult of efficiency that he could not comprehend why workers objected to his scientific management.[4]

Transportation and Time

The development of coach road and waterway at the beginning of this period, and of railroad and steamship by the mid-nineteenth century is a familiar story.[5] It was a response to the demands of industrialization and urbanization, and in turn further stimulated them. Changes in transportation added two important facets to the contemporary experience of time, namely, the need to standardize time, and the connection between travel time and distance.

In the late eighteenth century, stagecoaches averaged only a few miles an hour, so there was no need to keep a very exact schedule. By the middle of the next century, trains were regularly averaging forty miles an hour, and the volume of rail transport increased enormously. Therefore, scheduling became necessary, in order to coordinate the multitudes of arrivals and departures. Previously, most towns had had their own local times; but now a standard railroad time was necessary.

Three

The use of telegraph signal in 1852 made possible the synchronization of local times with Greenwich Mean Time. Finally, in 1884, an international agreement was signed on standard time and time zones.

With increased speed in transportation, less time was required to cover the same distance. In 1780, stagecoach covered the distance between London and Manchester in four to five days. A hundred years later, trains traveled the same distance in four to five hours. Conversely, in the same amount of time, one could now travel more distance. It has been said that, with the new means of transportation, the world became smaller. Actually, the world was enlarged by new experiences of travel and tourism.

Communication and Time

Communication by means of typography increased throughout this period. The manufacture of paper became less costly; literacy increased; and reading became a more popular pastime. More specifically, in the second half of the nineteenth century, the invention of cylinder and rotary presses, of stereotype and linotype made the newspaper a mass medium. Simultaneously, the use of telegraph and cable speeded up news reporting.[6]

Newspapers had a different perceptual impact on the reader than the printed book. Unlike the linear development of a plot or an argument in the book, the concurrent reporting of news from different parts of the world made newspapers a mosaic of unrelated events. Newspapers contracted time to the instantaneous and the sensational, expanded space to include anything from everywhere. The present became much more diverse and complex, no longer containable within a single chronological framework. And the reader had to provide the connection behind the different news items. Therefore, with the speeding up of communication, perception of the present became more disconnected, begging for explanation or interpretation.

Visualization and Time

The photographic revolution in the mid-nineteenth century made communication even more visually oriented than before. Typography had already emphasized visuality, and engraving and lithography had standardized visual information. However, photography provided detail and accuracy which prints could never attain. With photography, one could see a trace of what had happened at another place, another time. Thus, greater reliance was placed on visual information. By the last quarter of the century, photography tried to capture animals and humans in motion, and birds in flight. In the early twentieth century, photography assisted in the science of time-and-motion study.[7]

Photographic information made people more aware of speed and time. Even a fast shutter can never really capture motion, because each photo is a static instantaneity from a specific angle. However, a succession of slightly different static traces enabled the bourgeois viewer in the age before film to infer motion. Such perceptual interpretation would have been incomprehensible to people from other cultures. They would have had to acquire the bourgeois perceptual emphasis on visual information in discontinuous, mechanical time, before they could have translated static traces into motion.

Urbanization, mechanization, rationalization, transportation, communication, visualization—these were concurrent, interdependent developments in bourgeois society. Mutually reinforcing, they made the bourgeois experience of the present much more mechanical, discontinuous, and external than before. And as compensation to this linear, segmented present, there emerged in bourgeois society new, different experiences of the past and the future.

Distances from the Past

There is no past in itself. It is forever lost. But each present symbolizes a past on its own terms. A past is therefore the intentional retrospection by a present. As the experience of the present became more mechanical and external, the past appeared more distant. New efforts were therefore made to recapture it.

Symptomatically, the increasing sense of distance from the past was evident in the changing meaning of "revolution."[8] Until the seventeenth century, revolution was an act or state of revolvement. Only in that century did it begin to mean the political overthrow of an established order. But even then revolution still meant restoration, as for example in the "Glorious Revolution" of 1688. By the eighteenth century, people became much more aware of the radicalism and innovation implied in the act of a political overthrow, although the American Revolution still claimed to be a restoration of the rights of Englishmen. Finally, the French Revolution made it impossible for anyone to claim that revolution could be the restoration of anything time-honored. The present had become so different from the past that it could no longer be bound by any past.

39

Three

The Consciousness of Tradition

Even before modern times, tradition was never static, but changing, albeit slowly.[9] However, the inhabitants within the slow-changing continuum of a premodern tradition believed their values to be absolute, transcending time. The inhabitants of bourgeois society, having experienced the discontinuity between the present and the past, approached tradition from the outside as a romantic other. Formerly, tradition contained time; now, tradition cut off from the mechanical, linear present became mere "traditionalism," an idealization of past tradition as a romanticized other.

Traditionalism was a new word in bourgeois society. So were such other -isms as "antiquarianism," "classicism," "medievalism," "orientalism," "primitivism."[10] People now believed that each period in the past possessed its own distinct set of values and styles. The experience of discontinuity in time made them aware that values were time-bound.

The Temporalization of Nostalgia

The Renaissance longing for classical antiquity sought a fundamental resemblance between that past and its own present; it was an exercise in similitude. "Nostalgia" was a word coined in the second half of the seventeenth century, to denote a form of melancholia induced by prolonged absence from one's home or locale, i.e., homesickness, the longing for a familiar space.[11] It was not yet the longing for a familiar time, since the continuity from the past into the present was still a seamless web. However, in bourgeois society, with the break between past and present, nostalgia was temporalized to be the longing for a former, more familiar time. And this nostalgia for the past soon became a widespread phenomenon.[12] The sentimental longing of the estranged bourgeois was now directed toward many pasts. Old documents and records were discovered and preserved; museums and antiquarian societies proliferated. New disciplines such as anthropology, archeology, and mythology developed out of the interest to recapture the past.[13] In addition, the art styles and motifs of other periods were idealized as "neoclassicism," "romanticism," "medievalism," "orientalism," "primitivism"—all nineteenth-century words. That century saw a series of imitation and revivals of these styles. Bourgeois society tried to consume the past, in order to attenuate somewhat its estrangement in the mechanical, segmented present.

Temporality

The Historical Novel and Internal Time

Walter Scott was fully aware of the problem of temporal discontinuity which led to nostalgia for the past. In the introduction and postscript to his *Waverley; or 'Tis Sixty Years Since* (1814), a work which popularized the genre of the historical novel, Scott discussed how he had wanted to avoid both a romance of distant chivalry and a tale of modern manners. Too great a distance would make his novel appear venerable, whereas too recent a setting would emphasize novelty for its own sake. Therefore, he set it in the Scotland of the mid-eighteenth century, not too far removed from the industrial England of his early-nineteenth-century readers, yet distant enough to arouse their nostalgia. Within that ideal distance, Scott believed he could direct the reader's attention to the internal development of the actors' characters and emotions.[14] He would thus be able to move the reader from mere interest in the external setting of an exotic era, to the internal time of human passion. In this manner the past would become alive for the reader.

Scott's historical novel had a few precedents. But the instant success of *Waverley* led him and others both in England and elsewhere to write other historical novels.[15] It was to Scott's credit that he was quite conscious of the prospect of a historical novel. But we need to credit the popular reception of the historical novel to the time-consciousness peculiar to bourgeois society.

The historical novel integrated the external time of a historical setting with the internal time of the actors' emotions. The inner conflicts of the actors were enhanced by the historical setting of the plot. On the other hand, nostalgia in bourgeois society was provoked by spatio-temporal dislocation, when the bourgeois was confronted with a lack of coherence between internal sensibility and external surroundings. Thus a new reservoir of unstructured sentiment was available, which could potentially be mobilized in many directions. The historical novel became popular, because in this case the reader's sentiment was directed to another time, another place, where he or she could esthetically, i.e., vicariously, enjoy the meaningful outcome of human passions and aspirations. The past was put to use in the historical novel, to restore that temporal coherence lacking in the reader's present.

Extension of the Temporal Landscape

Interest in the past extended the historical landscape of bourgeois society. That landscape included different periods from antiquity up to the recent past, as well as other societies. But the nineteenth century was especially interested in the Middle Ages. People were fascinated by medieval literature, folklore, and religion. Medieval scenes were favorite topics for painting; and Gothic revival was the leading nineteenth-century architectural style.[16] The romantic longing of the century looked back to the medieval past, a period not yet tainted by any tinge of modernism. This idealization of the Middle Ages enabled some to ward off the threats of technology and industrialization. Once more, historical representation of a past was governed by present motive.

In addition to history, geology and archeology also extended their studies of the past. From Buffon and Hutton in the eighteenth century to Lyell in the nineteenth, the study of the formation of the earth assumed a much more extended time framework. Finally, geologists were able to overcome the former concerns with original creation and providentialism, as well as the limitation of the biblical time span. Instead, they associated the formation of different strata of rocks and fossils with different ages. By the middle of the century, they had defined the major stages of geological time.[17] Influenced by this development in stratigraphic geology, archeologists in the first half of the nineteenth century extended the antiquity of the human species back to the three ages of stone, bronze, and iron cultures.[18] Thus all three disciplines—history, geology, and archeology—extended the time scale of society further and further back into the past.

Despatialization of Historiography

In the estate society of the seventeenth and eighteenth centuries, representation-in-space restricted the historical study of other societies. With the major exceptions of David Hume and Giambattista Vico, most historians did not realize that the modality of time was fundamentally different from the modality of space. Instead, they believed time to be merely another extension of space, and likened the study of history in time to the study of nature in space. In this, they followed the dictate of Descartes who had insisted that the study of nature, being more exact and mathematical, was superior to the study of history. In addition, they believed that human nature and reason were constant, everywhere the same. If in the past that same reason did not triumph, then Voltaire, for instance, would attribute its failure to the prejudices of religion and other nonrational opinions. They could not realize that reason was historical, and that the understanding of one age by another was a problem. In spite of its professed interest in distant lands and ages, historiography in the Enlightenment was a series of judgments, based on the belief that other ages were either identical with or different from the eighteenth century. The noble savage and the wise mandarin were not concepts derived from the study of America and China, but the stereotyped projection of eighteenth-century ideals, useful in criticizing the less-than-ideal in contemporary France. Seventeenth- and eighteenth-century historians lacked understanding of other ages. They were unable to penetrate to the specific, changing motivations and mentalities of those other ages. History appeared as a series of ups (rationality) and downs (irrationality), as in Voltaire's *Age of Louis XIV*. But they were unable to ask the question, why?[19]

In bourgeois society, development-in-time despatialized historiography. With the extension of the historical landscape, time now possessed a depth and diversity which it previously had lacked. It was now much more difficult to maintain that human nature and reason were constant, universal. The Renaissance had already discovered the concept of anachronism, i.e., each age possessed its own coherence, integrity. But bourgeois society discovered the concept of historicism, i.e., how could one age know another, if each, including our own, were distinct and self-contained? This was the central problem of historiography in the nineteenth century. In addition, since neither human nature nor reason was universal, then the products of human endeavors also acquired a new, hitherto unrealized dimension of time. Thus, language, art, myth, religion, etc., all developed in time. The change in approach was not a result of mere accumulation of information, but the result of the displacement of representation-in-space by development-in-time. Within this new historical landscape, the formerly neglected Vico was now appreciated for what he had to say concerning the history of human mental activities and products.

The changing meaning of "revolution," traditionalism as the consciousness of a tradition that was no longer absolutely binding, nostalgia as longing for the past rather than another place, the historical novel as a popular genre, the extension of the temporal landscape, as well as the despatialization of historiography—all these developments were new efforts to recapture a past which had become more fleeting and distant, as bourgeois society experienced a more mechanical, segmented present. Past and present needed to be consciously reconnected, now.

Visions of the Future

There is no future; it has not yet happened. Instead, every present projects different visions of the future. In bourgeois society, as the present became more disconnected from the past, visions of the future became more material, secular, and immanent.

Three

Expectations of Material Improvement

By the second half of the nineteenth century, technology and industrial production had altered the urban landscape, and the expectations of those who lived within it.[20] By then, the urban scene outside of the slums began to improve. A fresh water supply and plumbing were available; the use of electricity spread; the ideals of sanitation and cleanliness became popular. In addition, the railroad, streetcars, and bicycles made transportation more convenient; and the invention of the telegraph, telephone, typewriter, fountain pen, and even the lead pencil altered communication. These plus many other innovations gave the upper and middle classes a sense of material improvement and well-being. However, the poor, as the studies of Mayhew, Booth, and Rowntree repeatedly showed at the time, remained untouched by the new prospects.

Even more significant for the outlook of the upper and middle classes was the new development in retail marketing and advertisement. Previously, retail shops were specialized, individually owned, craft-oriented establishments, where one went to buy specific items. But by the second half of the nineteenth century, mass production of commodities brought about an entirely new trend in retailing. Large numbers of standardized manufactured goods were sold either in the English-type multiple chain stores, or in the French universal department stores. In these new retail outlets, customers were exposed to a wide variety of well-packaged, mass-produced commodities on display. They were stimulated to buy more than what they had originally intended. Moreover, large-scale advertising of standard brand products was put in newspapers and magazines to further stimulate sales. This kind of advertising had not been possible before the era of mass production of commodities. In effect, both the new retail marketing and the new advertising worked to whet the public's appetite for material goods.

This new appetite was evident in the furnishing of the bourgeois household. The home had become a center of conspicuous consumption. But there was a limit to the necessities which one could consume. Hence the ideal of comfort emerged to justify all the unnecessary purchases, as compensation for bourgeois toil. Furniture and devices of various sorts cluttered the upper- and middle-class homes, all in the name of comfort. In addition, international exhibitions, from the Crystal Palace Exhibition of 1851 to the Paris International Exposition of 1900, celebrated the material achievements of the bourgeoisie. Both domestic household and public exhibition testified unabashedly to the new cult of material progress.

Temporality

Expectation of material improvement and the ideal of comfort constituted an ideology of consumption. This emphasis on consumption was unprecedented. It altered the conscious, perceived motives of the upper- and middle-class consumers, whose vision of the future was increasingly defined by the lure of new, manufactured commodities. The ideology of consuming the unnecessary was necessary to sustain the ever-mounting capacity of industrial production.

From Millennium to Progress

In Christian eschatology, the millennium was the end of time, when all things would come to a standstill and the kingdom of God would be established on earth. It was an impending expectation, the outcome of which depended entirely on God. On the other hand, the idea of progress posited changes within time. Progress as a gradual improvement depended on rational, human effort. The former, an apocalyptic vision, belonged to a traditional, religious world and stood in opposition to life on earth; whereas the latter, an immanent ideal, was distinctly a part of the modern, bourgeois world, where rational expectation was projected into the foreseeable future. They were two disparate approaches to reality, denoting two entirely opposing senses of the future. There was no development from one to the other, i.e., the apocalyptic vision was not secularized to become the immanent concept. Rather, each belonged to a different world. The change from millennium to progress implied the transformation of a traditional, religious world into a modern, bourgeois one.

During the Renaissance, millennial expectations apparently increased. That world was more self-contained than medieval Christendom, and the problem of the end of time loomed larger than before. In the estate society of the seventeenth and eighteenth centuries, the belief in scientific progress did affect some millennial visions, i.e., it was believed that there would be some human improvements on earth before the coming of the millennium. Nevertheless, human improvement on earth and millennial end were not really reconcilable, since they involved two entirely different horizons of expectation. On the other hand, the idea of progress in estate society was still a limited one, not yet universalized into a philosophy for all humankind. It was concerned with the recent past and immediate future of Europe. The more distant ages and places did not figure in its expectation.

However, in bourgeois society, beginning with Condorcet's *Sketch of a Historical Survey of the Progress of Human Spirit* (1795), the idea of progress was universalized. The order of development-in-time has engulfed the world, with progress as its major article of faith.

45

The history of that world was a continuous, progressive development from the remote past into the future. Only by the end of the nineteenth century did some fall away from that faith to voice doubts and misgivings.[21]

The transformation from millennium to progress was not merely a shift from a religious to a secular outlook, but a fundamental change in the experience of time. The chiliast expectation of the millennium posited a goal transcending time, rather than a continuous improvement into some distant future. Millennial time would come to an abrupt, unexpected end. It was as if the leap beyond time would consume the entire person. That expectation was a total involvement, psychically much more intense than the futurist orientation of any idea of progress. On the other hand, the idea of progress presupposed immanent temporality, and provided a rational vision of the future to its bourgeois believers. No one within this progressive development could leap beyond time. Thus, as the future widened its prospect, the temporal horizon became more immanent. Though psychically less involving, the idea of progress was more optimistic than any chiliast expectation. One could calculate progress with the intellect and verify its accomplishment with the eye; but the human emotion was left behind, unfulfilled, a potential ready for other kinds of mobilization.

From Utopia to "Euchronia"

From the famous treatise of Thomas More in 1516 to the French Revolution, the concept of utopia was a spatial critique of the status quo. Although literally meaning no-where, utopia was in the present. The critical distance between utopia and the status quo was a spatial rather than temporal one. However, in bourgeois society, a new type of utopia, or "euchronia," as Frank Manuel has termed it,[22] appeared, which was more an anticipation of the future than a critique of the present. From the phalanges of Fourier to *Looking Backward, 2000–1887* by Edward Bellamy, the new temporal utopia transcended the spatial restriction of its predecessor, to project a development from the present into the future.

The transformation from spatial utopia to euchronia was a shift of focus from a spatial critique of the present to a temporal anticipation of the future. The present was still seen as imperfect; but contemporary experience with rapid economic changes had generated the prospect of a better future. Euchronia or temporal utopia projected the vision of an institutionally better organized community, along either a hierarchical or an egalitarian formation. Moreover, being immanent rather than millennial, euchronia pointed to an immediate, calculable future. The new utopian imagination reflected the hopes and expectations of bourgeois society.

Scientific Romance and the Ambivalent Future

In the second half of the nineteenth century, the scientific imagination captured the reading public.[23] The series of extraordinary voyages written by Jules Verne from the sixties on was highly successful; and the imaginary air battle of Dorking captured the public fancy in the seventies. These were the best-known examples of the new scientific romance. As the future became more immanent and secular, scientific romance epitomized the bourgeois anticipation of the future, just as the historical novel was its nostalgia for an increasingly remote, specious past. In the imaginary worlds of scientific romance constructed by Bulwer Lytton, Samuel Butler, and W. H. Hudson, the future did not appear entirely hospitable to human inclination and frailty. Instead, there was a contrast between the tangible human present and that supposedly perfect, yet all-too-bland future. For every Edward Bellamy looking back from an idealized future, there was the reply of a William Morris which criticized the scientific vision for its lack of human proportion.

The future in scientific romance was a revelation of things to come. On the basis of the scientific, materialist trends in the present, the bourgeois envisaged an even more rational future. Scientific romance nourished the intellectual imagination of its readers, but neglected their emotional sensibility. Characters in scientific romance usually lacked psychological depth or sophistication. This lack was not due simply to any preference for adventure, but rather to the inherent difficulty of extrapolating human emotion into a rationally constructed world. The visualization of a scientific future inevitably impoverished the subjective, human dimension. And that led to an ambivalence about the future in some scientific romances.

This ambivalence was the underlying motif in the works of H. G. Wells, the most successful writer of the genre in bourgeois society. Wells was an ardent advocate of the scientific vision of the future. Yet, even in his earliest works, e.g., "The Discovery of the Future" (1902) and *A Modern Utopia* (1905), he admitted that this vision of the future was limited to the general and the determinable; it could not comprehend the individual, the specific. Wells, throughout his life, was aware of the limitation in the scientific vision of the future. The ambivalence came out in the jarring vision of *The War of the Worlds* (1898), and in his even more pessimistic, devastating *Mind at the End of Its Tether* (1945), written near the end of his long career.

Three

The Amelioration of Death

With changing attitudes toward the future, even the concept of death underwent transformation. Previously, ritual functioned as a preparation for the dying; it enabled the dying person to undertake the passage from this world to the next. But in bourgeois society, there was more concern for the ones left behind. Wills became more worldly and secular in their provisions. Death occasioned an entire etiquette of costumes and mourning, including even the use of death calling cards. Funerals were less a baroque procession, and more a social display. And burials were shifted from the churchyards to individual, private plots in the newly established cemeteries, where a cult of tombs and monuments developed to commemorate the dead. The unresolved grief of the bereaved was now a pressing problem. Therefore, sentimentalization of death for the benefit of the bereaved now displaced rituals for the dying. This sentimentalization was also quite evident in contemporary portraiture of dying.[24]

In estate society, rituals for the dying had implied the prospect of a deliverance beyond time. The transcendent symbols associated with those rituals, although more baroque and visual than before, were still meaningful to the contemporaries, both the dying and the ones left behind. However, in bourgeois society, these symbols could no longer induce catharsis, because now the future was foreclosed within immanent time. Thus death became a greater threat, stripped of the prospect of any relief beyond time. The helpless grief of those left behind expressed a sense that death was now the ultimate barrier which could no longer be overcome. The threat of a more immanent end had to be ameliorated in order to relieve that grief. Sentimentalization fulfilled the purpose of providing a means of expression for the new reservoir of helpless, unfocused emotion. Thus, the change from ritual preparation for the dying to sentimentalization of death indicated a much more immanent sense of the future.

In bourgeois society, the expectation of material improvement was widespread among the upper and middle classes, as the future became more immanent within time, less eschatological, and as progress became more continuous. Instead of being a spatial critique of the present, utopia posited a vision into the not-too-distant future. Nevertheless, that future was ambivalent, as revealed in the new scientific romance. Death within immanent, secular time was also a problem, which baroque rituals could no longer handle; therefore death was sentimentalized for the sake of the bereaved. Somehow, as the past became more distant in bourgeois society, the future became more enclosed and threatening. Therefore, the visions of the future had to be more rational and explicit.

Temporal Process and Immanent Dynamics

With the present more mechanical in tempo, the past more distant, no longer contained by tradition, and visions of the future more immanent and rational, reality has become a temporal process. Anything and everything took time to develop. Time without end, rather than just infinite space, was the outermost limit of bourgeois perception. The new epistemic order was development-in-time, displacing that of representation-in-space. The temporalization of reality underlay such new conceptualizations as the evolution of species, the ages of human life, and the development of society. In addition, since reality was a temporal process, the changes in that reality had to be accounted for immanently, i.e., by causes from within the process itself. "Dynamics," a nineteenth-century keyword meaning "the moving physical or moral forces in any sphere, or the laws by which they act,"[25] displaced teleology and eschatology.

The Evolution of Species

In the seventeenth and eighteenth centuries, the science of natural history had classified species and genera by their identical and different characteristics. These characteristics might not necessarily be the functionally essential or important traits of an entity; but they were the visible evidence for a system of classification. That system ordered the species and genera in a spatial, not a temporal field. The knowledge which resulted from the visible identification was a taxonomic order. It was not concerned with organic life or function. Within a presupposedly uniform and continuous spatiality, questions of gradation and connection among species and genera, which subsequently were answered in bourgeois society as development-in-time, simply did not emerge. Natural history was a discontinuous taxonomic order within a continuous spatiality. By the second half of the eighteenth century, a few outstanding theoreticians did speculate that the earth was much older than biblical chronology had allowed. However, their concept of time was merely an analogy of space: within an enlarged space plus time, all the observable species and genera, all equally static, would find their proper locations. Such tentative speculation regarding time did not overthrow the fundamentally spatial framework of taxonomy. Within that framework, neither organic life nor development was possible. However, by the late eighteenth and early nineteenth centuries, historical geology and the organic study of life superseded taxonomic order.[26]

Formerly, scientists explained geological changes as the result of either water erosion (the theory of Neptunism) or heat (the theory of Vulcanism). Both types of change were equally catastrophic, not requiring a prolonged period of time. However, in 1785, James Hutton proposed that changes of the earth were gradual, resulting from various mechanical agents. This marked the beginning of the theory of uniformitarianism, as opposed to those of catastrophism. Hutton conceived of the earth as a self-evolving machine, endowed with its own laws. He maintained the belief in a providential God; but that God was conceived of by Hutton in deistic terms. Therefore, nature, once created by and separated from God, possessed its own regularity, consistency, and wisdom. Changes in nature were uniform and gradual, stretching over a tremendous expanse of time. Quite appropriately, Hutton conceived time to be without beginning or end, in sharp contrast to biblical chronology. In the 1790s, William Smith founded the science of stratigraphy to study the correlation of geological strata and fossil remains. Finally in 1830, Charles Lyell consolidated the theory of uniformitarianism, in his *Principles of Geology*. Lyell was more empirical and comprehensive than Hutton, and in his work proposed a far greater variety of mechanical agents for geological changes. Development-in-time had arrived on the geological scene. Nevertheless, both Hutton and Lyell still believed that species were fixed and nondevelopmental.

In the last third of the eighteenth century, natural history made a new distinction between the organic and the inorganic. It proposed that the characteristics of organic entity were the ones necessary for an organism's life and constituted a hierarchical structure. The conceptual principle of structure made possible the new science of biology, which appeared in 1802 as the study of organic life. Initially, the divergent views of Jean-Baptiste de Lamarck and Georges Cuvier dominated that study. Lamarck posited spontaneous generation from the inorganic to the organic, and transformation among the organic species. The pressure of environment would modify the characteristics of species; these modifications were directly passed on to subsequent generations. Hence, over prolonged time, species were transformed. The species continually strove for life; and the world itself was constantly in flux. Lamarck's theory of transformation still assumed a great chain of being. But his chain was no longer merely spatial in extension; it developed across time. Cuvier, on the other hand, believed that species were fixed and discontinuous, and that their changes were catastrophic. In contrast to Lamarck's theory of organic life extending throughout a temporalized continuum, Cuvier's paleontology focused on the co-

herent, dynamic function of each organism. For Cuvier, organic function was the basis for a comparative anatomy. Life did not pervade the
universe, as Lamarck had insisted; instead it resided within the organism. Both Lamarck's transformism and Cuvier's paleontology separated the study of organic life from the natural history of the
seventeenth and eighteenth centuries. Yet neither succeeded in extending geological uniformitarianism to the new biological science.

It remained for Darwin, in his theory of evolutionary biology, to
combine the geological principle of uniformitarianism with the study
of organic species. The new combination presupposed an absolutely
immanent temporal framework. Within this self-contained temporal
process, the Darwinians explained development in terms of three immanent causes. As Marjorie Grene said:

> In short, three concepts, *evolution,* in the minimal sense of 'de-
> scent with modification' (no 'emergence', no 'higher and lower'
> allowed), *variation,* in the sense of Mendelian micromutation,
> tiny fortuitous changes in the structure or arrangement of the
> genes, the ultimate material of heredity (no sweeping or sudden
> alterations allowed), and *natural selection,* the decrease in fre-
> quency of those variants that happen in each successive gener-
> ation to be less well adapted than others to their particular
> environment: these three form a tight circle within which, in happy
> self-confirmation, neo-Darwinian thinking moves.[27]

Each concept was already a hypothesis concerning an intermediate
level of development-in-time, not deducible from evidence alone, but
within which the visible evidence assumed significance. The three concepts together constituted the immanent dynamics to explain the evolution of species. Changes were not due to any transcendent causation
or teleology, or contained by any great chain of being. Instead, concept
and evidence reinforced each other to form a perceptual circuit. Within
the order of development-in-time, this perceptual circuit could cover
any apparent discontinuity in visible evidence. Darwinism believed that
were one to dig back in time, the evolution of species and genera would
be proven. Therefore, it has been an effective theory, pushing for further scientific discovery.

The Ages of Human Life

Parallel to the evolution of organic species, a lifespan in bourgeois
society, especially the bourgeois lifespan, consisted of different, dis-
tinguishable ages.[28] Already in estate society, the bourgeois family per-

ceived childhood as a distinct age between infancy and adulthood. In dress, games, mores, and moral teaching, the child was different from the adult. Concurrently, among the bourgeois, sentiment and loyalty began to shift from kinship to the nuclear family. The family was the institutionalization of a private, emotional space, as a safeguard against the new rationalization and objectification of economic life. And the new sentiment toward children occupied an important place in the privacy of the family. The concept of childhood began as an urban, bourgeois phenomenon, and thence spread elsewhere.

In bourgeois society, youth became yet another age separating childhood from adulthood. Previously, youth had been not so much an age, but a semidependent status in society, when one had already left the family to become an apprentice, a servant, a page, or a student elsewhere, but had not yet gotten married or set up an independent household. It had been, in effect, an intermediate space between family and society at large. But industrialization and urbanization both strengthened and prolonged the bourgeois family. Bourgeois youth now reverted from that intermediate space into the family. One stayed at home much longer after childhood, and had to go to school to acquire the necessary virtues of rationality and discipline, in preparation for the mature, adult world. In oppostion to this newly enforced dependency, youths sought other outlets in student organization and bohemian lifestyle.

Then, by the late nineteenth and early twentieth centuries, the prolonged training and delayed gratification which bourgeois youth had to undergo led to the phenomenon of adolescence. Adolescence was youth with all its problems of puberty, sexuality, and restlessness running rampant. Parents and educators promoted public schools, sports, and cold showers to cope with these problems. Novels and studies of adolescence became popular. The problems of adolescence were new, in the sense that family and other social institutions now made greater efforts than before to discipline youth. Finally, by the early twentieth century, Freud traced this turbulence all the way back to infantile sexuality. Not the child, but the infant had become the father to the man.

From infancy to childhood, from childhood to youth and adolescence, from youth to adulthood—life in bourgeois society was increasingly segmented into phases of development-in-time. The nuclear family, age-graded school, voluntary and law enforcement agencies, and contemporary literature all promoted this segmentation of life. In the apt characterization of J. H. van den Berg, contemporaries experienced life as a developmental escalator, with maturation an unrealizable goal.[29] This phenomenon of the segmentation of human life began with the bourgeoisie, then gradually infiltrated the lives of the aristocracy and eventually the lower classes, as it spread slowly from the urban center into the countryside. Finally, in the twentieth century, adulthood was further segmented into young adulthood, middle age, and old age. Life itself has become a developmental process which ends not in maturity, but with death.

The Evolution of Society

Contemporaries in the seventeenth and eighteenth centuries had experienced estate society as a vertical hierarchy. They had greater familiarity with all ranks and orders of people in their own community than with those of their own kind in distant places;[30] and to them this hierarchically ordered society seemed to persist in time. In other words, estate society was an order in space, which did not develop in time; and every fall from such order needed a "revolution," i.e., a restoration.

From within this spatialized hierarchy, objective reason represented society as a social contract founded on natural law. The theory of social contract was a rational critique of existing society, and challenged its claim of special privileges and prerogatives. Instead, the theory posited a contractual act in the transition from nature to society, with the contract as the foundation of society. Nevertheless, the theory of social contract was pre-evolutionary. It conceived of the transition from nature to society not as an event in time, but as a distinction in space.

However, the industrial and political revolutions of the late eighteenth century shattered the belief in a stable, spatialized hierarchy. The inhabitants of bourgeois society experienced it as being quite unstable, obviously changing, and sometimes even in conflict. Instead of a hierarchy of ranks and orders, society by the early nineteenth century became a horizontal stratification of classes, founded on the institutionalization of labor. "Class" came to mean social class, rather than hierarchical rank or order.[31] Throughout the nineteenth century, the deep chasm separating upper from lower classes reconfirmed the horizontal stratification of bourgeois society,[32] unlike the vertical hierarchy of estate society.

The new experience of horizontal class stratification required a change in the justification of societal order. Society itself has become problematical.[33] The previous natural law critique of society had not had to worry about whether or how society would hang together, since that world was experienced as a set, compact one. But in bourgeois society, both order in space (social statics) and change across time (social dynamics) required conscious explanations. In addition, there was the insoluble problem of explaining the transition from an order in space to change across time.

In the third quarter of the eighteenth century, the Scottish school of empirical philosophy began to discuss the problem of rank and class, of labor and wealth, in its study of society. By the end of the century, Thomas Malthus had written the influential *Principle of Population,* in which he argued that populational increase would always outstrip the growth of production, thus leading inevitably to increased poverty. Malthus's argument with its emphasis on deterministic laws was an exercise of social Newtonianism. In fact, it was the immanent dynamics of his argument which later so impressed Alfred Russell Wallace and Charles Darwin. But the Scottish empiricists and Thomas Malthus remained within the bounds of an objective reason in space—a reason modeled upon the mechanical sciences, not yet open to the new challenge of development-in-time. Jeremy Bentham and James Mill, the utilitarians, accepted the same spatial reason. The dimension of change in time was of secondary importance. But Lamarck's and Lyell's arguments for change in time became increasingly influential in the first half of the nineteenth century. In addition, both Condorcet's belief in the perfectibility of the human race and Henri de Saint-Simon's scheme of a reorganized social community presupposed a linear time framework. Evolution was in the air; and reality became a development-in-time. By the middle of the century, not only had Darwin and Wallace worked on evolutionary biology quite independently of each other; Auguste Comte in France and Herbert Spencer in England were separately writing on social evolution.

Both Comte and Spencer saw society as a rational system lodged in two separate compartments of space and time. Society in space was a functional structure with all the forces cohering to structure an order of social statics. Yet the same society was also a social dynamics, in the sense that it necessarily underwent the stages of an evolutionary development in time. Herein lay the contradiction. How could the same forces, identified by objective reason as the cause of social statics, also be the cause of social dynamics? Objective reason was unable to comprehend the different realities, with their different ongoing motives, in the different periods of a society. Nevertheless, the epistemic order of development-in-time contained that contradiction. Most contemporaries believed that objective reason was sufficient in accounting for development in time. In accepting the objective development-in-time, Comte and Spencer were representative thinkers of their time.

However, the gap between objective reason and social totality subsequently led most academic thinkers to shy away from the temporal dimension in their studies. On the one hand, Emile Durkheim concentrated on the explanation of social solidarity in space; on the other, the British anthropologists emphasized the rationality of functional structure within a given society. Neither were concerned with explaining society in transformation, for a proper account of the dynamics of society through time had to begin with a fundamental critique of objective reason.[34]

Rationality and Temporal Dynamics

Bourgeois society placed a premium on objective reason. Archimedean reason posited quantifiable mass in objective space and time, rather than the intersubjectivity of conscious, embodied life. By emphasizing the visual, the nonreflexive, this reason enabled the bourgeoisie to triumph over the "irrational" value orientation of the other classes. It located the conscious calculation of action in an impersonal space, where all nonobjective considerations would be discounted. In that space, knowledge of both the world and the human being became more objective and specialized. However, this objective reason would reduce the intersubjectivity of the world, as well as the reflexivity of embodied life. Objectification therefore opened new voids in knowledge, unknown in previous societies.

Development-in-time enlarged this objectification from a strictly spatial order to a temporal continuum. That was the significance of evolutionary biology and social evolution in the nineteenth century, when both species and society were symbolized as developmental processes. However, the reason that informed this development was still objective. The result was that the life of species as well as the prospective reality of society was eliminated by objective development-in-time. Objective reason flattened both life and prospective reality. As compensation, the explanation for both species and society was extended back into the remote past. The unanswerable aspects of the question "what is it?" were displaced by another question, "how did it evolve?" This was the fundamental contradiction in the epistemic order of objective development-in-time. However, objective development was so crucial to bourgeois ideology that its inherent contradiction was largely ignored. The criticism of objective development-in-time had to come from the outside, namely, from romanticism, Hegelian idealism, and historical materialism, as well as Nietzsche's concept of eternal recurrence.

Unlike the uniform, homogeneous space of objective reason, romanticism in the late eighteenth and early nineteenth centuries posited an immanent life world. Within this spatio-temporal immanence, the human being and nature retransacted the former supernatural symbols. "For the fact is that many of the most distinctive and recurrent elements in both the thought and literature of the age had their origin in theological concepts, images and plot patterns which were translated, in Wordsworth's terms, to men 'as natural beings in the strength of nature,' living in 'the world / Of all of us, the place in which, in the end, / We find our happiness, or not at all.' "[35] Thus, romanticism has been most aptly characterized as natural supernaturalism. In the world of the romantics, everything was more intimate, alive, and illuminated. Yet in its resymbolization of the supernatural, romanticism differed fundamentally from Christian anagogy which had presupposed the penetration of immanence by transcendence, as well as from Renaissance similitude which had assumed a correspondence between microcosm and macrocosm. For the romantics, the world was thoroughly immanent and natural. They emphasized the illumination of the moment, whether that moment in time was a mere present or an intimation of eternity.[36] The intensity of that moment in time provided romantics with the prospect of transcendence within immanence. The romantic moment was a rejection of the objective development-in-time; instead, time was to be overcome from within.

Hegelian idealism, unlike Platonic idealism, was a thoroughly worldly philosophy. From the present within time, it sought the reconciliation of idea and actuality. Idea was eternal; but that eternity was not a negation of time. Instead, idea actualized itself in time as spirit. Or, to put it the other way around, spirit in its self-consciousness could grasp the immanent development of idea, from the abstract to the concrete. This self-consciousness was possible because spirit in the present could know all the dimensions of time. Time itself, as the unity of past, present, and future, was eternal; and knowledge of this unity would transform the present into the eternal present. The present could therefore mediate between time and eternity. In the eternal present, spirit ascends to absolute knowedge, i.e., knows itself as spirit. Therefore, time was both the necessity and the freedom of spirit.[37]

In contrast to Hegelian idealism, Marx grounded social dynamics in historical materialist forces. The Marxian critique of objective development-in-time began with the concept of alienation, and its corollary, estrangement. Alienation defined the necessary interaction between the human being and the world. From the world, the human being derived sustenance; to it, the human being alienated, i.e., externalized, a part of the self, namely, labor.[38] Alienation as an economic necessity resulted in the estrangement of the human being. The degrees of alienation differed in different stages of historical materialist development, becoming most acute in industrial capitalism. Society, according to Marx, was a totality, a multi-level structure developing at various paces. There were the material forces of production; the economic structure (i.e., the social relations of production); the legal and political superstructure; and the corresponding forms of social consciousness. Therefore, alienation/estrangement infiltrated the human being at all the different levels and stages of structured social existence. Developmental time was not external to the human person. From within this structured, historical materialist totality, Marxian critique pointed to objective reason as a bourgeois ideology. "It is not the consciousness of men that determines their existence, but their social existence that determines their consciousness."[39] Instead of an objective reason, Marx posited a critical theoretical consciousness of totality, which could be the basis for revolutionary *praxis* to overcome human alienation/estrangement. From within the ongoing totality, the unity of theory and practice could accelerate historical/materialist development. As opposed to objective development-in-time, Marxism posited a dialectic of the subjective and the objective, consciousness and structure, critique and *praxis*.

In an entirely different way, Nietzsche also rejected objective development-in-time. For Nietzsche, "consciousness *is* a surface,"[40] a mere epiphenomenon which reduced the multiplicity and dynamics of life. "Everything of which we become conscious is a terminal phenomenon, an end—and causes nothing."[41] From within consciousness we made the errors of mistaking cause for consequence; of false causality; of imaginary causes; of free will.[42] Thus, the bourgeois concept of objective development-in-time was another reduction by consciousness. Life had its onward thrust, its force. Zarathustra had said: "And life itself confided this secret to me: 'Behold,' it said, 'I am that which must always overcome itself.' "[43] This transcendence within immanence, beyond all good and evil, Nietzsche would symbolize as will to power. "Life is not the adaptation of inner circumstances to outer ones, but will to power, which, working from within, incorporates and subdues more and more of that which is 'outside.' "[44] Beyond will to power, however, the intimation of absolute immanence culminated in Nietzsche's prophecy of Eternal Recurrence:

> This world: a monster of energy, without beginning, without end;
> . . . a sea of forces flowing and rushing together, eternally changing, eternally flooding back, with tremendous years of recurrence, with an ebb and a flood of its forms. . . ; this, my *Dionysian* world of the eternally self-creating, the eternally self-destroying, this mysterious world of the twofold voluptuous delight, my "beyond

good and evil," without goal, unless the joy of the circle is itself a goal.[45]

The illumination of the romantic moment, the eternal present of the Hegelian spirit, the dialectic of the Marxian unity of theory and practice, and Nietzsche's eternal recurrence—each in a different way rejected objective development-in-time. Temporal dynamics was not mere developmental series. It was multi-dimensional as well as inter-subjective, involving both body and mind, individual and society. Hence, it could not be symbolized by objective reason alone.

Spatiality

Spatiality as lived, humanly oriented space is a perceptual, horizonal extension. It is more fundamental than any objective, measurable space. Yet it is not just personal and private, but intersubjective. Society provides for certain symbols and institutions to organize spatial orientation, within which perceptual connections then become possible. In any given period, there are a variety of spatial organizations, providing for different, complementary perceptual prospects. In estate society, immanent, rational spatial representation was the dominant epistemic order, putting pressure on the traditional symbols and institutions. However, within the bourgeois perceptual field constituted by typographic culture, the primacy of sight, and the epistemic order of development-in-time, spatial organizations had to reflect and encompass the new dynamics of bourgeois society. In this chapter, I shall describe the new space of political economy; the authorization of political space; planning and urban space; the family and private space; the novel and typographic space; as well as painting and visual space, in bourgeois society.

The New Space of Political Economy

Estate society in the seventeenth and eighteenth centuries did not have a science of political economy. Instead, it analyzed wealth within a much more restricted, nondynamic space of circulation and exchange. According to its analysis, cultivated and manufactured goods could be exchanged for one another, or for money. Therefore, in addition to their usefulness, they acquired an exchange value in relation to each other. The circulation and exchange of goods generated wealth within this systematized space. Money itself did not possess any intrinsic value, but was a representation of wealth in circulation. The system presupposed an agrarian economy with limited manufacture, where production had not yet displaced circulation as the economic center of gravity. And contemporaries believed that the circulation should be as simple and comprehensive as possible, rather like William Harvey's mechanical model for the circulation of the blood in the human body. The state could facilitate the circulation of wealth by either the physiocratic policy of fostering agriculture, or the mercantilist policy of promoting export over import. Both physiocracy and mercantilism accepted the validity of this system of circulation and exchange. The system did not comprehend production, supply and demand, banking and monetary policy, since these phenomena were not yet amenable to the analysis by spatial reason.[1]

Then, for almost a century in bourgeois society, from approximately 1776 to 1870, the new science of political economy carved out a new, enlarged space quite different from that of the seventeenth- and eighteenth-century analysis of wealth. Instead of circulation and exchange, the new discipline comprehended production and exchange. Political economy proposed a much more dynamic spatiality to analyze industrial capitalism.

For Adam Smith, political economy was *"An Inquiry into the Nature and Causes of the Wealth of Nations,"* the title of his work published in 1776. The wealth of a nation was a ratio between what its labor produced and what its population consumed. The ratio depended on the skill and judgment with which a nation's labor was applied, as well as on the proportion between those employed in useful and those in nonuseful labor. The labor theory of value was the all-important factor linking production and exchange into a single system. The natural price or exchange value of a manufactured commodity, around which fluctuated its market price, was the cost of its production. This cost included both the wage paid to the worker for his or her sustenance and the profit paid to the capitalist in return for the use of capital stock. The exchange value of farm produce, on the other hand, included the wage and profit of the tenant farmer as well as the rent, which was a price paid for the use of the land. Political economy promoted wealth through the efficient allocation and use of wage, profit, and rent. Ideally, this allocation and use depended on the workings of an unfettered market, wherein all commodities competed openly.

The space of political economy as defined by Smith extended beyond that of the seventeenth and eighteenth centuries' analysis of wealth. Instead of being restricted to the space of circulation and exchange, wealth in political economy resided within a much more dynamic system linking production and exchange. The labor theory of value was the underlying factor which made possible that linkage. Smith assumed that "equal quantities of labor must at all times and places be of equal value to the laborer" (1st ed., book I, chapter v). Production and exchange now became analyzable phenomena within an enlarged, common space. Political economy perceived the system of production and exchange within this space as being autonomous, self-contained, much less dependent on the state than the old analysis of wealth. However, it extracted a human price for the workings of the new system. The human being became a mere "economic man" to political economy.

David Ricardo, in his *Principles of Political Economy and Taxation* (1817), refined Smith's system of production and exchange. Ricardo's theory also dealt with the distribution of rent, profit, and wage. However, he criticized Smith for basing exchange value on the cost of labor in production. Instead, Ricardo insisted that it was the relative quantity of labor in production, not its cost, which determined the relative value of a commodity in the market. With his concept of quantitative labor, he then undertook a calculus of rising and falling rent, profit, and wage, "depending mainly on the actual fertility of the soil, on the accumulation of capital and population, and on the skill, ingenuity and instruments employed in agriculture" (Preface). The result was a much more rigorous and quantifiable system than that of Adam Smith. However, Ricardo still restricted his system to production and exchange. He still presupposed a Malthusian, mechanistic interaction between populational growth and growth in production. Supply and demand were of no account.

John Stuart Mill, in *Principles of Political Economy* (1848), implicitly criticized the restricted mathematical system of Ricardo by going back to the system of Adam Smith. At least Smith had recognized that political economy was intertwined with other branches of social philosophy, so that no practical question could be decided by mathematical calculation alone. Nevertheless, much in Smith's system was obsolete by the mid-nineteenth century and had to be brought up to date. Most significantly, Mill placed political economy within a historical framework (preliminary remarks and book IV)—a dimension neglected by Smith and Ricardo. The system of political economy, according to Mill, was not entirely spatial. The laws of production might resemble the physical laws of nature; but those of distribution, upon which exchange value was based, depended on institutional, psychological, and ideological considerations, and therefore varied over time. Within an enlarged spatio-temporal framework, Mill cautiously revised the concept of exchange value, as well as downgraded its importance. He typically began by agreeing with Ricardo that exchange value depended on the quantity of labor required for the production of a commodity. However, he went on to qualify that, by saying it also depended on wage and profit. In fact, Mill subtly shifted the entire basis of exchange value from the laws of production to the laws of supply and demand. By enlarging the space of political economy to include supply and demand, he necessarily brought in many more social, historical considerations. Thus Mill could proceed to downgrade

Smith's and Ricardo's preoccupation with exchange value. He separated exchange value from the physical laws of production, and made it dependent on social, historical changes. In fact, he even anticipated the need for a regulatory, if not an outright welfare, state. Nevertheless, Mill's diffident revision did not overthrow the theories of Smith and Ricardo. Political economy restricted itself to the analysis of production and exchange, girded by the Malthusian vision of growing populational pressure on a not too dynamic economy.

However from 1870 to 1914, first with the works of Jevons, Menger, and Walras, then finally with Alfred Marshall's *Principles of Economy* (1890), the theory of supply and demand displaced that of production and exchange. Marginal utility succeeded political economy. By then, a much more dynamic market economy put to rest the old Malthusian demographic pessimism. But marginal utility's analysis of this market economy was highly specialized and technical. In a sense, it was even more restrictive than political economy, in accepting without question the existing social and economic institutions which supported the market. Marshall correctly emphasized that marginal utility was a continuation of political economy. His analysis was the heir to the positivism of Smith and Ricardo. According to Marshall, supply, in terms of production, and demand, in terms of final utility, were the two blades of a pair of scissors. But he did not ask who wielded that pair of scissors, for whose benefit.

Political economy confined itself to the analysis of production and exchange, and marginal utility to that of supply and demand. Both theories accepted without question the existing social and economic institutions; both assumed the psychology of economic rationality, i.e., that the human motivation underlying production and exchange as well as supply and demand would conform to the rationality of "economic man." Therefore political economy and its successor, marginal utility, were the ideologies of industrial capitalism. It remained for Marx to undertake the most thorough critique of the limited rationality of political economy.

Already in *The Economic and Philosophic Manuscripts of 1844,* Marx had criticized political economy for merely expressing the general abstract formulas of the material process of production, without exposing the human alienation which underlay production. Capitalist production approached both labor and the worker as commodities in a freely competitive market. The object produced by labor confronted the worker as something alien, with a power quite independent of the producer.

The alienation of the worker in his product means not only that his labor becomes an object, an external existence, but that it exists outside him, independently, as something alien to him, and that it becomes a power on its own confronting him. It means that the life which he has conferred on the object confronts him as something hostile and alien.[2]

By transcending the space of political economy, Marx pointed to the alienation which underlay it. The *Grundrisse* of 1857–58 located that alienation in the very process of capitalist production. Capitalist production necessarily had to extract the difference between the use value of labor power, which went into production, and the exchange value of labor power, which was the wage paid to the worker, in order to obtain surplus value. And in the well-known preface to *A Contribution to the Critique of Political Economy* (1859), Marx replaced the uni-level space of political economy with the multi-level structure of a spatio-temporal totality: At the bottom were the material forces of production; in accord with these forces were the appropriate social relations of production, or economic structure; on that foundation arose the legal, political superstructure; to which corresponded definite forms of social consciousness.

Political economy presupposed the alienation of "economic man." Marx exposed that alienation as the foundation of estrangement in bourgeois society. This estrangement, as I shall argue, was the perceptual dynamics which brought about changes in the authorization of political space, the planning of urban space, the family in private space, the novel in typographic space, and painting in visual space.

The Authorization of Political Space

Political space in the estate society of the seventeenth and eighteenth centuries was a formalized hierarchy, founded on the special prerogatives given by God and by birth, not amenable to objective reason. The major concerns within that formalized hierarchy were with precedence, honor, and territoriality, and the money necessary to wage war in order to maintain them. The space, though traditional and pre-rational, was by then visually enhanced by the grandeur of baroque symbolization. In contrast, the natural law critique of that space replaced the tradition of special prerogatives with a theory of social contract: There was no political space in the state of nature, but in civil society the social contract authorized such a political space, within which constitutional discourse and political exchange then became possible. The extent of this space was bounded by Hobbes's absolute monarch, Locke's private property, or Rousseau's general will. These were not open to question. The foundation of political space by social contract however was not an event in time, but a logical necessity. The intent of the logic of social contract was to criticize the traditional, prerational space of the *ancien régime*. Development-in-time was not yet a perceivable order. A fundamental gulf separated the immemorial tradition of *ancien régime* and the rationality of social contract.

In bourgeois society, the French and the industrial revolutions transformed the authorization of political space. The political revolution put an end to the formalized hierarchy of the *ancien régime*. In its place, revolutionaries realized for the time being an atemporal space of social contract. Theory has become reality. Having cut their ties with the past, revolutionaries relied on reason to anticipate the future. And the rationality of the new political authority presented the problem of continuity to both revolutionaries and their opponents. Concurrently, the industrial revolution subverted the social hierarchy upon which the old political space was based. It transformed the experience of society from one of vertical hierarchy to one of horizontal class stratification. The horizon of politics had widened to include new social issues which affected classes of people beyond the limited experience of one's own local hierarchy. Thus the two revolutions exposed the problems of temporal continuity and social depth for the new political space in bourgeois society. We can sample the different approaches to these problems by Robespierre, Burke, J. S. Mill, and de Tocqueville.

Robespierre the incorruptible revealed, in a number of speeches made during 1791–94, his Rousseauesque approach to the political space.[3] The human heart could comprehend the eternal laws of justice and of reason which transcended space and time. Nevertheless, false understanding and poor social customs had often in the past led to bad laws and maladministration. Tyranny and republic were typologies of bad and good political orders, with the former founded on human principles, the latter on eternal principles. Between the bad and good orders, i.e., between the *ancien régime* of the past and the revolutionary present, there could be neither continuity nor comparability. Robespierre had a tremendous sense of discontinuity in time. For him, the world had changed drastically, and was bound to change again. Hence history taught nothing, although one could learn lessons from the examples of other places. Nevertheless, changing circumstances justified different applications of the eternal laws. Robespierre recognized the great pressure of revolutionary events on political space. He distinguished revolutionary government from an eventually more permanent type of republican government. The former, according to him, was so new that no theory could anticipate its problems. Revolutionary government was subject to less binding and uniform regulations, since the circumstances surrounding it were so tempestuous and unstable. The political space of Robespierre was a present intimation of eternity, cut adrift from the tyrannical past.

In contrast, Edmund Burke, in *Reflections on the Revolution in France* (1790), questioned the very rationality of the new political space. Instead he conceived of political space as a continuous chain in time, within which the action and interaction of opposing, conflicting interests across the generations drew out the harmony of the universe. If history taught Burke anything, it was that human miseries were brought on by such disorderly appetites as pride, ambition, avarice, lust, revenge, sedition, hypocrisy, and ungoverned zeal. According to Burke, one should not view human actions in abstraction, since their outcomes depended on changing circumstances. Political wisdom therefore should take into account the spatio-temporal continuum. Society was a partnership among the living, the dead, and the yet to be born: "Each contract of each particular state is but a clause in the great primeval contract of eternal society, linking the lower with the higher natures, connecting the visible with the invisible world, according to a fixed compact sanctioned by the inviolable oath which holds all physical and moral natures, each in their appointed place."[4] The interest of no single group or generation should prevail over the rest. Therefore, rational change was always hazardous, to be avoided at all cost. The American Revolution was for Burke only a reformation to preserve ancient laws and liberties; it did not break with the past. On the other hand, the French Revolution was an innovation which broke the bounds across time. The new rational spirit, according to Burke, had transformed France into a play table for gamesters; and those accustomed to day-to-day calculation, such as "the burghers and the monied directors," would seize the advantage, to the detriment of all others.

Yet what Burke feared most regarding the fragmentation of political space had already been advocated by Jeremy Bentham in *An Introduction to the Principles of Morals and Legislation* (1780). There, Bentham justified all human actions by his principle of utility, or the greatest happiness of the greatest number as the measure of right and wrong. Primarily a critic of the *ancien régime,* Bentham was not concerned with the foundation of a new political space. However, half a century later, John Stuart Mill, his erstwhile disciple, had to rethink the implications of the Benthamite principle of utility. For Mill, political space could not be founded on any abstract, rational contract. As he pointed out in *Considerations of Representative Government* (1861), it had to rely on the willing support of the people. The form of a government was therefore relative to a particular people, and should be approached in that way. Besides, politics was not an absolute end; it had to be balanced and limited by other ends and considerations. In *On Liberty* (1859), Mill tried to balance the end of the individual with the end of authority. The latter, he feared, could very well become the morality of an ascending class, and degenerate into the tyranny of a majority. To guard against such danger, that liberty of the individual which did not prejudicially affect others should always be considered inviolable. The political space of Mill reflected the growing pain and adjustment of bourgeois society in the mid-nineteenth century. Within that space, Mill, always a self-conscious, empirical rationalist, tried to promote progress.[5]

Against the background of repeated political upheavals in France, an increasingly more harried and conservative Alexis de Tocqueville had a more acute sense of the tension and limitation of poitical space in bourgeois society than did Mill. From his conservative standpoint, de Tocqueville extended the analysis of the political space to include civil society. The freedom and liberty which he always treasured, de Tocqueville admitted, were possible only in a community where the ties of family, caste, class, and craft fraternity were strong. On the other hand, the new principle of equality and democracy presupposed a leveling of all ideas, sentiments, morals, and customs in society. Yet, de Tocqueville admitted, equality was inevitable in the modern world, as the old community ties were broken up by bourgeois money and individualism. In America, equality had been the operative principle since the late eighteenth century. In France, even before 1789 the separation and isolation of aristocracy, bourgeoisie, and peasantry had already subverted the principle of freedom; and the struggle between aristocratic freedom and bourgeois equality since 1789 ended with the decisive triumph of the bourgeois principle in 1830. De Tocqueville's political analysis comprehended both spatial extension and temporal continuity. He claimed that political authority stemmed from civil society, and that the origins of modern egalitarianism could be traced back to prerevolutionary days. Nevertheless, de Tocqueville feared that equality by itself, unchecked by aristocratic freedom, would degenerate into despotism. Therefore, he felt justified in upholding the concept of freedom in bourgeois France.[6]

Robespierre, Burke, Mill, and de Tocqueville, each from a different vantage point, dealt with the problems of social depth and temporal continuity in the new political space. Each, in varying degrees, still regarded this space as the preeminent, self-contained domain of bourgeois society, possessed of its own rationality. It remained for Marx to question the very integrity of this space, and reveal it as a superstructure founded on an underlying economic structure. In both

Critique of Hegel's Philosophy of Right (1843) and *On the Jewish Question* (also 1843), Marx reversed Hegel's relation between civil society and political state. In theory, civil society might appear to be a stage leading to the rational state; but in actuality, the former was the presupposition of the latter, and membership in civil society was prior to citizenship in the state. The development, according to Marx, always took place at the actual, rather than the theoretical, level. Then, in the 1844 introduction to his *Critique,* Marx singled out the proletariat as the negation of civil society. From within civil society, the proletariat would be the immanent force to transcend the status quo. The Marxian dialectic of class struggle undercut the limited rationality of political space in bourgeois society.

Planning and Urban Space

Town planning, in the sense of comprehending and coordinating all the different aspects of an entire urban community, was absent before the period of bourgeois society. In the Renaissance, visual perspective founded on mathematical ratio restricted itself mostly to the symmetry and proportion of buildings and piazzas. In estate society, both monarchy and the church utilized visual perspective to create the impression of monumentality and infinite power in their palaces, churches, and gardens. The preindustrial town changed gradually over time; and the demographic, economic forces which led to the growth or decay of a town were invisible to contemporaries. However, in bourgeois society, industrialization and urbanization transformed the urban landscape so drastically as to provoke new, conscious responses to the problems of spatial extent and social depth in urban space.[7]

Initially, during the late eighteenth and early nineteenth centuries, the traditional baroque and neoclassical styles remained in fashion. The uniform crescent facades at Bath, the rue de Rivoli facade in Paris, the Regent Street development in London, the series of enclosed garden squares with surrounding housing in London from Bedford Square (1776) to Gordon Square (1860)—all typified the traditional approach. These limited urban developments maintained a standard of esthetic visuality which catered to the taste of the upper classes. But they either ignored or fended off the threat of the new demographic, economic changes in the cities.

The really new response was the entirely new communities established by a few paternalist manufacturers or by utopian socialists outside of the existing urban centers. Examples of the former were the model villages of Copley, Saltaire, and Akroydon in the West Riding of Yorkshire; examples of the latter were the utopian communities inspired by Robert Owen, Charles Fourier, and Étienne Cabet. Both types of communities were sporadic, highly individualist responses to the impact of the industrial revolution, and never led to any sustained development. Nevertheless, they were noteworthy as conscious attempts to set up small, integral communities apart from the urban industrial centers. Instead of mere esthetic or financial considerations, town planning by paternalist manufacturers and utopian socialists took into account the needs and activities of the inhabitants of these communities. Each community was functionally divided into living and working areas, with empty spaces separating them. In addition, there were recreational areas. These planned, standardized communities were an alternative to the congested, chaotic urban centers. Yet by being apart from the latter, they testified to the difficulty of improving on the existing urban sprawl.

In the expanding urban centers, reformers agitated for and eventually got better sanitation, sewage, and transportation. But these efforts did not represent town planning in any holistic sense. The prime example of city planning in the nineteenth century was Haussmann's modernization of Paris, in the fifties and sixties. Haussmann provided the sprawling growth of Paris with an arterial network of broad boulevards, water supply, sewage and gas lines. Although he also included greenery and promenades in his modernization, the visual esthetic element was secondary. Primary was his concern for the efficient circulation grids of Paris, which catered basically to the financial interest of the upper-bourgeois supporters of Napoleon III. Joseph Paxton in 1855 proposed a somewhat similar Great Victorian Way for the east-west traffic flow of London. Though never carried out, Paxton's route anticipated that of the London underground developed in 1863.[8] Neither Haussmann nor Paxton set out to transform the city. They wanted only to streamline it, in order to facilitate the existing economic, demographic forces. Both left untouched the social problem of large urban sprawl. Only at the end of this period, in the late nineteenth and early twentieth centuries, did town planning finally emerge as a holistic, dynamic proposition. This could be seen in the works or projects of Tony Garnier, Ebenezer Howard, and Patrick Geddes.

Garnier's *cité industrielle* project of 1901–4 was the leading example of urban, industrial planning which took into account all the economic and demographic factors, as well as the latest technology in reinforced concrete and electricity. Garnier adopted a regional approach to town planning. He distributed the different spatial zones in his planned medium-size industrial city according to the topography of the land; separated industries, public buildings, residential area, and schools by means of greenery; and integrated the architecture, landscaping, and interior design within each zone. Although he was never able to carry out the project, the *cité industrielle* with its emphasis on the importance of industry, the separation of urban functions, and the consideration of arterial circulation did eventually influence the development of urban planning.[9]

Howard's garden city was the culmination of the English tradition of integrating town with countryside. This tradition had earlier led to the development of Bourneville, Port Sunlight, and Birkenhead Park; and in turn the tradition was reinforced by the social criticism of Ruskin and Morris. Howard's idea itself later led to the construction of Letchworth and the Hempstead Garden Suburbs by Parker and Unwin, in the 1890s. In his *Garden Cities of To-morrow* (1898, revised 1902), Howard spoke of a town-country magnet which could combine the attraction of urban society with rural setting. A garden city of approximately a thousand acres, with a population of 30,000, surrounded by a green belt of five thousand acres was his ideal. The city would have sufficient manufacture to support most of its population. But the city municipality would own and control urban development, in order to prevent undue growth. Howard's garden city was not socialism, but a community controlled by an aroused public.

Geddes, in his *Cities in Evolution* (written in 1909–10, enlarged in 1915), placed town planning in a total spatio-temporal framework. Not only would he involve the geographer, hygienist, and sociologist in studying the "hows," or spatial dynamics, of a city; but he also envisaged such temporal questions as the "whence" and "whither" of a city, i.e., its past and future. The present, according to Geddes, was a transition from the paleotechnic to the neotechnic city. Paleotechnic competition had led to "conurbation" and slums, with the corresponding depletion of energy and resources, and the deterioration of human life. The neotechnic order of the future held out for Geddes the prospect of a balance between humanity and environment, between beauty and utility, the rural and the urban. In order to obtain that balance, town planning had to be total. Each city possessed its own life history. In order to capture that civic personality, the plan for the neotechnic city would take into account such diverse factors as situation, topography and natural advantages, means of communication, industries, manufacture and commerce, and population, as well as conditions in the past and in the future.

The new economic and demographic forces in bourgeois society had dynamically transformed the urban landscape. Although the effects of blight, congestion, and slum were all too visible, town planning initially did not go beyond the visual level of esthetic consideration, and did not grapple with the new forces. The tradition of visual perspective in town planning sought merely to preserve the taste and value of the upper classes. Then, some paternalist manufacturers and utopian socialists began to found new communities apart from the urban, industrial sprawl. The works of Haussmann and Paxton attempted to modernize the urban center. But Tony Garnier, Ebenezer Howard, and Patrick Geddes extended the perceptual framework of urban space to include all the invisible forces as well as visible features which went into the planning of a modern city. (We should also mention the *ciudad lineal* of Arturo Soria y Mata [1882] and the *Städtebau* of Camillo Sitte [1889].) By the twentieth century, urban planning finally transcended visual perspective.

The Family and Private Space

Family occupies a different space from that of kinship; the former is one of privacy, whereas the latter is a communal solidarity. There was no continuous development from traditional kinship to the modern family.[10] In estate society, as it became more involved in rational, commercial activities, the bourgeoisie began to emphasize the privacy of the family as a compensatory space. Rationality invaded this private space. The home now had private, special rooms for different purposes, rather than general, all-purpose rooms. Birth control became a method of family limitation. Moreover, a new ideal of domesticity emerged within the family. Childhood became an intermediary age between infancy and adulthood, when cuddling and protection were needed. However, the new privacy of the family had not yet displaced the old solidarity of kinship, but existed alongside it. Parents still apprenticed their children to other households as servants, apprentices, and pages, rather than keeping them at home. Nevertheless, by the eighteenth century, especially in France, the bourgeoisie began to substitute formal education for in-service training.[11]

Bourgeois society consolidated the privacy of the family. It promoted the separation of the workplace from the home, so that the bourgeois family, financed by the new industrial wealth, did not have to confront its operation. The differentiation of sex roles paralleled the separation of workplace and private family. The male went out to work, whereas the female stayed at home.[12] However, the family was not immune to the influence of economic values, and its ideals were increasingly defined in material, monetary terms.[13] By the second half of the nineteenth century, the bourgeois family lived the myth of social mobility through conspicuous consumption. The prosperity of the fifties and sixties not only improved the bourgeoisie's standard of living, but enhanced its expectations. Young adults delayed marriage in order to maintain and improve their standard of living. The bourgeois family spent an increasingly higher percentage of its income to maintain a larger number of servants, so that the mistress of the house could be idle. Quite revealingly, in the late nineteenth century feminists did not advocate birth control as a part of the liberation of women. Instead, housewives practiced it in order to maintain a proper standard of living.[14]

The emphasis on the privacy of the family in bourgeois society led to two phenomena: a particular style in interior decoration and a "Victorian" ideal of femininity. The bourgeoisie had a compulsion to fill up the visible space of the home with excessive furnishing and intricate decoration. They cluttered every room in the house with objects. The eye seemed to abhor any visible, empty space.[15] In addition, a sentimentalized, asexual eroticism pervaded the invisible space of the home, through the conduct and ideology of the proper Victorian lady. Beginning in the thirties and forties, the literature concerning the proper behavior of the bourgeois housewife became popular in England. In France, the clerics supplemented that literature with their counseling both inside and outside of the confession booth.[16] Both interior decoration and "Victorian" femininity were means by which the private space of the family could compensate for the estrangement in the public world.

The sharpened demarcation of the public and private spaces in bourgeois society institutionalized the contemporary opposition between reason and sentiment, between man and woman. In effect, the bourgeois home became the space for feminized sentiment as well as sentimentalized female. This private space supposedly would make up for all that was lacking in the outside world. But neither sentiment nor femininity was whole; each was a bourgeois bifurcation, the other side of the coin to the equally deformed concepts of reason and masculinity.

Against this background, the ideology of the family and its guardian angel becomes understandable. Take, as a typical example from the vast literature, Ruskin's lecture "Of Queens' Gardens" (1864). According to him, each sex had what the other lacked and complemented the other. Man was active and progressive; he was the doer, the creator. Woman, on the other hand, ordered and arranged; her great function was to praise and appreciate. "The man, in his rough work in the open world, must encounter all peril and trial. . . . But he guards the woman from all this; within his house, as ruled by her . . . enter no danger, no temptation, no cause of error or offense. This is the true nature of home—it is the place of Peace; the shelter." Therefore, "she must be enduringly, incorruptibly good; instinctively, infallibly wise." The education of a woman's mind should "confirm its natural instincts of justice, and refine its natural tact of love." To accomplish that end, "all such knowledge should be given her . . . not as knowledge . . . but only to feel, and to judge."[17]

The ideology of the family was a bit too shrill. It tried to camouflage repressed tensions in the family, as well as compensate for the family's estrangement from the outside world. Any critique of the bourgeois family had to take into account that private space which sustained it, and the impact of society at large upon the private space. Feminist critique, utopian critique, socialist-anarchist critique—each became more thorough, as it rejected the private-public spatial separation in bourgeois society.

Mary Wollstonecraft, in *A Vindication of the Rights of Woman* (1792), concentrated on the equal education of woman, but indirectly discussed the issue of the family. Though accepting the necessity of the family as an institution, she thought it was deformed by the separate, unequal education for man and woman. Instead, she would have liked to have had a family based on natural reason, fostered by equal education. Wollstonecraft had great faith in the effectiveness of that education. With man and woman in common, equally educated in regard to their rights and duties, they would become better partners and parents. John Stuart Mill, in *The Subjection of Women* (1869), pointed out that woman's legal subordination made her a slave of the father and the husband. At home she was taught self-negation; outside, she was kept ignorant. In turn, the husband often became willful and self-indulgent. Thus the family turned into a despotism. Only with the establishment of legal equality for women, so argued Mill, could the family proceed to cultivate the virtues of freedom. In France, Maria Desraismes, in *Eve dans l'humanité* (1869), argued in a similar vein. She saw the family as the means for the education and cultivation of the individual. However by legitimizing the existing inequality of the sexes, the family actually perpetuated the double standard for man and woman. The wife, supposedly dedicated to the family, knew no civic virtues and could not be a good citizen. Hence family as an existing institution operated against the civic needs of society. According to Desraismes, only equal rights for man and woman could end this contradiction.

Feminist critique of the family was limited and indirect. Though critical of the existing family arrangement, Wollstonecraft, Mill, and Deraismes were primarily concerned with the equality of education, law, and civic rights for women in the public space. They did not challenge the institution of the family itself, or criticize the separation of public and private spaces in bourgeois society. Instead they believed that if women were treated equally in the public space, the family would right itself in the private space. Feminist critique contributed little to the solution of the problem of the bourgeois family. A notable exception was Charlotte Perkins Gilman, who, in *Women and Economics* (1898) and *The Home* (1902), criticized the confinement of woman to the private, domestic space, thus restricting her to a life of hypersensitivity, pleasure, and consumption. However, Gilman believed that with the recent mechanization and socialization of domestic work the sphere of the home would contract and woman be liberated to participate in the economic progress of society. And, in general, the feminist movement for equal rights in the late nineteenth and early twentieth centuries kept rather aloof from the issue of the family.[18]

Utopian critique of the family stemmed from a perspective which sought to transcend bourgeois society. Hence it was more throrough in its rejection of the separation of the public and private spaces in bourgeois society. William Thompson, in *Appeal of One Half of the Human Race* (1825), criticized political economy for not only encouraging individualist competition, but also excluding and enslaving one half of the human race, namely, women. The man, with his control of money and justice, dominated over the wife. Thompson attacked the family as being the husband's house, but the wife's prison. Instead of the bourgeois system of political economy, Thompson advocated an Owenite system of association, or labor through mutual cooperation. In the new system of equal, communal ownership and living, man and woman would pair with each other on the basis of natural affection, and raise children cooperatively. However, in the meantime, argued Thompson, women should demand equal rights and justice. Charles Fourier attacked the institutions of bourgeois society throughout his life.[19] Instead of a society of competitive commerce and private family, Fourier envisaged an order of phalanges which would permit men and women of different characters, passions, instincts, and tastes to intermingle freely both at work and in pleasure. Here, everyone could have variety, in order to satisfy his or her inclinations. Fourier believed that fidelity was against human nature, and that the restriction of monogamous marriage led to unhappiness and deceit. The husband tried to escape from it; the wife was oppressed by it; and the children rebelled against it. Forced into this constricted space, members of the family fled from each other, in search of companies to their own likings. Hence, the family was not a pivot of, but rather a very crude, unworkable clog in, existing society.

Utopian critique of the family posited an all-encompassing, integral space, founded on rational cooperation or the harmonizing of human passions and needs. The new spatial organization would replace the bourgeois separation of the public and private spaces, which utopian critics believed to be contrary to human nature. In their critique, they saw a close connection between competitive individualism and the privacy of the family. They were equally critical of both. The problem was soluble no longer by piecemeal reform, but by total social reorganization. Only in an integral space of the future could human aspirations be fulfilled.

Socialist critics like Engels and anarchist critics like Emma Goldman exposed the economic structure underlying the institution of the private family. Engels, in *The Origins of the Family, Private Property and the State* (1884), placed the development of the family within the framework of an evolutionary anthropology. From savagery through barbarism to civilization, the family evolved from group marriage through pairing to monogamy. The monogamous family was founded on private property and male supremacy; therefore the subjection of woman coincided with the appearance of class struggle. Capitalism transformed the monogamous marriage even more blatantly into a business transaction involving private property. Nevertheless, within the confines of bourgeois marriage arose the ideal of sexual love. Engels predicted that, with the abolition of private property, the economic foundation of the family would disappear; and under socialism, both housekeeping and child rearing would become public concerns. Then marriage, freed from its economic fetters, would be truly based on sexual love. Goldman, in a number of articles written in the late 1900s, especially "Marriage and Love," advocated the true emancipation of woman.[20] Marriage, according to her, was primarily an economic arrangement, which condemned the woman to lifelong dependency and parasitism. With its barren monotony and sordidness, marriage had failed to achieve harmony and understanding between man and woman. Love and marriage, Goldman believed, were contradictory. One could have either, but not both. Only in a free, unrestricted love, unhampered by the inevitable economic considerations of a marriage, could one achieve true companionship.

Both Engels and Goldman saw the bourgeois family as being a captive of the economic structure; and both valued sexual love. For Engels, that love would belong to the family in a socialist society, free from the necessity of economic exploitation. Goldman's ideal of love would depend on no institutional support. It was a personal attainment in the present.

The Novel and Typographic Space

Printing made possible a typographic space. Within this space, a communication between the writer and the reader unfolds. That communication is neither oral, nor chirographic, nor yet electronic. It is a silent, detached one-way address by the writer, using linguistic signs, which the reader receives through the eyes. From the late eighteenth to the early twentieth century, the bourgeois novel provided a hierarchical structure of perspectives within this typographic space of communication.[21]

The novel tells a story. But that telling is not an unchanging form. Narrative in the bourgeois novel was a three-level structure of perspectival consciousness: at the basic level, the first- or third-person narrator, whose point of view, whether subjective or omniscient, gave coherence to the story; at the second level, characters with their conflicting perspectives, emergent and changing as they lived the development of the plot; and at the third level, the horizon of the fictional world, with its institutions, values, and prospects. None of the three levels coincided. Instead, their hierarchical structure enabled the bourgeois novel to present a meaningful, connected development which often was not available in the real world of everyday life.

Before this period, the novel had not yet realized the hierarchical structure of multi-level perspectival consciousness. It appeared in bourgeois society as an antithesis to the increasing objectification of the world by Archimedean reason. The novel's topic was always the conflict of characters as seen from a single, consistent point of view, against the background of a fictional world whose values were no longer unquestioned. The reader, with an estranged subjectivity disconnected from the real world, would silently, vicariously enjoy the meaningful, connected development of a subjectivity in the novel. However, by the end of this period, as linear perspective itself became problematical, the hierarchical structure in the novel fell apart.

The narrative of estranged subjectivity had begun shortly before this period, with Samuel Richardson's epistolary novels *Pamela* (1740) and *Clarissa* (1748). Neither the aristocratic world of passion in Mme. de La Fayette's *La Princesse de Clèves* (1678), nor the bourgeois world of money in Defoe's *Moll Flanders* (1722), produced characters with estranged subjectivity. In a sense, Marivaux's *La Vie de Marianne* (1731–41), with its use of the memoir to undertake character analysis and social commentary, anticipated Richardson's epistolary novels. But Marianne's retrospective memoir lacked the immediacy and sensation of Pamela's and Clarissa's "instantaneous" letters. However, in *Pamela,* Richardson had not yet been able to separate the fictional world from the heroine's view of it, since she was both the narrator and leading character. Thus, there was only one prevailing perspective, namely, Pamela's; and the reader could not find out how accurate or exaggerated her view of the events was. In *Clarissa,* Richardson employed a number of letter writers, in order to open up the dimensions of subjectivities in conflict. Clarissa and Lovelace in correspondence with other characters, "written to the moment," revealed new depth of character in their seemingly fated sado-masochistic conflict. However, even in *Clarissa,* Richardson failed to achieve the distinction between the characters' perspectives and the narrator's point of view. Without that distinction, there could be no irony in the novel. Nevertheless, the innocent, nonironic subjectivity narrated in Richardson's epistolary novels was a revelation and led to many imitations, notably Rousseau's philosophical study of sensibility and utopian space in *La Nouvelle Héloise* (1761) and Choderlos de Laclos's brilliant dissection of sexual mannerism in *Les Liaisons dangereuses* (1782).

It remained for Laurence Sterne to point out the complexity of narrative, and to anticipate the subsequent hierarchical structure of multi-level perspectives. In *Tristram Shandy* (1759–67), the hero who was the first-person narrator attempted to reconstruct his own birth and early life, via the reminiscences of his father and uncle. But Sterne presupposed a Lockean type of free association of consciousness; therefore, the hero-narrator as well as his father and uncle was repeatedly bogging down the narrative with his reminiscences and asides. In addition, the author himself stepped into the narrative to point out that there was a difference between the time it took to write a narrative and the time it would take to read it. Thus, instead of a structured narrative, Sterne played upon the dissociation of the diverse perspectives of narrator, characters, author, and even reader.[22]

By the late eighteenth and early nineteenth centuries, in bourgeois society, the novel had succeeded in structuring a hierarchical relation among narrator, characters, and fictional world, in order to present the theme of characters in conflict with their world. A prime example of such a structure can be found in the novels of Jane Austen. Though she restricted herself to the protrayal of "three or four families in a country village" in each novel, Austen was perfectly aware of the connection between characters and their world. Society in transition from gentility to moneyed wealth was the background for all her novels. Each of them examined different qualities of the characters in that transitional world, such as pride and prejudice, sense and sensibility, persuasion, and so on. There was no alternative world for these characters; hence they had to learn to accept the dictates of the world with grace. In *Sense and Sensibility* (1811), for example, Austen dealt with the worldly problem of freedom of the heart. Both Elinor and Marianne, the two leading characters, had strong feelings; but sense, or Elinor, tempered her heart with her mind, the self, and the world, whereas sensibility, i.e., Marianne, was exclusively preoccupied with feeling.

Sense and sensibility were not fundamentally in opposition, since Elinor and Marianne had the same set of values, though they possessed different temperaments. The novel plotted the necessary trials and tribulations through which Elinor came to terms with her feeling, and Marianne with social and moral sense. Moreover, their perspectival growth in time was accomplished by means of a spatial movement—from their original estate at Norland, to the new family community at Barton, to the attack upon sense and sensibility in London, and finally to Barton again via a partial recovery at Cleveland. Irony in Jane Austen's novels resulted from the interplay between the perceptual growth of her characters and the precise, absolute certainty of the narrator's judgment regarding the fictional world.

In contrast, the characters in Stendhal's novels were entirely estranged from their world, and had to fall back upon their own resources. In *La Chartreuse de Parme* (1839), the omniscient narrator half whimsically presented the story in the guise of an operatic farce, thus creating an ironic distance between the reader and that world of fiction. Parma, as a political microcosm, belonged to neither the bourgeois present, nor the prerevolutionary past. Yet, its court intrigues and secret police contained the worst features of both. None of the three leading characters, Fabrice, Count Mosca, and the Duchess of Sanseverina, really belonged in Parma. Against the languor of that isolated world, they each acted decisively upon their own needs. In so doing, each discovered his or her own integrity. Through the hierarchical interplay of ironic narrator, estranged characters, and caricatured world, Stendhal showed how impossible the connection between subjectivity and the world was. Fabrice, the antihero who drifted irresolutely from one crisis to another seeking genuine passion, finally in the prison tower of that antiworld, Parma, discovered that happiness was within himself.

Both Balzac and Dickens viewed bourgeois society as overwhelming and inescapable; and their novels presented visions of the fate of subjectivity in that world. Balzac in the 1842 preface to his *La Comédie humaine* saw his effort as a panoramic history, which portrayed the two or three thousand character types with their passions caught in everyday life. Each novel in the series presented an aspect of that world, whether provincial or Parisian, upper or lower class. Balzac emphasized the interrelatedness of that world by having some characters appear and reappear in different novels. Dickens, on the other hand, in his social novels of the 1850s, saw a schism between the human being as an orphan and urban, industrial society. It was a hostile, confused world which reduced human beings to stereotypes. Dickens enhanced this somber picture by using certain recurrent symbolisms, such as the fog in *Bleak House,* the "fact" in *Hard Times,* and the prison in *Little Dorrit.* While Balzac's characters desiring the world were driven by monomaniac passions, Dickens's were metaphysical personae for worldly values. Both authors have been charged with creating fixed and one-dimensional characters; but it is more appropriate to say that they portrayed the reduction of subjectivity by the material forces of bourgeois society.

Flaubert's *L'Education sentimentale* (1869) was an anti-*Bildungsroman,* where time could no longer be the means to reconnect subjectivity and the world. The foreground of the novel was the idealized love of Frédéric Moreau, the background the revolution of 1848 in Paris. However, there was no progress in either love or politics. Instead, Flaubert portrayed a parallel series of private and political crises all leading nowhere. In this sense, character in love paralleled society in revolution; each reflected the other. And both seemed lost in a dreamlike haze, without climax. The omniscient narrator reinforced that pervading quality of inertia and dissolution, because the narrative only appeared to be linear, but was actually degenerative. It began in 1840, yet ended with nostalgia for the best times of 1837. Time had no development in *L'Education sentimentale,* only retrogression.

Middlemarch (1871–72) by George Eliot was a study of the intersubjective web in a provincial world. Set in the era of the reform of 1832, it protrayed a number of characters caught up in four or five interwoven plots. These characters were all in search of something; and some of them had high ideals. Yet, they all succumbed eventually to "the rush of unintended consequences." For instance, Dorothea in her marriage and Lydgate in his medical career each started with high hope, though both their hopes ultimately came to naught. Failure was the fate of these characters. Yet it was not an externally imposed fate, but, rather, one due to the perceptual gap between the subjective awareness of the characters and the reality of their world. The only character who seemed able to escape the fate of Middlemarch was Will Ladislaw, the romantic alien, who did not belong to it.

By the late nineteenth century, the vision of a deterministic world loomed even larger, making an even greater impact on the characters than it had in the novels of Balzac and Dickens. In his Rougon-Macquart cycle (1870–93), the natural and social history of a family under the Second Empire, Zola portrayed groups of characters determined by both heredity and environment. The characters' lack of freedom was offset by melodramatic scenes of violence, lust, and riot. The cycle of novels was a broad social panorama, undertaken by Zola in the name of "naturalism." Hardy, on the other hand, in *Tess of the d'Urbervilles* (1891), pointed to a mythic pattern beyond social determinism. Both

Spatiality

Tess and Angel were marginal characters seeking in vain to escape their fate. Their personal encounters, motivated by unfulfilled desire, took place beyond the pale of their communities. Yet the semidetached narrator was able to provide their acts of passion and vengeance with a symbolic pattern of timeless truth, in sharp contrast to their earthbound lives. While Zola's naturalism acquiesced to the determination of characters by their world, Hardy's symbolism eternalized that determinism.

By the end of this period, particularly with Henry James, the problem was no longer estranged characters versus an overwhelming world, but rather how the perspective of the narrator could intersect with that world. The third-person, omniscient narrator could no longer give meaning and coherence to a massive, disconnected reality. James in his late-nineteenth-century novels was concerned with a center of consciousness in the novel, an angle of vision from which to illuminate the story. By the early twentieth century, the immanent point of view in James's novels became even more dramatic. In *The Wings of the Dove,* the central character was mirrored in the consciousness of the others. In *The Ambassadors,* the story was told through the consciousness of Strether, who eventually reversed positions with the protagonist, Chad Newsome. And the narrative of *The Golden Bowl* alternated between the viewpoints of the Prince and the Princess. Finally, in 1905–8 prefaces to the New York edition of his works, James discussed the need for an indwelling point of view within the novel which could intensify the plot. That point of view would dramatize the reality of James's private world, where characters withdrew from society. In experimenting with shifting centers of consciousness, James sensed the collapse of the omniscient narrator capable of penetrating the complex, contemporary world and giving it coherence. With that collapse, the modern novel of the twentieth century abandoned the hierarchical structure of multi-level perspectives, to explore other prospects and sensibilities.[23]

Painting and Visual Space

If the bourgeois novel was a perspectival structure in typographic space, then bourgeois painting provided a perspectival structure in visual space.[24] Bourgeois painting presupposed a hierarchical structure of three levels of visual connection. At the first level, the convention of visual perspective founded on mathematical ratio gave the illusion of three-dimensional depth to the two-dimensional canvas. This convention of visual perspective had been established since the Renaissance. At the second level, the pictorial image, constructed by color and line, light and shade, occupied the three-dimensional spatiality opened by visual perspective. Together, visual perspective and pictorial image gave the viewer the illusion of a realistic representation. However, the meaning or iconography of the image depended upon a third level of referential values shared by both painter and viewer. Both attributed a symbolic value to the pictorial image, so that iconography controlled the representation of the image. Seeing is never a mere reception; it anticipates and projects, in terms of what culture has taught. In bourgeois painting, there was always more than what met the eye. A multi-level structure of visual perspective, pictorial image, and iconographic symbol determined what the eye would see. That structure corresponded to the structure of narrator, characters, and fictional world in the bourgeois novel. As the eye became more estranged and critical, it successively questioned the iconographic value, then the pictorial image, and finally visual perspective itself. Thus, by the early twentieth century, the collapse of this hierarchical structure had put an end to a tradition of painting; in its stead emerged modern painting. In this development, bourgeois painting paralleled the bourgeois novel.

The iconographic framework for pictorial images was already a problem before the start of bourgeois society. The symbolic reference for images depended on the perceived values shared by both painter and viewer. As perception in estate society became more visual, objective, and nonreflexive, a new sense of spatial void appeared, beneath the overblown, mannerist styles of the baroque and the rococo. As one critic pointed out, "During the eighteenth century the idea of distances comes to be based more fully than heretofore upon first-hand experience with perception and upon observation of how the mind works than upon . . . convention."[25] The discontinuity introduced by the late-eighteenth-century revolutions further exacerbated this problem of iconographic reference.

Both neoclassicism and romanticism confronted the problem of how to resymbolize pictorial images, though they differed in their approaches. David proudly claimed that "supported by the study of antique models, [the arts can] turn once more to moral and political preoccupations."[26] In other words, the value of a painting resided not in its images per se, but in its classical reference. On the other hand, Delacroix wrote in his *Journal:* "These figures, these objects, which seem the thing itself . . . are like a solid bridge on which imagination supports itself to penetrate to the mysterious and profound sensation for which the forms are, so to speak, the hieroglyph, but a hieroglyph far more eloquent than a cold representation."[27] Therefore, "in the presence of nature herself, it is our imagination that makes the picture.''[28] Delacroix appealed to imagination, while David appealed to antiquity. The fundamental significance was that both saw the need to reinvest the pictorial image with an extra level of iconographic meaning. Romantic painting might be more explicitly emotional than neoclassical painting; but that was a difference only in degrees. Sometimes, it was even difficult to say which painter or painting had shaded from neoclassicism into romanticism. Both were conscious efforts at resymbolizing the pictorial image.

In an entirely different way, William Blake was also concerned with the problem of iconography. However, Blake's images referred to his own unique vision. As Northrop Frye said, Blake was neither a mystic nor a romantic, but a visionary who used painting, engraving, and poetry to convey his personal vision. For Blake, the world had become too rational and visual. Visual, rational knowledge had led to division and disintegration, with the various arts becoming compartmentalized and specialized. Instead, he argued in *The Marriage of Heaven and Hell* (1789–90),

> Man has no Body distinct from his Soul, for that called Body
> is a portion of Soul discerned by the five Senses, the chief inlets
> of Soul in this age.
> Energy is the only life and is from the Body; and Reason
> is the bound or outward circumference of Energy.
> Energy is Eternal Delight.[29]

Blake was not interested in painting for the sake of painting; nor in image for its own sake. To him, painting with its images, engraving with its designs, and poetry with its words all combined to work upon imagination, in order to create that vision. In his pictorial image, Blake emphasized the importance of line over color. With distinct, wiry lines, he drew nonsubstantial figures effusing energy. Moreover, his figures were allegorical, visually complementing the words of his poetry to celebrate the vision of a reawakened, integrated human being. Blake's pictorial image played a part in his synesthetic vision.

By the mid-nineteenth century, the concern with the iconographic framework for the pictorial image was broken, when Constable and Turner, the English landscapists, as well as Corot, Millet, Courbet, and the Barbizon school in France appealed directly to nature. These painters believed that the image should be derived from nature, instead of being loaded with classical, romantic, or visionary significance. Courbet wrote:

> Painting is an essentially CONCRETE art and can only consist of the representation of REAL AND EXISTING objects. It is a completely physical language that has as words all visible objects. . . . Imagination in art consists in knowing how to find complete expression of an existing object, but never in imagining or creating the object itself.

Therefore, "the beauty based on nature is superior to all artistic convention."[30] Without appeal to nature, imagination would degenerate into mere convention. The appeal to nature gave these painters' images a new vigor, a freshness—no matter whether we call their styles realist or naturalist. The image was disencumbered of symbolic value.

Although divested of iconographic reference, the naturalist or realist image still had a definite subject or theme, namely, nature. The image, in conveying the meaning of a subject or theme, continued to possess a representational function. In this sense, Turner in the last phase of his career began to free pictorial image from the burden of representation. For example, in *Sunrise, with a Boat between Two Headlands,* the boat was hardly recognizable, suffused with color and light. In emphasizing the play of color and light, the later Turner was decomposing pictorial image itself. Thus, he brilliantly anticipated the development of impressionism.

The significance of the impressionists and postimpressionists was their preoccupation with color and light in the presentation of pictorial image. They shifted focus from the representational function of the image to the presentation of the image itself. It did not matter what the subject was. The image was no longer governed by an extra-pictorial consideration. As Renoir said: "Nature knows only colors."[31] The impressionists concentrated on how color and light presented themselves to the retina of the eye, how brush strokes and color pigments could capture the immediacy of that presentation. Monet described himself as chiefly "experimenting with the effects of light and color."[32] Behind the impressionists' experiment was the theory that objects did not possess inherent colors, but under different light and shade reflected changing colors. The image resulted from the play of color and light on the eye. Thus the radiancy of the impressionist image. Later, van Gogh and Gauguin claimed that colors in themselves possessed emotional, expressive qualities, without the need for a specific subject or story. In their preoccupation with color and light, impressionist and postimpressionist painters downgraded all the other elements in pictorial composition. A young painter told of the following advice from Seurat: "Look for the kind of nature that suits your temperament. The motif should be observed more for shape and color than for drawing.

Spatiality

There is no need to tighten the form which can be obtained without that. Precise drawing is dry and hampers the impression of the whole, it destroys all sensations. Do not define too closely the outlines of things; it is the brush strokes of the right value and color which should produce the drawing.''[33] Visual perspective itself was now under pressure.

Cézanne carried this investigation of the pictorial image further. Nature, according to him, presented to the eye color sensations. But the eye received these sensations as concentric patches. Therefore, he advised,

> treat nature by the cylinder, the sphere, the cone, everything in proper perspective so that each side of an object or plane is directed towards a central point. Lines parallel to the horizon give breadth. . . . Lines perpendicular to this horizon give depth. But nature for us men is more depth than surface whence the need of introducing into our light vibrations, represented by reds and yellows, a sufficient amount of blue to give the impression of air.[34]

In Cézanne's later paintings, pictorial image and spatial background converged as color patches. By merging the two, he destroyed the underlying visual perspective in bourgeois painting. This convergence of image and space evoked a vibrant, dynamic strength, which faithfully reflected Cézanne's sensation of nature.

At the start of bourgeois society, the visual space of painting was a hierarchical structure of symbol, image, and perspective. Neoclassicism and romanticism each sought to resymbolize the pictorial image by providing it with classical or imaginative value. Blake sought to provide it with visionary value. However, by the mid-nineteenth century, the pictorial image in the English landscape and the French naturalist schools appealed no longer to iconographic value, but to nature directly. This removed the symbolic reference for pictorial image. Impressionism and postimpressionism then concentrated on presenting the color/light composition of the image itself, and downgraded the representational function of the image. With Cézanne, the decomposition of the image led to the collapse of visual perspective itself. Finally, the hierarchical structure of visual space in bourgeois painting was destroyed. That destructuring of visual space made possible the cubism of Picasso and Braque, and all the other modern paintings to follow.

Embodiment

Life is embodied existence. Body and mind are a psychosomatic unity, mutually directing and affecting each other. But what we mean by "mind" is also the content of perception. And perception is the intentional connection between an embodied being and the environing world—a world which is always cultural and historical. Therefore, embodiment is not only a psychosomatic unity of body and mind, but also a historical formation of the self in the world. Changing perceptual fields in different periods lead to different prospects for bodily or even disembodied existence. Within the bourgeois field of perception constituted by typographic culture, primacy of sight, and the order of development-in-time, embodiment became more disconnected than before, with different parts or aspects of it being visually, rationally analyzed. In this chapter, I shall examine the changing perceptual connections for embodied life, sample four divided lives in bourgeois society, and then describe the bourgeois perception of the body, emotion, sexuality, and the unconscious—i.e., the bourgeois compartmentalization of embodied life.

Changing Perceptual Connections

In each period, embodied life was located in a different perceptual field, leading to a differently perceived connection for the lived body.[1] The Middle Ages had inherited from classical antiquity a theory of humoral equilibrium. The four humors, i.e., phlegm, blood, choler (yellow bile), and melancholy (black bile), corresponded to the four elements, i.e., water, air, fire, and earth. Phlegm was like water, moist and cold; whereas blood and air were moist and hot; on the other hand, choler was dry and hot, like fire; and melancholy, like earth, was cold and dry. Contemporaries used these different qualities to categorize all the perceivable phenomena in the world, since all things partook of them in some combination. A correspondence therefore existed between the elements in the cosmos and the humors in the person, in effect between macrocosm and microcosm. The universe from their point of view was a qualitative, hierarchical chain of being from top to bottom, with the emphasis placed on the macrocosm. It was energized and alive; the whole sustained by God. Within this perceptual framework, embodiment was not a unique phenomenon. The bodily being was a temperament based upon a combination of the four humors. Like all other active, physical entities, it too was sustained by the anagogy pervading the universe. Macrocosm and microcosm both depended on God. In that sense, the order of humoral equilibrium in the person was like that of the universe. The human person did not possess a self-contained, coherent, individual personality, but rather was a character of different qualities whose stability was continually threatened by outside forces. "Personality" had meant the quality or character of being a person as distinct from a thing. Not until the late eighteenth century, at the start of bourgeois society, did it come to mean the quality or character of being one person as distinct from other persons, i.e., being an individual.

The Renaissance continued to uphold the theory of humoral equilibrium. However, in substituting the order of similitude for the anagogy of signs, the Renaissance world shifted the emphasis from macrocosm to the human microcosm. The human being was now considered the center of a self-contained universe, located at the intersection of the divine and the mundane, the spiritual and the material. A few contemporaries began to probe the microcosmic order of the human person on its own terms. Leon Battista Alberti and Leonardo da Vinci empirically studied human anatomy; and Vesalius even performed anatomical dissection. Painters and sculptors portrayed the temperament and physiognomy of outstanding figures, and showed greater appreciation for the vitality and sensuality of the nude. Humanists such as Juan Luis Vives in his psychological studies and Montaigne in his essays opened new paths into the recesses of the human psyche. These new, tentative probings detached the human being from the macrocosmic analogy, and tried to locate the being in a new, visual, rational space. Nevertheless, that space was still overshadowed by the neo-Platonic, Hermetic cosmology of the Renaissance.

In estate society, the scientific revolution defined a new spatiality. No longer concentric and enclosed, space was a linear extension, to be approached from an Archimedean perspective. Within this spatial extension, scientific reason could measure and classify in terms of identity and difference. A new kind of knowledge emerged, which appealed to visuality and quantity. In this spatialized order, embodiment was flattened out. One approach, which extended from Descartes's *Treatise on the Passions* (1649) to La Mettrie's *L'Homme-machine* (1747), likened the human body to a machine, and characterized its movement as mechanical. A second approach, from Robert Boyle's *The Sceptical Chymist* (1661) to Buffon's *Natural History*

(1749ff.), explained the body and its movement as the property and activity of tiny corpuscles. Both approaches accepted the visual, rational assumptions which underlay the new mechanistic science. As a result, both substituted a materialist body for the psychosomatic unity of human embodiment.

The materialist reduction of the body in the seventeenth and eighteenth centuries created the corollary problem of a disembodied mind. Human embodiment was split by the compartmentalization of mind and body, so that philosophy or philosophical psychology had to explain the genesis of knowledge of the material world within the disembodied mind. Cartesian rationalism and British empiricism dealt with the problem from opposite poles. Rationalism from Descartes to Leibniz posited an active mind, which constructed knowledge on the basis of innate ideas. On the other hand, empiricism from Hobbes to Hume posited a blank mind as passive receptor: simple ideas were immediate sense impressions; complex ideas were associations of simple ideas. Both rationalism and empiricism approached the concept of mind from within an objective, spatialized framework. Hence "mind" was solipsistically trapped by the logic of identity and difference, never able to obtain on its own the necessary connection with matter. Cartesian rationalism maintained a sort of psycho-physical parallelism, whereas British empiricism ultimately led to philosophical skepticism.

In bourgeois society, the new perceptual field incorporated time as an extra dimension, unlike space, thus extending perception from the visible present to the invisible past and future. Knowledge was no longer a visible table of taxonomy; rather, new invisible relations emerged in the spatio-temporal field, such as "organism," "function," "structure," and "development"—all new keywords, indicating problems which would have been meaningless in the order of representation-in-space. The difference between microscope and stethoscope signaled the transformation from that order to the new order of development-in-time. The microscope in the seventeenth century enlarged the field of visuality; but the stethoscope in the nineteenth century penetrated beneath the visible surface in order to probe organic function.

In bourgeois society, the new sciences of biology and physiology displaced natural history. "Biology" was a new word coined in 1802 to denote the new study of organic life. Instead of being flattened in a spatial, taxonomic field, the lived body assumed an organic unity in a spatio-temporal field, and was perceived as a dynamic entity. The new sciences understood life as the function and development of an organism. The human body had always been visible; but biological development and physiological function were invisible concepts in the new spatio-temporal field. The organism was a species in evolutionary time; and its function was explained by the biochemistry of the cell. Biologists and physiologists searched for missing genes and links as visible evidence to support the invisible concepts of development and function.

Successes in the biological and physiological fields influenced the development of psychology. Throughout this period, contemporaries used hypnosis, theosophy, and the occult to explain psychic phenomena. However, in the mid-nineteenth century, psychology abandoned its philosophical orientation and assumed the experimental technique of biology and physiology. By the 1890s, psychiatry began to study the unconscious dynamics of the human psyche in the spatiotemporal field.

Instead of the dualism of body and mind trapped in a spatial, taxonomic field, both body and mind in bourgeois society emerged as autonomous, separately functioning propositions in the new spatio-temporal field. Biology, physiology, and psychology divided up bodily life, with each discipline comprehending only an aspect of the human psychosomatic unity. There were, in bourgeois society, three significant efforts to study the body-mind connection. One was vitalism, the theory which opposed mechanistic explanation in biology with a natural yet life-enhancing principle. Another was Mesmerism, which explained psychic phenomena with the concept of animal magnetic fluid. And the third was phrenology, which localized character and personality traits in different parts of the brain. All three popular approaches originated before this period, although they now assumed a scientific guise. Nevertheless, all three proved abortive as science, because they raised issues of body-mind connection which the scientific logic of identity and difference could not resolve. In bourgeois society, objective reason continued to segment bodily life.

Four Divided Lives

The compartmentalized study of embodiment by the life sciences refracted and reinforced the phenomenon of the divided self in real life.[2] At the very time when bourgeois society posited the individual personality as an ideal, life was really a multiplicity, fragmented by the spatial dichotomy between the public and the private, by the sexual bifurcation of "masculinity" and "femininity," and by the scientific-philosophical dualism of body and mind. Under the pressure of visuality and objective reason, an invisible, disconnected subjectivity loomed ever larger, seeking connection and expression. In such circumstances, the bourgeois compartmentalized perceptions of the body, emotion, sexuality and the unconscious were at once cause and effect of the new division of embodied life. Before proceeding to describe these perceptions, let us examine briefly how division and multiplicity dominated the lives of two leading thinkers, Comte and J. S. Mill, as well as two leading novelists, George Eliot and Flaubert.

August Comte (1798–1857),[3] a child of the Revolution, was born of a royalist, Catholic family in Montpellier. At an early age, he renounced the values of his parents to pursue scientific studies. Comte had a strong emotional tie to his mother; yet this tie was broken off during his teens, as he went first to boarding school, then to Paris. Only many years later, influenced by an idealized love, did he regret that he had not properly appreciated his mother's love. In Paris, at the age of nineteen, he met the utopian thinker Saint-Simon and became his protégé. That relation lasted for about seven years, until it was torn by rivalry and quarrels. In 1822, Comte met and married a woman who was registered as a prostitute. Though the marriage lasted only two years, a fighting relation dragged on for years afterward between them. She became for Comte the evil woman incarnate. In 1826, he suffered a psychic collapse, and in the following year tried to commit suicide. Nevertheless, he recovered, persevered and produced his comprehensive *Cours de philosophie positive* (1830–45). The *Cours* systematized the organization and development of human knowledge, from the early stage of theologism, through that of metaphysics, to the present age of positive reason. It was a brilliant work of synthesis, and made Comte's reputation as the philosopher of positivism. Yet he remained deeply unfulfilled, and was dissatisfied with his own system. Meanwhile, in 1844, he had met his angel, Clothilde de Vaux, a sensitive, intelligent, and unhappy woman who had been abandoned by her husband. Their stormy, unconsummated romance lasted a little over a year, until her untimely death. In retrospect, Comte felt that that fatal romance had been his "one incomparable year" of happiness. It was Clothilde, so Comte claimed, who had opened his eyes to the union of heart and intellect, which he had not been able to achieve by himself. The union was to be the centerpiece in his positive religion of humanity, as expounded in his *Système de politique positive* (1851–54). The *Système* superseded the *Cours* by adding a religion of humanity to positive philosophy. In the new positive religion, of which he was the high priest and Clothilde the Virgin-Mother, Comte finally found what he had been striving for all his life, namely, a comprehensive, integral system which could incorporate all human aspirations. His former philosophical supporters were appalled; but Comte ended his old age happily, in harmony.

A man of strong affection and an imaginative, analytical intellect, Comte was torn by emotional need and the craving for order. He lived a wide-ranging, discontinuous life—switching his allegiance from his father to his patron, Saint-Simon, with whom he eventually broke; transferring his love from his mother via the wife-whore to the Virgin Mother; altering his outlook from his Catholic family background through positive philosophy to the religion of humanity. During his psychic breakdown, he even experienced the three stages in his own theory of the development of human consciousness, namely, theology, metaphysics, and positive reason. Though tortuous, constricted, and discontinuous, his life was ever-changing. What held the disparate phases together was his will to unity. For Comte, that unity had to comprehend the totality of the world, with himself located at its center. The *Cours* was a theoretical synthesis, but quite understandably it could not resolve the peculiar tension between emotion and order within Comte. The second synthesis, the *Système,* finally resolved that conflict. By recognizing the fundamental importance of affection, his religion of humanity provided for the union of heart and intellect. Not only was it a comprehensive system, but within it Comte and his beloved Clothilde became the two principles incarnate, he positive reason, she love. It was quite an accomplishment! The *Système* smothered the existing division between man and woman, mind and body, in the name of a postponed, idealized love. However, Comte achieved his synthesis at a tremendous cost, namely the gulf which separated his system from the world of everyday reality.

John Stuart Mill (1806–73), was the child of utilitarianism, born of a disciplined, striving father and a loving but submissive mother.[4] The father displaced the mother and monopolized the boy's education, by cultivating an analytic, utilitarian reason, to the neglect of emotion, fancy, and play. In effect, the young Mill never had a childhood. Throughout his life, he had a longing for the family which he believed he had not had, one where womanly influence would prevail. At the age of twenty, Mill suffered a mental crisis, and realized that he could not live by reason alone. It was then that he read the poetry of Wordsworth, and cultivated a number of friends with temperaments and outlooks different from his own. In 1831, he wrote "The Spirit of the Age," in which he characterized his time as one of conflict between the old and the new, of consciousness of the change from the past to the present. It was an age of transition! Later, in the essays "Bentham" (1838) and "Coleridge" (1840), he paid tributre to the two seminal thinkers of this transitional age. Bentham with his empirical method and Coleridge with his transcendental philosophy necessarily complemented each other from Mill's point of view. This was the time when Mill sought the reconciliation of reason and emotion in his private life. In 1830, he had met Harriet Taylor, a spirited, intelligent, and dominant woman, who was already a wife and a mother. The two soon established an intensely emotional, intellectual partnership, in which Harriet would lead and John Stuart obey. Theirs was a strictly Platonic relation. Throughout, Harriet held on to her husband, while shunning sex with both; and Mill lived at home with his family. This delicate triangle lasted until the death of Mr. Taylor in 1849. After observing a proper mourning for two years, the two were married, but continued apparently to lead chaste, Platonic lives, rising above what they believed to be mere animal inclination. When his father had died in 1836, Mill had assumed responsibility for his family's household. But immediately upon his marriage with Harriet Taylor, Mill quarreled and broke with all the members of his parental family. When Harriet Taylor Mill died of consumption in 1858, it was the end of a perfect romance; Mill bought a house near her grave and spent at least half a year there annually. Nevertheless, throughout this romantic private life, Mill maintained an active, public career as speaker and writer, in addition to his job at the East India Company. Later, after retirement from the company, he even served a term in the House of Commons, though he disliked the life of a politician.

Mill saw himself primarily as an intellectual in the age of transition. His *Autobiography* (1873) dealt only with his intellectual development; herein lay his limitation. Out of his mental crisis, he admitted that poetry was higher than logic, and that philosophy ought to be a union of the two. He had tried to modify the utilitarian education which he had gotten from his father, but never succeeded in transcending its limitation. In *A System of Logic* (1843), he had asked for a science of character formation, or "ethology"; but he never returned to realize it. He was familiar with Comte's philosophy of the three stages of human rational development; yet he never wrote any history or philosophy of history, although his *Principles of Political Economy* (1848) did add a time dimension to the spatial analysis of Smith and Ricardo. Somehow he was too much the son of his father to transcend utilitarian reason. His relationship with Harriet Taylor was a conscious attempt to unite reason and emotion: but Harriet did not entirely displace his father; rather she activated the latent emotion in him. That was why she had to lead. Theirs was an idealized relation of complementarity, which did enable Mill to realize that every person possessed both "masculine" and "feminine" attributes. This realization led Mill and Harriet Taylor to advocate an advanced view on sexual equality, in *The Subjection of Women* (1869). Nevertheless, their idealized love could not accommodate the sex act. In a fundamental sense, John Stuart Mill never trespassed the boundaries set by his father and Harriet Taylor. Instead, he juggled and balanced the two.

George Eliot (1819–80), was born Mary Anne Evans, in War-
wickshire, of a well-to-do land agent and his second wife.[5] She possessed ardent affections and a forthright intellect, two traits whose war-
ring combination fueled her through the many phases of her emergent
self. As a child, she was shy and overly serious, closer to her father
and brother than to her mother, and apparently not too happy. Though
slow in learning how to read, she soon became an omnivorous reader,
engrossed in the world of imagination. In her teens, under the influence
of a teacher, she was converted to evangelicalism. However, by her
twenties, she had ceased to believe in revelation, and came under the
influences, successively, of pantheism, positivism, and science. These
changes occasioned a rupture with her father and brother. Nevertheless, she lived with her widower-father and dutifully attended him until
his death in 1849; only then did she move on to the literary world of
London. There, under the sponsorship of some friends, she translated
Strauss, Feuerbach, and Spinoza, wrote essays and reviews, and was
for a while subeditor of the *Westminster Review*—a considerable
achievement for a young woman, at that time. But she still felt like a
pent-up demon, full of dissatisfaction, despairing of achieving anything
worthwhile. She must realize her potential, in order to justify the break
with her father and brother. Her character chafed at the restriction
which bourgeois society had placed upon women. She had by then
already turned down the marriage proposal of a young man, for fear
of jeopardizing her intellectual pursuits. Yet her need for and depen-
dence upon male companionship led her to a series of indiscrete in-
fatuations. In 1853, she finally met in the writer George Henry Lewes
a person she could lean on. The following year, she defied Victorian
social convention by openly living with Lewes, who was already un-
happily married. They had a full, complementary, androgynous relationship. Lewes had a wonderful sense of her talent and needs; and
with his encouragement she began to write fiction in 1856, at the age
of thirty-six. The following year, she assumed the pen name of George
Eliot, and embarked upon her true vocation. Within the span of some
twenty years, she wrote and published all her fiction, from *Scenes of
Clerical Life* to *Daniel Deronda*. She was soon greeted with critical
acclaim and financial success. Yet throughout, whenever she was giving
birth to a novel, her deeply ingrained self-doubt manifested itself in
symptoms of cold and headache, depression and anxiety. Lewes had
to mother as well as protect her. But gradually she assumed the persona
of George Eliot the renowned writer, an impressive, harmonious presence worshiped by her followers. In 1878, Lewes died, and George
Eliot's novel-writing career came to an abrupt end. In her solitude, she
turned once more to another man, this time twenty years younger than

herself, and married him. She died shortly after, at the age of sixty-one.

In the Prelude to her masterpiece, *Middlemarch* (1871–72), George Eliot spoke of present-day Saint Theresas, who "were helped by no coherent social faith and order which could perform the function of knowledge for the ardently willing soul. Their ardor alternated between a vague ideal and the common yearning of womanhood." This struggle was true for herself, as well as the heroines in her novels. In the various phases of her life, from childhood to evangelicalism to secular immanentism, she revealed an ever-widening awareness of a world without God. She willed herself to overcome her innate self-preoccupation, what she had called egoistic imagination and vague ideal, in order actively to engage the world. The common yearning of womanhood was not enough, for she found out that it was necessary to her not simply *to be,* but to *utter.* In other words, the integration of an ardent affection and forthright intellect must lead to creative expression—an expression in the form not of abstract philosophy, but of the more vivid and concrete novel. Her novels were the form wherein she reworked her past and projected a comprehensive vision of human passions in a deterministic world. That vision was nurtured by her human sympathy as well as by her analytical intellect—a combination attested to by her peculiar style of interspersing narrative with omniscient judgment, as well as by the long, involved structure of her sentences filled with qualifying participial phrases. Her realistic novel was a moral art which lived up to her own ideal of social responsibility, artistic integrity, and popular acclaim. That was her true vocation. Nevertheless, her life was a succession of multiple phases. The persona that sustained and in turn was sustained by the novels was not the whole person, for the Mary Anne Evans who became George Eliot went on to be briefly Mrs. John Cross. Each phase was a different persona in a divided, multiple life.

Gustave Flaubert (1821–80) was born in the commercial, industrial town of Rouen, the second son of a prosperous surgeon and an indomitable, reticent mother.[6] Precocious and sensitive, he was from an early age influenced by romanticism and wanted to be a writer. He rejected the successful medical careers of his father and older brother, and failed repeatedly to pass the examination for the legal profession. Happily an epileptic attack in 1844 ended all prospect of a profession, so he could devote the rest of his life to writing. Ever since childhood, he had cultivated a close camaraderie with a number of male friends. Women, on the other hand, were a threat. At the age of fourteen, he had fallen in love with a married woman eleven years older. The affair was not consummated; but she, like Mme. Arnoux in *Sentimental*

Education, kept returning to his life and memory. His later affair with the poetess Louise Colet, again eleven years older than he, was a tempestuous romance. They were more apart than together, and fought even in their correspondence. To Flaubert, love was not a fulfillment, but an aspiration. He compartmentalized sex and love, classified women as either whore or angel. Yet he saw "feminine" traits within himself, and sought a hermaphroditic ideal. Flaubert never married; after the death of his father he lived with his mother near Rouen, until her death in 1872. Only then did he admit that she was the person he had loved most. There was in Flaubert a deeply ingrained ambivalence; a sort of active passivity pervaded his entire being. He had always hated the banalities of Rouen; yet throughout his life, he lived in or near that town. Travels, like his extended tour in the Near East, and periodic visits to Paris for social and sexual excursions were liberating. But it was in the refuge of his home, on the outskirts of bourgeois Rouen, that he undertook his antibourgeois art.

Flaubert's life and novels epitomized that peculiar dialectic between bourgeois society and art. He abhorred everything that was bourgeois; and by rejecting the values of that society, he steered his own life away from the expected, bourgeois pattern of maturation. Time had neither continuity nor development for Flaubert. Instead, in his walled-up chamber at home, Flaubert discovered a profound boredom, an emptiness in which the memory of the past was more alive than the past experience itself. This boredom provided him a freedom with which to create a stylistic *rapport,* a consistently impersonal way of describing the world. Each of his literary works was composed of a series of scenes; and in constructing them, he was invisible yet all powerful, everywhere felt but nowhere seen. That was his ideal of art. Just as his life lacked a pattern of maturation, so his works provided no clue to any growth, but instead revealed repetition and variation. He returned three times to his favorite theme, the temptation of Saint Anthony. Switching back and forth between exotic, romantic themes, and mundane, present-day topics, each of his works was a new, distinct effort. But in his most successful works, such as *Madame Bovary* (1856), *Sentimental Education* (1869), and "A Simple Heart" (1877), Flaubert did not turn away from bourgeois society. Rather, transcending both romanticism and realism, he focused his pure, impersonal style upon that world which he so detested. His art refracted the world, as he had claimed, like the sun which put gold on the dungheap of reality. But that art was made possible only by the sacrifice of a life which neither entirely rejected nor entirely accepted bourgeois society.

The lives of these four "individuals," Comte, Mill, George Eliot, and Flaubert, revealed neither unity nor coherence. Instead, each went through different phases of a multiple life, divided by the dichotomy between mind and body, reason and emotion, "masculinity' and "femininity." Only their respective projects in life enabled them to persist through the different phases of their divided lives. Although they cannot be considered typical representatives of their society, their divided lives illustrate the problem of embodiment in bourgeois society.

The Body

Perception of the body has a history which changes from period to period. In the Renaissance, "the proportions of the human body were praised as a visual realization of musical harmony; they were reduced to general arithmetical or geometrical principles."[7] That perception of the human body was governed by the fundamental similitude between microcosm and macrocosm. But, with the coming of the typographic revolution, the sensing hierarchy was in transition from hearing to seeing.[8] By the latter half of this period, there emerged a new, visual consciousness of the human body. In 1530, Erasmus wrote a treatise on outward, bodily propriety which became quite popular. The new reading public possessed a new sense of delicacy and shame, and were concerned with bodily carriage, gesture, dress, and facial expression. I would attribute this consciousness of the body to a change in the hierarchy of sensing from the primacy of hearing and touching to the primacy of seeing.[9] With the emphasis on visuality, contemporaries became more conscious of their own bodies. Subsequently, in estate society, visuality and Archimedean reason detached the human body from macrocosmic analogy and mathematical ratio. Instead, contemporaries dissected and classified the body in an objective, taxonomic field. Finally, within the enlarged spatio-temporality of bourgeois society, visuality and objective reason made the human body an autonomous entity in itself. The body had become self-conscious.

The new, self-conscious autonomy was evident in several different yet related changes in perception of the body. Medicine in estate society had dissected the human body within the framework of a spatialized order. Doctors identified and taxonomically classified visible symptoms of disease in the body. However, in bourgeois society, medical perception approached the body via a combination of seeing, touching, and hearing. The three senses together enabled the doctor to penetrate beneath the surface of the body, in order to diagnose an illness which was perceived against the spatio-temporal background of organic life. With organic life displacing the taxonomy of human anatomy, the human body became an irreducible entity, an opaque density which sight by itself could not penetrate. The body as an organized life had acquired a new perceptual autonomy in the world, which it had previously lacked. As the embodiment of life, it became a mysterious entity, quite different from other matter.[10]

Not only in the clinic, but also in everyday life, there was a new awareness of the body.[11] Personal hygiene or the care of one's own body was a new virtue. In estate society, the upper and middle classes gradually became more aware of what they saw and smelled, in regard to such bodily functions as spitting, farting, urinating, and defecating. By the eighteenth century, caring for the body had led to revived interest in the bathing cultures of other societies. Bourgeois society saw the advocacy of various bathing methods, such as hot air, vapor, douche, tub, or shower. In addition, the hydrotherapy of cold water and the heliotherapy of sunbathing became popular; and public beach bathing was a new pastime, undertaken by those who could not afford to go to the spas. Concurrently, the bathroom received more attention in the bourgeois home. The late eighteenth-century home began to have the washstand. In the nineteenth century, there was the flush toilet, supported by improved plumbing and sewage systems. Finally, by the early twentieth century, the bathroom was completely mechanized. Cleanliness was the foremost virtue for the bourgeois body.

Parallel to the concern for personal hygiene was the growing interest in physical education. At the beginning of this period, Rousseau, in *Emile* (1762), had urged the natural cultivation of the child's physical prowess. Other reformers in the late eighteenth century introduced physical education into the child's educational curriculum. By the nineteenth century, physical education in the schools consisted of either gymnastics or organized sports. The masses undertook gymnastics, which required a minimum of space and equipment; whereas the elite practiced organized sports, which cost more. In England, public schools promoted organized sports, to discipline the body of the gentleman. Meanwhile, gymnastics prevailed in the French schools. Not until the late nineteenth century was there any movement for organized sports in France; and there, too, it took on an upper-class connotation.[12] Both gymnastics and organized sports complemented personal hygiene to cultivate the autonomous, self-conscious body.

As it became more self-conscious and autonomous, the human body began to assume a new ideal type, both in posture and in fashion. Previously, the ideal body type was heavy and set; but by the latter half of the eighteenth century, the favored type for both men and women was slender and sentimental. In the nineteenth century, the well-to-do bourgeois borrowed the rococo furniture from the aristocrat, and with it ease of sitting posture. Subsequently, an even freer posture was advocated, namely, that of inclined relaxation, neither sitting nor lying, but halfway in between. For this self-conscious body, fashion was now more functionally related to the spatial organization of society. There had always been changing fashions for both men and women. However, in bourgeois society, the bourgeois male attire became less fanciful in color and style, more utilitarian and somber, to reflect the man's rationality in the public space. On the other hand, bourgeois female fashion underwent a series of stylistic revivals, sometimes decorative, sometimes *décolletée,* but always antiutilitarian, in order to indicate the woman's embellishing function in the private space.[13] Previously, fashion denoted one's rank and order within a formalized hierarchy; but now it revealed the different functions of the body in a more rationally organized society.

Painting in bourgeois society represented the human body less from the standpoint of iconographic reference than for the sake of the image of the body itself. Renaissance painting had idealized the body in terms of classical mythology and Christian allegory. In estate society, this idealization lessened somewhat. Underneath the iconographic reference, the human body became more sensuous and erotic. More often than not, the body was female. Iconography maintained the convention of the nude, so that the public could enjoy the naked body of a woman without shame. By the period of bourgeois society, the nude was always appearing under the guise of a classical or romantic theme, or an academic pose. Though they differed in styles and techniques, the leading painters of the nude, such as Etty, Delacroix, Ingres, and Bouguereau, all followed the same trite convention. Their nudes were usually passive and submissive, though sometimes mysterious and threatening. The nudes possessed neither energy nor inner life, only surface sensuality. Yet the naked body is not erotic in itself, but only appears so to the mind of the male viewer; and the convention of the nude permitted the erotic enjoyment of the naked female body. The shock came when Manet in *Luncheon of the Grass* (1863) and *Olympia* (1865) discarded the convention of the nude to portray naked women without pretense. Without the convention of the nude, the representation of the naked female emphasized delight in the texture and color of the skin, as in the women of Renoir. Nevertheless, the painter in bourgeois society, usually a male, represented the female body, whether nude or naked, for voyeurist consumption by other males.[14]

At the very beginning of this period, William Blake was fully aware of the problem of visualization and rationalization of the human body. According to him, the tyranny of Urizen, objective reason, led to the disintegration and compartmentalization of the five human senses, with sight becoming despotic. Visuality and rationalism destroyed the connection between the human being and the world, and approached the body as an isolated, externalized entity. To overcome that disintegration and compartmentalization, Blake in his painting drew the human body with lines, rather than colors. His figure was not a visual surface of color and texture, but an outline for visionary imagination. Synesthetically, his poetry and painting by combining words and images would reenergize perception with imagination, in order to renovate the human body.[15] But Blake was an isolated visionary.

In bourgeois society, the body acquired a new self-consciousness. It was no longer likened to something else, whether by anagogy, similitude, or representation. Instead, under the pressure of visuality and objective reason, the body became an autonomous development. Medical diagnosis, personal hygiene, physical education, fashion, and painting all promoted the concept of a dynamic, autonomous body.

Emotion

Emotion is neither mere physiological reflex, nor private impulse. It is a prereflective, perspectival consciousness of the person in the world, revealing a specific connection between the two. From his or her embodied location in the world, the human being experiences a spontaneous, deeply felt attitude toward the world. This attitude has its basis in sensing and feeling, but then penetrates the surrounding world, so that the world and everything in it are sustained for the person through that perspective. Emotion is prereflective; consciousness has not yet focused or stabilized it. Therefore, it is a true revelation of the specific connection between a person and the world, before analytic reason has torn them apart. Each emotion is different from another, every time, no matter how much they may seem alike in retrospect. They indicate different modes of embodied existence: whether being with someone or something, or being thrown back upon oneself; whether flowing on, extending out, or being subdued; whether expanding oneself, or being injured; whether taking, assimilating to oneself, or losing, abandoning a part of oneself. Such are the significations of joy, sadness, love, hatred, happiness, anger, hope, fear, etc., with each emotion revealing a specific lived experience of being-in-the-world, each a particular connection between the human being and his or her environing world.[16]

Changes in perceptual fields will alter the prereflective emotional connection between the person and the world. In bourgeois society, visuality and rationality made the person more discrete and autonomous than before. With the person thrown back upon the self, emotion became more pent up, a recoil from the world. This change had begun prior to bourgeois society.

Embodiment

In the Renaissance, "passion" had been any kind of feeling by which one was powerfully affected or moved; and "temperament" was a combination of the four humors which determined the physical and mental constitution of a person (OED). Human "character" possessed no internal coherence, but was open to outside forces displaying conflicting passions (OED). Renaissance passion was spontaneous and violent, made possible by the reflexive connection between the macrocosm of the universe and the microcosm of the person. But "emotion" was a new word in estate society, to describe an agitation or disturbance of the mind, feeling, or passion (OED). It was a vehement state of feeling. The person had become more detached in the spatialized world of estate society than previously, and began to have more of an inside as opposed to the outside. Emotion, unlike passion, resulted from the new oppositon between inside and outside, between mental and physical. It was a state of feeling cooped inside a person, not coming out spontaneously like passion. Emotion, being mental and on the inside, resulted from sense perception of the physical, of outside. To be "sensible" was a state of emotional consciousness; and "sentiment" became a mental feeling (OED). There was even a cult of "sensibility" by the eighteenth century, implying the quickness and acuteness of apprehension or feeling (OED). Seventeenth- and eighteenth-century emotion was more private and personal than Renaissance passion, less a spontaneous connection in the world.

Bourgeois society consolidated the new emotion and sentiment of estate society. On the basis of this emotion and sentiment, "personality" in the late eighteenth century acquired a new prospect, i.e., the quality or assemblage of qualities in a person as distinct from other persons (OED). By the early nineteenth century, the ideology of "individualism" supplemented that new personality. As the person possessed more of an inside, emotion rather than objective reason accounted for his or her individuality. This emotion was disconnected from the visual, rational world. In bourgeois society, "sensitivity" and "sentimentalism" were new concepts, while "sensitive" and "sentiment" acquired new meaning, to indicate emotion as the *ressentiment* of a more autonomous, pent-up being.

J. H. van den Berg, the existential psychologist, has even claimed that, in this period, sensitivity to pain became more acute than before.[17] Earlier periods offered little evidence to indicate concern with pain as a problem. People evidently lived through their surgical operations and illnesses without too much complaint. However, in bourgeois society, pain had become enough of a conscious problem to demand some kind of anesthesia. In the early nineteenth century, doctors began to use hypnosis during surgery; by the middle of the century, they used ether. Earlier periods had known about hypnosis and ether, yet ignored their anesthetic property. Only in the nineeteenth century, when consciousness of pain became a problem, were hypnosis and ether used as anesthesia. As people became more autonomous and withdrawn, their sensitivity to pain increased.

Love as an emotional effervescence, a flowing outward of the self seeking union with an other, has different prospects in different periods. In bourgeois society, when visuality and rationalism tended to objectify the other, love became an emotional recoil. This love, more immanently directed in the world, could not be nurtured in the public spaces of business and politics. Even in the private space of the family, love led a precarious existence, since bourgeois marriage was founded on property and rank.[18] Meanwhile, the meaning of love underwent transformation. Formerly, love had implied both sentiment and sex; the two were connected. But in the eighteenth century, with the separation of mind and body, love came to denote the sentiment apart from sex.[19] Uprooted and disembodied, the new love in bourgeois society was an immanent ideal, to fulfill the need for transcendence in an increasingly visual, rational world. It was sentimentalized in the mid-eighteenth century, and romanticized by the late eighteenth and nineteenth centuries. The epistolary novels of Richardson discovered this new sentiment of love, for the voyeurist enjoyment of the bourgeois reader. Subsequently, romanticism saw in this love the new dynamic to overcome the rationalization of the world. Romantic love could serve as the integrative force in a now absolutely immanent universe.[20] Nevertheless, spiritualized, disembodied love could find no shelter in either the public or the private spaces of bourgeois society. Unable to overcome the visuality and rationalization of the world, it recoiled upon itself. Because the human being had become more estranged and disconnected, we find evidence of a subterrane of nervousness and anxiety in bourgeois society.[21]

Sexuality

As the human body became autonomous and self-conscious, as emotion recoiled from the world and became more cooped up, sexuality in bourgeois society emerged as an explicit phenomenon. At the beginning of this period, de Sade had asked in *Juliette:* "Can't you go to bed with a woman without loving her, and can't you love her without going to bed with her?"[22] Sex was now separated from love. In fact, "sexuality" itself was a nineteenth-century word, indicating the awareness of a new, discrete phenomenon (OED).

Embodiment

Even sex has a history. Sex is a fundamental connection between human beings. It is that act involving all the senses which culminates in a loss of the separateness of being. Sight is the threshold of sex; it introduces and stimulates. But sight always presupposes a distance between the viewer and the viewed. Hence the progress of sex inevitably shifts from sight to touching, smelling, tasting, and hearing, the four, more enwombing senses. At the moment of orgasm, one is liberated from the specific senses, as well as from one's own individuality. Sex is therefore human transcendence this side of death, when one experiences a primal connection. Georges Bataille sees sex as having a sacramental character, as being somewhat similar to mystical experience.[23] However, in bourgeois society, with the emphasis on sight, sex was approached much more visually. This was evident in the painting of nudity, and in pornographic literature. Both indicated a tendency to make sex more explicit and disconnected—thus contributing to the privatization of the person as well as the sublimation of sexuality.

The female body had usually been the subject in the portrayal of nudity, undertaken by males for male enjoyment. This tradition since the Renaissance reflected the underlying sexual politics in the West, where, in the apt words of John Berger, "men look at women. Women watch themselves being looked at." The male portraiture of the female made her appear passive and submissive, yet sensuous and inviting. The nude was not a real person with character or individuality, but a stereotype. The nude in painting was the naked woman clothed in the iconography of classical or biblical mythology, so that the viewer could enjoy the naked body without shame or guilt. By the eighteenth century, the nude in Fragonard and Boucher appealed more blatantly as sex object. In the nineteenth century, the nude was even more an eroticized object, in spite of the maintenance of that iconographic convention. Under the pressure of visuality, the convention had worn thin, a mere hypocritical pretense. But the public still insisted on it. In the 1860s, Manet exposed the hypocrisy of the conventionalized nude by portraying naked women in *Luncheon on the Grass* and *Olympia*. The public was shocked and outraged.[24]

Parallel to the demythologizing of the nude in painting was the visualization of sex in pornographic literature. Previously, literature had presented sex from within a context of folk humor, for the sake of satire and ribaldry. Even in estate society, writing on sex was usually associated with attacks on social or religious conventions. However, by then, writing began to discard literary metaphor and image, in order to concentrate on the explicit itineraries of the sex organ. From *Memoirs of a Woman of Pleasure* (1749) to *My Secret Life* (ca. 1890s), the literary portrayal of sex became more graphic and mechanical, in order to maintain the sensation of novelty. Sex without emotional involvement became a free commodity for the voyeurist reader. Yet visualized sex without emotion would soon lose appeal. Bourgeois pornography in its preoccupation with explicit sex revealed a grim, humorless world of supposed masculine virility and endless feminine availability. It was an exclusive, male fantasy, written by men for men, in which male sexuality became brittle and aggressive, embarking upon endless conquests. However, male virility could never outlast female availability. Behind the endless conquests in pornography was the male's fear of the insatiable female. The fantasy in bourgeois pornography revealed the isolation and privatization of the new economic man.[25]

The visualization of sex in painting and in pornography indicated an uprooting and isolation of human sexuality in bourgeois society. It was no mere coincidence that, at the very beginning of this period, two nonbourgeois outsiders, the aristocrat de Sade (1740–1814) and the peasant-artisan Restif de la Bretonne (1734–1806), wrote about the problem of uprooted, disconnected sexuality.[26] Though they approached the problem of sex from diametrically opposing standpoints, both de Sade and Restif realized that sex was an irrepressible force in life. De Sade considered sex to be the only genuine, personal force in an amoral, egalitarian world. Hence, sexual egotism was justifiable, because in this sort of amoral world only power could resolve the inevitable contest among individuals. In his vision of a sexually free, competitive society, the equivalent of Adam Smith's laissez-faire economy and Hegel's civil society, de Sade anticipated the reduction of all human bonds to "sadism," i.e., power alone mattered and sex itself was power. On the other hand, Restif saw the new, disconnected sexuality as an irrepressible, obtrusive factor, and very much wanted to reintegrate sex into society. He wrote voluminously on the education of man and woman, on the reform of social mores, with the hope that sex could be a part of a vitalist world of hierarchical order. Unlike de Sade's prophetic nightmare, Restif's vision was a conservative one. Nevertheless, de Sade and Restif from opposing perspectives were both acutely aware of the disjunction of sex in bourgeois society.

Smell is an integral part of sex, together with sound, taste, and touch. Visuality and objective reason must have led to a decline in the signification of smell in bourgeois society. In the late nineteenth century, psychologists and physiologists theorized about the connection between sex and olfaction; and Baudelaire, Zola, and Huysmans wrote of the nostalgia for smell in their poetry and fiction.[27] If smell were ever-present, few would remark on it. The theory and nostalgia for smell were conscious attempts to reconnect smell, implying a prior decline of its signification. That decline had contributed to the disjunction of sexuality in bourgeois society, since smell is so important a part of sex. Quite symptomatically, it was in this period that we have accounts of olfactory fetishism, i.e., the displaced desire for forbidden smell.

The narrowed focusing of sexuality implied also the stereotyping and polarizing of sexual roles and attributes in bourgeois society. Different societies had stereotyped woman for different cultural and ideological purposes; but it was in this period that the polarity between masculinity and femininity became most marked. Contemporaries considered reason to be masculine, and emotion feminine. Virtuosities in the public space, such as aggressiveness, discipline, calculation, self-reliance, and postponement of immediate gratifications, were all perceived as male virtues; "masculinity" itself was a nineteenth-century concept (OED). Their opposites were used to "feminize" the private space of the bourgeois home (OED). These sexual dichotomies were commonplace in the literature of the period, from Restif de la Bretonne to Coventry Patmore. Take, as an example, the following extract from the 1842 edition of *Encyclopaedia Britannica,*

> The man, bold and vigorous, is qualified for being a protector; the woman, delicate and timid, requires protection. Hence it is that man never admires a woman for possessing bodily strength or personal courage; and women always despise men who are totally destitute of these qualities. The man, as protector, is directed by nature to govern; the woman, conscious of inferiority, is disposed to obey. Their intellectual powers correspond to the destination of nature. Men have penetration and solid judgment to fit them for governing, women have sufficient understanding to make a decent figure under a good government; a greater portion would excite dangerous rivalry between the sexes, which nature has avoided by giving them different talents. Women have more imagination and sensibility than men, which make all their enjoyments more exquisite; at the same time they are better qualified to communicate enjoyment. Add another capital difference of disposition: The gentle and insinuating manners of the female sex tend to soften the roughness of the other sex; and wherever women are indulged with any freedom, they polish sooner than men. [Vol. 13, p. 577]

But there is no man that totally masculine, or woman so completely feminine. This sexual polarization was ideological and repressive; hence other stereotypes emerged to compensate for the distortion. According to Peter Cominos, the ideal types of *homo economicus* and *femina domestica* were supplemented by the counterstereotypes of *homo sensualis* and *femina sensualis*. Underneath the idealization of masculine/feminine opposition emerged the danger of sensuality. Nevertheless these two different sets of sexual stereotypes—i.e., *homo economicus/femina domestica* and *homo sensualis/femina sensualis*—did not comprehend the whole human being. They revealed instead the fundamental schism in bourgeois society between social roles and human desire. The schism prevented the expression of those tendencies in man considered to be unmasculine, and those in woman considered to be unfeminine.[28] This sexual stereotyping of social roles therefore further contributed to the fragmentation of the human being in bourgeois society. The passionate man and orgasmic woman in D. H. Lawrence's novels did not heal the schism; they were merely the romantic antinomy to bourgeois expectation.

The institutionalized demarcation between public and private spaces reinforced the sexual stereotyping of man and woman. The man in order to compete in the public space had to be aggressive and tight; his female counterpart was supposed to be the guardian angel of the private space of the home, where he could escape from the rigor of laissez-faire competition and be emotionally replenished. Since the angel had to be innocent and unchallenging, sex in the sentimentalized bourgeois home was only for the purpose of procreation. So an institutionalized underground of prostitutes and pornography flourished, where the whore could be enjoyed by *homo sensualis,* whether in person or in print. Both angel and whore served the bifurcated sexuality of the bourgeois male; meanwhile, the sexuality of *femina domestica* was repressed.[29] Sexuality had become more and more regulated and compartmentalized.

By the late nineteenth century, several criticisms of bourgeois sexuality had emerged. One was the homosexual dandyism of Oscar Wilde and Aubrey Beardsley, posited as an antithesis to bourgeois masculinity. For example, J. A. Symonds argued that Greek love was purer than heterosexual love. Another criticism was centered in the myth of Androgyne, in order to emphasize the fundamental bisexuality of the human person. And the third was the scientific study of sex, the outstanding example of which was Havelock Ellis's monumental *Studies in the Psychology of Sex.*[30] These criticisms did not change the contemporary bourgeois perception of sexuality. However, they did anticipate the new sexuality which came out after the catastrophe of the first world war.

"Sexuality" was more visualized, compartmentalized, self-conscious, and, therefore, less connected in bourgeois society than before. It lost a part of that fundamental sensuality which Bataille associated with the mystical experience. As Foucault has pointed out recently, since the seventeenth and eighteenth centuries

> there has been a constant optimization and an increasing valori-
> zation of the discourse on sex; . . . this carefully analytical dis-
> course was meant to yield mulitple effects of displacement,
> intensification, reorientation, and modification of desire itself. Not
> only were the boundaries of what one could say about sex en-
> larged, and men compelled to hear it said; but more important,
> discourse was connected to sex by a complex organization of
> varying effects, by a deployment that cannot be adequately ex-
> plained merely by referring it to a law of prohibition.[31]

At once more significant and less profound, the brittle sexuality of
bourgeois society led to an increase in anxiety, which manifested itself
in symptoms of impotence and hysteria.

The Unconscious

The unconscious is the antithesis of consciousness. Consciousness is intersubjective, not merely subjective. It is one's lived intentionality, perceptually directed in the world. Consciousness of self takes
place within a framework of consciousness of the world. However,
there is always more of the self and of the world than one's consciousness. In this sense, the unconscious is that aspect of being-in-the-world
not comprehended by consciousness.[32] Being-in-the-world bestrides
the boundary between consciousness and the unconscious. Since both
being-in-the-world and consciousness change, so does the unconscious.
Therefore, the unconscious has a history. In the eighteenth century,
"unconscious" had meant not being conscious of, unaware; by the
nineteenth century, "unconscious" came to mean not realized or
known as existing within oneself (OED). The unconscious turned inward, in bourgeois society. However, we cannot study the history of
the unconscious in itself; rather, it can be studied only in relation to
changing consciousness.

Being-in-the-world, under the pressure of visuality and objective
reason, divided and turned in upon itself. Bourgeois society was highly
compartmentalized; thus the articulation of the self took place in all
the many spaces and times of that world. However, there was always
more of the self than what could be realized in these compartmentalized
experiences. As a result, the person was disembodied into mind, body,
emotion, and sexuality. Each was a part of the person; but together
they did not constitute a whole being. With compartmentalization and
disembodiment, the phenomenon of divided personality emerged. First

discovered during the late eighteenth century, it became fairly well known by the middle of the next century, and was a popular topic among psychologists and philosophers from 1880 on. The phenomenon included simultaneous multiple personalities, successive multiple personalities (both amnestic and cognizant types), as well as personality clusters.[33] A concept of the unconscious was needed to explain how these multiple facets of a divided person held together.

In addition, bourgeois society showed a great deal of interest in psychic phenomena related to the unconscious. The most popular method for approaching the unconscious was hypnotism. In the 1770s, Franz Mesmer had discovered an invisible magnetic fluid which he claimed pervaded the universe. Illness was due to insufficient, faulty distribution or poor quality of the fluid in the patient. By harnessing it, Mesmer was able to establish a rapport with the patient and restore equilibrium. Subsequently, Amand-Marie Puységur discarded the theory of unseen physical fluid for one of unknown psychic forces. He was able to induce artificial somnambulism, which testified to his control over these psychic forces. Later still, the idea of psychic energy was conceived. In 1834, James Braid renamed magnetism hypnotism, implying that it was not a physical but a psychic phenomenon. However, during the latter half of the century, hypnotism seemed to have fallen from favor, until its revival as a psychotherapeutic technique by Hippolyte Bernheim and Jean-Martin Charcot, in the 1880s.[34]

Interest in hypnotism centered on both spontaneous and artificially induced somnambulisms. But related symptoms such as lethargy, catalepsy, ambulatory automatism, multiple personality, and hysteria also aroused contemporary interest. These phenomena of psychic dissociation led to a theory of the duality of the human psyche. In dipsychism, or the double ego, one part was mostly unconscious, and would manifest itself in a somnambulist state. Sometimes it was assumed that this unconscious part could be in communion with the spirits beyond. Somewhat later, the theory of a subpersonality cluster, or polypsychism, posited that all the subpersonalities were under a dominant, conscious ego; and the sum total of these subpersonalities constituted the unconscious.[35]

In addition, there were other approaches to the unconscious in the nineteenth century. Romantic writers and philosophers had speculated extensively on the importance of the unconscious. Then in the mid-nineteenth century, spiritism came into vogue, using mediums to communicate with the beyond via the unconscious. This subsequently led to interest in parapsychology, and the founding of a Society for Psychical Research in 1882. Other scientists, such as Jules Héricourt and Théodore Flournay, also did clinical and experimental studies of the unconscious. By the end of the nineteenth century, the unconscious was a fairly well-known concept, although it lacked a generally agreed upon definition. It could be the automatic or dissociated part of a person; it could be a storage of memory and perception; or it could be a creative, mythopoetic force.[36]

It was Pierre Janet who posited the psychological concept of the subconscious. During the late eighties and early nineties, Janet discovered what he called fixed ideas in hysterical patients. These were, according to him, usually the result of traumatic events, which had been forced into the subconscious and later manifested themselves as symptoms. There were levels of fixed ideas in the subconscious, some primary, others secondary; but all of them originated at different points in a patient's life. These ideas were both the result of mental weakness and the source for further deterioration. Difficult to identify, they appeared as disguised reenactments during hysteric crises. However, the therapist could with the help of hypnosis get at these fixed ideas, and destroy them by dissociation or transformation. Later, Janet explained mental weakness by the concept of psychic energy. In the human psyche, nothing was ever lost, but everything persisted in the subconscious. The tension and quantity of psychic energy in a person would determine whether consciousness or the subconscious would triumph in the continuous struggle between the two.[37]

Then, from 1895 to 1905, Freud in his studies of hysteria, dream, parapraxis, and joke gradually elaborated a theory of depth psychology. Psychic life, according to him, was both conscious and unconscious, with symptomatic manifestations at the conscious level and traumatic reminiscences at the unconscious level. Symptom was a cipher for trauma, and was caused by the latter. Owing to the mechanism of repression, the relation between trauma and symptom was not instantaneous. A symptom could be connected via a chain of memory to some traumatic reminiscence in puberty, childhood, or even infancy. Yet the conflict between consciousness and the unconscious lasted throughout life. The symptom could be therapeutically removed by forcing the trauma into consciousness and abreacting it.[38]

It is a prominent feature of unconscious processes that they are indestructible. In the unconscious nothing can be brought to an end, nothing is past or forgotten. The unconscious path to thoughts, which lead to discharge in a hysterical attack, immediately becomes traversible once more, when sufficient excitation has accumulated. A humiliation that was experienced thirty years ago acts exactly like a fresh one throughout the thirty years, as soon as it has obtained access to the unconscious sources of emotion.[39]

The Freudian unconscious was the timeless dynamic of the human psyche. Unlike Janet's subconscious, it was sexual, therefore was repressed and had to be released.

In 1909, at the Sixth International Congress of Psychology, Janet tried to make a distinction between the clinical concept of the subconscious and the more general, philosophical-psychological concept of the unconscious. But Janet's distinction went unheeded.[40] With the objectification of the world, the unconscious had turned inward; there was no unconscious beyond, only the subconscious within. Therefore, contemporaries could not appreciate Janet's attempt to distinguish between these two terms, and instead accepted Freud's position that the two were identical. The triumph of the Freudian unconscious over Janet's subconscious attested to the interiorization of the unconscious in bourgeois society.

My argument is that the unconscious as the antithesis of consciousness was that aspect of being-in-the-world (excluding mind, body, emotion, and sexuality) which could not be visually or rationally connected in bourgeois society. It was the unrealized aspect of the human psyche which needed connection and expression. The project of expression undertaken by a Comte, Mill, George Eliot, or Flaubert utilized a part of the self's unconscious; and to the extent that the project was meaningful, an aspect of the unconscious did connect, so that what remained still unconnected and inexpressible was a different psychic unconscious than before. The unconscious is not an autonomous something in itself, but the antithesis to changing consciousness of being-in-the-world. In bourgeois society, with the visualization and rationalization of the world and also of much of the self, the unconscious had to assume the burden of a dynamic which was absent everywhere else. However, the various practices such as hypnotism, spiritism, psychotherapy approached the unconscious as something in itself, and thus unwittingly reconfirmed the existing boundary between consciousness and the unconscious set up by visuality and objective reason. For example, the Freudian unconscious was a mythic symbolization of the inexpressible aspect of being-in-the-world, couched in the language of dynamic mechanics.[41] It accounted for conscious life. But the language itself was a part of the prevailing scientific objectification of the world; and the Freudian unconscious as a concept masked the inexpressible aspect of being-in-the-world. In this sense, Freudianism reconfirmed and further perpetuated the existing opposition of consciousness/unconscious in bourgeois society.

From Linearity to
Multi-Perspectivity

The perceptual transformation from bourgeois society to the bureaucratic society of controlled consumption, during the decade of 1905–15, was as fundamental as that from the Renaissance to estate society in the early seventeenth century, or that from estate society to bourgeois society in the last third of the eighteenth century. There is no continuity from one period to the next; each is a different world.

Linearity was the chief characteristic of perception in bourgeois society. Visual primacy and objective reason, supported by typographic culture, isolated certain perceived phenomena as cause and others as effect. The linear connection from cause to effect imposed a positive order on intersubjective reality. Bourgeois society had inherited this linear perspective from estate society. However, the institutionalization of labor in bourgeois society brought forth new, different problems for linearity to resolve, such as "dynamics," "function," "structure," "organism," "evolution," and so on. Instead of a taxonomic representation-in-space, visuality and objective reason now extended the perceived connections among phenomena from the visible present to the invisible past and future, as a development-in-time. What could not be so ordered within consciousness was then symbolized as the unconscious, the cause of consciousness. Bourgeois ideology posited objective time and space as the limit of perception, and individual personality as an autonomy.

However, this linearity broke down in corporate capitalism. By the early twentieth century, correlative to the concentration and control of the leading industries by trusts and cartels, three altered relations characterized the multi-level structure of corporate capitalism, namely, those between production and consumption, between the economy and the state, and between economic structure and ideology. Consumption now became more manipulable, and production and consumption could be somewhat more closely coordinated in line with the inevitable prosperity and recession of the market. Government now played a greater role by cooperating with capital to promote a public sector of the economy, as a supplement to the private sector. And ideology through communications media played a greater role in facilitating the workings of advanced capitalism. Because of these structural changes, corporate capitalism can best be termed a bureaucratic society of controlled consumption. Within this new, more structured totality, linearity fell apart, no longer competent to deal with all the diverse, interacting forces.

We have seen that some philosophical and esthetic critics in bourgeois society had already pointed out the limitations of linear perspective, with its emphasis on visual primacy and objective reason. Blake in using the synesthesia of the five senses to free imagination; Nietzsche in rejecting any causation from within consciousness; Henry James in experimenting with shifting focuses of consciousness in his later novels; and Cézanne in depicting both objects and distances as geometric color patches were all trying to point to a reality beyond the bounds of linearity. In addition, others by the late nineteenth century also chafed against the rigidity of visual, rational perspective: Baudelaire had in *Les Fleurs du mal* (1857) used the correspndence of the five senses to free imagination from ordinary association, in order to point to a new reality. That reality as revealed in symbolist poetry from Mallarmé to Yeats could be either an immanent esthetic or a transcendent religious absolute, but definitely was not visual or rational. In philosophy, Henri Bergson had in *Time and Free Will* (1889) and *Matter and Memory* (1896) criticized the objectification of time by science. He distinguished the intuition of duration from mechanical time. The former, according to him, was the source of our reality. Finally, by the end of the nineteenth and beginning of the twentieth century, the revolt against visual, rational perspective by such avantgardists as Henri Rousseau, Erik Satie, Alfred Jarry, and Guillaume Apollinaire had resulted in the rejection of maturation in their own lives, and the acceptance of juxtaposition in their work. This juxtaposition, in the sense of "setting one thing beside the other without connective."[1] anticipated twentieth-century modernism.

However, the perceptual revolution of 1905–15 transformed the bourgeois field of perception. In a number of quite different, unrelated disciplines, visual, rational linearity was overthrown. What emerged in its stead can best be characterized as *multi-perspectivty*, i.e., the acceptance of different perspectival relations within a single discipline. Multi-perspectivty ushered in a new perceptual field in the twentieth century, to reflect the transformed structure of the bureaucratic society of controlled consumption. A number of historians believe that somewhere between the fin de siècle to the end of the first world war Europe underwent a fundamental transformation: R. Shattuck showed the years from 1885 to 1918 to be the origins of the avant-garde in France; H. S. Hughes considered the period from 1890 to 1930 as one of reconstruction in social thought; J. Romein pointed to the span from 1890 to 1914 as "the watershed of two eras"; and H. Lefebvre said: "Around the years 1905–10 the referentials broke down one after another under the influence of various pressures. Common sense and reason lost their unity and finally disintegrated.''[2] My contention is that during the decade of 1905–15 certain changes and discoveries in perception led to the displacement of linearity by multi-perspectivity. This new perceptual field, constituted by an electronic culture superimposed over typographic culture, by the extrapolation of hearing and seeing, as well as by a new epistemic order of synchronic system, is prevailing over the old bourgeois field of perception, although most of us still like to look at the twentieth century from pre-twentieth-century standpoints.

With the displacement of linearity by multi-perspectivity, time, space, and the individual are no longer the absolute coordinates in perception. Therefore, in this chapter, instead of continuing to describe further development in temporality, spatiality, and embodiment in the present century, I shall discuss first the perceptual revolution of 1905–15; then three of the distinctly new perceptual prospects in the bureaucratic society of controlled consumption, namely the semiology of the sign, the spatio-temporality of film, and the meta-communication of the image. These new perceptual dynamics are transforming the temporality, spatiality, and embodiment we inherited from bourgeois society.

The Perceptual Revolution of 1905–15

In the winter of 1904–5, Edmund Husserl gave a series of lectures at Göttingen, on the phenomenology of internal time-consciousness.[3] In these lectures, he distinguished phenomenological time from objective time. The former is the immanent time of the flow of consciousness. Within this flow, consciousness is characterized by an intentional structure, with its protention and retention. The intendedness of consciousness makes possible the connection of perceived phenomena in our experience. The significance of the lectures was that Husserl moved the analysis of temporality from mechanistic analogy to a hermeneutic, phenomenological description, i.e., analyzed consciousness on its own terms, rather than reducing it to be like something else. Then in 1907, Husserl lectured on the idea of phenomenology, and previewed the major themes of his philosophy. In that same year, Bergson published his *Creative Evolution,* in which he criticized the mechanical conceptualization of evolution from the standpoint of time as lived duration. Evolution, according to Bergson, was not a mechanical process but a creative becoming, during which the development from instinct to intelligence altered the very process itself. Evolution therefore could be characterized as *élan vital*. In different terminologies, both Husserl and Bergson inaugurated the twentieth-century concern with the philosophy of time-consciousness.

In 1905, Einstein published a number of far-reaching papers in the *Annalen der Physik*. In one, he used Max Planck's quantum hypothesis to explain the photoelectric effects of metals under the influence of light. According to Einstein, light instead of being radiation was composed of quanta or photons of energy traveling through space. In another paper, entitled "On the Electrodynamics of Moving Bodies," he introduced what subsequently was known as the special theory of relativity. The theory predicted that astrophysical events which appeared to be simultaneous to one observer in a particular state of motion would appear to take place at different times to other observers in other states of motion. The special theory of relativity revealed the limiting character of the speed of light, as well as challenging our commonly held concepts of space and time.

By 1908, the mathematician Herman Minkowski, who had been Einstein's teacher, said: "Henceforth space by itself, and time by itself, are doomed to fade away into mere shadows, and only a kind of union of the two will preserve an independent reality."[4] Instead of objective space and time, Minkowski worked out the mathematics of a four-dimensional space-time continuum.

In 1911, the first Solvay Congress of physicists was held at Brussels, attended by the leading theoreticians of the time. The congress was convened to consider the revolutionary impact of Einstein's theory; and its topic was "The Theory of Radiation and the Quantum of Energy." In the same year, Rutherford proposed a new model for the structure of the atom. He conceived of the atom as a positively charged, massive nucleus, with negatively charged electrons circling around it. The atom, in fact, was an electromagnetic field. Then in 1913, Niels Bohr, with the help of the quantum theory, explained the stability of the nuclear atom, as well as its emission of light.

In 1916, Einstein published his general theory of relativity, which extended the concept of relativity from electromagnetic field to gravitational field. Within the gravitational field, mass and energy are equivalent, an equivalence which presupposes the four-dimensional space-time continuum to be a curvature. This continuum, far from being rigid and homogeneous, "has geometric properties that vary from point to point and that are affected by local physical processes. Space-time ceases to be a stage . . . for the dynamics of nature; it becomes an integral part of the dynamic process."[5]

Within the span of 1905–16, the mechanistic universe posited by Newtonian physics was displaced by Einstein's theories of relativity.

It was a revolution in the perception of physical events. In the words of Werner Heisenberg, two important consequences ensued from that revolution: "The first was . . . that even such fundamental concepts as space and time could be changed and in fact must be changed on account of new experience. . . . [Secondly] the idea of the reality of matter . . . had at least to be modified in connection with the new experience."[6]

In this period, the foundations of mathematics also went through a fundamental crisis, out of which emerged three new, major approaches. The first was the logicism of Russell and Whitehead, as exemplified in their *Principia Mathematica* (1910–13), which argued that all mathematical notions are reducible to the idea of abstract property, and that mathematics is derived from basic logical principles concerning these properties. The second was the formalism of David Hilbert, which held that mathematics consists simply of the manipulation of finite configurations of symbols, in accordance with prescribed rules. Hilbert's work on integral equations in 1909 led to twentieth-century research in functional analysis. And the third was the intuitionism of L. E. J. Brouwer who, in his basic works from 1909 to 1913, approached mathematics as a self-sustained intellectual activity that deals with mental constructs governed by self-evident laws. Brouwer made fundamental contributions to the modern study of topology.[7]

Art, too, underwent transformation in this period, though no artist seemed too conversant with the contemporary developments in physics and mathematics. In 1906–7, Picasso painted his *Les Demoiselles d'Avignon,* a work which finally broke the confines of single-eye, visual perspective. The painting had no visual depth, but instead was a collage of angular shapes and color patches. Nor did it possess internal coherence, since the figures were rendered in different styles. Under its influence, Braque painted his *Grand Nu* in 1908. Then in close collaboration, the two produced a number of works, which critics subsequently called cubist. Cubism immediately affected the works of such other painters as Gleizes, Metzinger, Léger, La Fauconnier and Delaunay, whose exhibitions in 1910–12 attracted widespread attention, and made it a most influential movement.

Cubism was as important a revolution in the history of painting, as had been the introduction of visual perspective in the Renaissance.[8] It destroyed the very foundation of three-dimensional representation on two-dimensional canvas. Instead of Dürer's window looking into the world, painting now became an artistic conceptualization of the world. The change was from representation to presentation. As Metzinger pointed out in 1910, cubism was endowed with "a free and mobile perspective."[9] It could present reality from different perspectival angles. With that, the object in painting was liberated from the restriction of linearity. In fact, pictorial space itself became an element in cubist conceptualization. Both object and space fused as a collage of shapes and planes. Cubism was not realistic representation from a single perspective, but a multi-perspectival conceptualization of reality.

By destroying visual perspective, cubism became a liberating force in stimulating and accelerating other developments in modern art. After 1910, Italian futurism, the expressionism of the *Blaue Reiter,* the abstract art of Malevich and Mondrian, the fantastic art of Chagall, Klee, and Miro—each in a different way transcended the representation of visual perspective.[10] They were all indebted to the pioneering work of cubism. The only major exception was Kandinsky, who quite independently, in "Concerning the Spiritual in Art" (written in 1910) and "On the Problem of Form" (written in 1911), called for the subordination of form to the inner necessity of artistic content. Since form is only an expression of content, and content would differ from artist to artist, there could be many different forms.[11]

In architecture, according to Sigfried Giedion, a new "space conception set in at the beginning of this century with the optical revolution that abolished the single viewpoint of perspective. This had fundamental consequences for man's conception of architecture and the urban scene."[12] Previously, architecture had worked out the spatial contour of buildings and the "hollowing-out" of the interior space. But now it introduced a hitherto unknown interpenetration of inner and outer space, and of different levels. Around 1910, Peter Behrens in Germany, with his use of steel and glass in industrial architecture, and Auguste Perret in France with his work in reinforced concrete, were training an entire new generation of architects to tackle the new architectonics made possible by the new materials. In that year, Adolf Loos in Vienna designed the modernist Steiner house; and an important exhibition of the works of F. L. Wright was held in Berlin. In 1911, Gropius built the Fagus works, the first modern glass-and-iron-walled factory, with emphasis on the plane surface. And in 1915, Le Corbusier drew a ferroconcrete skeleton for a dwelling, which revealed a new relation between structural space and material.

In musical composition, Arnold Schönberg in the single year of 1909 wrote three piano pieces, five orchestral pieces, plus a song cycle, *Das Buch der Hängenden Gärten,* and a one-act, monodramatic opera, *Erwartung.* These were revolutionary works, which broke with the old system of tonality, where everything was ordered in relation to a fundamental perfect triad. Instead, dissonance liberated from tonality attained its full range of expression. In the short period from 1909 to 1913, Schönberg and his disciples, Alban Berg and Anton Webern, produced a new "decentralized system in which cadence or resolution was achieved partly by tone, color, rhythm, texture, and phrasing, and partly by the new importance given to chromatic saturation."[13] As he had written in a program note of 1910, Schönberg, in breaking with the restrictions of tonal harmony, was conscious of obeying an inner compulsion.[14] The form of atonal music was to him the expression of that inner necessity which determined for Kandinsky the form of nonperspectival, abstract painting. In fact, Kandinsky in his "Concerning the Spiritual in Art" quoted Schönberg to support his own position. Meanwhile in Paris, Igor Stravinsky, in collaboration with Diaghilev's Ballets Russes, wrote and conducted *The Firebird* in 1910, and *The Rites of Spring* in 1913. The latter with its unfamiliar African rhythms created a furor among the audience.

Around the same time, the form of the novel was transformed. In his later novels, especially in *The Golden Bowl* (1904), Henry James was concerned with "a certain indirect and oblique way" of presenting the action.[15] Rather than an unquestioned spatio-temporal framework, the story was focused through the sensibility of the narrator(s). However, in 1909, Gertude Stein went beyond that, with the publication of her *Three Lives*. In "Melanctha," the second of the three lives, she employed a series of repetitious words, phrases, sentences, and paragraphs, in order to recreate the monotonous rhythm of the protagonist's life. The emphasis was upon the recurrent, insistent present, rather than any development in time.[16] The next year, 1910, Raymond Roussel published his *Impressions d'Afrique*. The events in the book were uprooted from any specific time and space, being a series of imaginative, playful revelries. Nor were they approached from a specific perspective, but were rather presented in an impersonal, visual, i.e., cameralike, manner.[17] *Impressions d'Afrique* was a preview of the *nouveau roman* of Alain Robbe-Grillet. And in 1915, Dorothy Richardson published the first installment of her lengthy novel of interior monologue, *Pilgrimage*, where everything was rendered through the consciousness of the heroine.[18] It was a solipsist world.

Marcel Proust, following the death of his mother in 1905, went through a deeply troubled period in his life. After many false starts, he finally conceived in 1909 the main theme and general structure of *A la recherche du temps perdu*.[19] He devoted the rest of his life to completing the work. *Swann's Way,* the first volume, was published in 1913; but *Time Regained,* the seventh and last volume, did not appear until 1927, five years after his death. Not only did Proust in real life withdraw from society; but within the novel itself, the fictional world possessed no objectivity. Everything in the novel was a reworking of his memory. *In Search of Lost Time,* as pointed out by Proust in a 1913 interview, was a study of psychology in time.[20] Proust's own sensibility furnished all the elements in the novel. They were the raw material of his involuntary memory. However, Proust the author in retrospect had provided an esthetic re-cognition for them, so that the involuntary memory in life became the "time regained" in art. *In Search of Lost Time* was at once the means as well as the result of achieving a reflexive consciousness within the depth of subjective time.[21]

James Joyce left Dublin in October 1904, with his lover Nora Barnacle, to lead a life of exile on the Continent. In 1914, with sufficient distance in both time and space, he began to write *Ulysses,* a tale of Dublin on June 16, 1904, that crucial day, he erroneously believed, when he had first met Nora. For the next seven years, Joyce was at work on the novel, parts of which were serialized in 1918–20, but which was not finished until 1922. *Ulysses* was a complex, highly structured work, that put to an end the traditional bourgeois novel of chronological narrative. Ostensibly, it was the story of Stephen, Bloom, and Molly on a single day, rendered through interior monologues. But the novel was set under the aegis of the Ulysses myth of eternal search, thus implying a Viconian cycle of repetition. It was divided into eighteen scenes, each of which corresponded to a different hour of the day, a different art/muse, a different symbol, a different episode in the *Odyssey,* and each written in a different literary style. In addition, some scenes also corresponded to different colors, as well as different bodily organs. Joyce poured into the work all the metaphors, allusions, references, and plays upon words of which he was capable. The result was what Hugh Kenner called a novel of discontinuity, unfolding in the technological space of the typographic book, rather than being a continuous narrative in time.[22] By breaking with the convention of objective space and time and stable narrative perspective, Joyce created a work at once prismatic and microcosmic. The peculiar Joycean portrayal of a single day in Dublin refracted the universal human drama of quest.

In the field of historiography, Oswald Spengler in 1911 first conceived the idea for his *The Decline of the West.* By the time the first world war broke out, Spengler had completed the initial draft, which he then revised and which was ready for publication by 1917.[23] Spengler's ecentric, jumbled work of interpretation is not much appreciated by academic historians. Nevertheless, his vision of the morphology of culture was a definitive break with the linearity of chronological narrative. According to him, every culture was an autochthonous organic whole, informed with its own destiny, undergoing a life cycle of birth, growth, maturity, and decay. In fact, the arts, sciences, and mathematics, as well as the polity, economy, and social organization of each culture were uniquely and integrally interrelated, different from those of other cultures. Spengler's history presupposed spatio-temporal discontinuity. This presupposition marked him as one of the generation of 1905–15.

In sum, looking back from the vantage point of the 1920s, the hypersensitive Virginia Woolf said

> on or about December, 1910, human character changed. . . . The change was not sudden and definite like that. But a change there was, nevertheless; and, since one must be arbitrary, let us date it about the year 1910. . . . And when human relations change, there is at the same time a change in religion, conduct, politics, and literature.[24]

The concurrence of all these new approaches in the philosophy of time-consciousness, physics, mathematics, painting, architecture, music, the novel, and historiography in this decade of 1905–15 is remarkable. (We shall discuss below the lectures of Saussure on linguistics from 1906 to 1911, and the films of D. W. Griffith from 1908 to 1914.) There were internal factors in each discipline or art to account for its transformation, regardless of whether they had influenced each other. But what is significant is that they all rejected the linear perspective of visuality and Archimedean reason, in that crucial decade of 1905–15! Of course, even at present some people still work under the old presuppositions. But the new, multi-perspectival approach expresses an entirely different sensibility. For space and time in the twentieth century can no longer be the unquestioned, objective framework of perception, but have themselves become aspects of a functional system and change along with it. Instead of a developmental order within objective space-time, twentieth-century perception posits synchronic system without temporal continuity.

Sign, Structure, and Semiology

With the collapse of objective development-in-time, language was studied as a synchronic system rather than a historical formation. From 1906 to 1911, Saussure delivered his lectures on general linguistics at the University of Geneva. The key concepts proposed by him in these lectures set the stage for twentieth-century studies of linguistics, structuralism, and semiology. These lectures were subsequently reconstructed from students' notes and published as *Cours de linguistique générale*, in 1915.[25]

Saussure proposed a new science of linguistics, distinct from nine-teenth-century comparative philology. He criticized comparative philology for being insufficiently systematic and scientific. Instead, Saussure envisaged linguistics as a systematic science, with a clearly defined objective and procedure. The object of linguistic study would be different from the objects of other scientific studies. In all the other sciences, Saussure claimed, the objects were given in advance, then studied from different viewpoints. However, in linguistics, the object did not antedate the science. In fact, linguistics created its own object. It was therefore a totally self-contained science. The object of linguistic study is language (*langue*), as opposed to speech (*parole*). Language was social and necessary, with a set of binding rules which enabled people in a society to communicate. Speech, on the other hand, was many-sided and heterogeneous, varying from person to person. But language as the foundation of speech was a homogeneous system, a self-contained whole, amenable to scientific study.

The unit of linguistic study, according to Saussure, is the sign; and language is a system of signs. Each sign is an arbitrary combination of a sound-image and a concept. The sound-image is the signifier, whereas the concept is the signified. A signifier or sound-image is pho-netically different from other sound-images; and the signified or con-cept is what it is because it is different from other concepts. Language has "only differences *without positive* terms."[26] The relation between each signifier and signified, which constitutes a sign, is neither natural nor consciously derived. It is in this sense that Saussure insisted that the linguistic sign is arbitary. The sign resulting from the arbitrary combination of signifier and signified has no value in itself, but only in relation to all other signs in a language system. "Language is a system of interdependent terms in which the value of each term results solely from the simultaneous presence of the others."[27] In fact, the relations among these terms resemble algebra.

The intervention of time creates a peculiar difficulty for linguis-tics. Language, so argued Saussure, is a complex system, which pos-sesses a collective inertia, yet necessarily changes through time. It is impossible for one to study simultaneously the systematic relationship of the signs as well as their changes across time. Hence, linguistics has to be divided into synchronic and diachronic studies. Synchrony ap-proaches the terms in any state of language as a systematic whole. Since each system is strictly atemporal, synchrony cannot deal with any problem of change. On the other hand, diachrony approaches the problem of change as a specific event; so it in turn cannot be systematic. To the former belongs the study of general grammar; to the latter, phonetic transformation.

Semiology as defined by Saussure studies the life of signs in society.[28] Since language is a system of signs, it is a semiological system. The semiological system differs from other social institutions in that it utilizes signs for expression. Signs are characterized by the fact that their relationship always eludes the individual or social will. There are many systems of signs besides language, such as writing, sign language for the speech and hearing impaired, symbolic rites, polite formulas, military signals, etc. But language is the most universal of all such systems. "In this sense linguistics can become the master-pattern for all branches of semiology although language is only one particular semiological system."[29]

Saussure assumed the binary oppositions between synchrony and diachrony, between *langue* and *parole,* between signifier and signified. The synchrony/diachrony opposition intersected the epistemic order of development-in-time. Instead, linguistics studied the spatial relations of signs; and diachronic event was subordinated to synchronic system.[30] The *langue/parole* opposition systematized language at a level other than that of intersubjective communication, since linguistics was not concerned with speech. And the signifier/signified opposition revealed the signifier to be that order amenable to systematic analysis, at the expense of the signified. The Saussurean concept of system was concerned with only synchrony, *langue,* and signifier. It posited a functional, differential relationship, beneath or beyond that of intentional, intersubjective reality.

Although Saussure himself never used the term structure, his concept of system was the basis for twentieth-century structuralism. As Roman Jakobson said in 1929:

> The leading idea of present-day science in its most various manifestations [is] *structuralism.* Any set of phenomena examined by contemporary science is treated not as a mechanical agglomeration but as a structural whole, and the basic task is to reveal the inner . . . laws of this system. What appears to be the focus . . . is no longer the outer stimulus, but the internal premises of the development; now the mechanical concept of processes yields to the question of their function.[31]

The structuralism of Claude Lévi-Strauss utilizes Saussure's concept of the double articulation of the sign to study kinship, myth, ritual, art, religion, etc. These are symbolic relations of exchange based upon concrete terms, which one can analyze as semiological systems. For example, myth, according to Lévi-Strauss, employs such concrete terms as raw and cooked, fresh and decayed, moistened and burnt, to express the abstract binary opposition of nature/culture. The structural analysis of myth considers these categories not as the signified, but as signifiers. The delineation of the paradigmatic/syntagmatic relations of these signifiers reveals an underlying system or structure of correlations. Paradigmatic relations are synchronic, whereas syntagmatic relations are diachronic. Among the various definitions given by Lévi-Strauss, the simplest and most direct is that "structures are models, the formal properties of which can be compared independently of their elements."[32] This method of analysis consists of the following steps:

> (1) define the phenomenon under study as a relation between two or more terms, real or supposed;
> (2) construct a table of possible permutations between these terms;
> (3) take this table as the general object of analysis which at this level only, can yield necessary connections.[33]

Lévi-Strauss, following Jakobson, criticized the fundamental opposition made by Saussure between synchrony and diachrony. At the level of structural analysis, he argued, this opposition can no longer apply. For example, the bundle of relations constituting a myth may appear in different combinations in different places and times. However, the structure of that myth persists through spatio-temporal variations, and cannot be said to be strictly synchronic or diachronic. It transcends that binary opposition.[34]

Structure is therefore constant and universal, according to Lévi-Strauss. It is the mental pattern which governs the manifest content of symbolic exchange. At the beginning of *Totemism,* Lévi-Strauss quoted from Auguste Comte that the laws of logic which ultimately govern the world of the mind are essentially invariable, common to all periods and places, as well as all subjects.[35] Hence, structure is unconscious; and structural analysis has nothing to do with the intersubjective world of human meaning. It does not ask questions of why and how, which fall into the provinces of ethnography and history. Summarizing his various works, he said in *The Raw and the Cooked:* "Throughout . . . I have always aimed at drawing up an inventory of mental patterns, to reduce apparently arbitrary data to some kind of order, and to attain a level at which a kind of necessity becomes apparent, underlying the illusions of liberty."[36] Beneath the determinism of his structural analysis, we detect a melancholy.

Lévi-Strauss believed that von Neumann and Morgenstern's *Theory of Games and Economic Behavior,* Wiener's *Cybernetics,* and Shannon and Weaver's *Mathematical Theory of Communication* have provided a mathematical basis for Saussure's ideal of semiology. Structuralism can apply their systems of communication to society.[37] For example, language is the exchange of messages, kinship the exchange of mates, and economy the exchange of goods and services. Structural analysis can uncover the formal systems which govern the exchanges that occur in language, kinship, and economy and draw relations of homology and transformation among them.[38] "Everything is different when the system consists of *classes of relations*. . . . The ultimate units of the system are no longer single member classes . . . but classed relations."[39]

If for Lévi-Strauss structure is unconscious, then for Jacques Lacan the unconscious is structured as a language. According to Lacan, the subject is never a unifying whole. Being is radically ex-centric to itself, characterized by a fundamental gap at the center. Instead of *cogito ergo sum*, for Lacan, "I am not, wherever I am the plaything of my thought; I think of what I am wherever I don't think I am thinking."[40] Being and consciousness are always at odds with each other. Freud had introduced the concept of unconscious to explain this elusive, ex-centric tendency of being. "But," Lacan insists, "the unconscious has nothing to do with instinct or primitive knowledge or preparation of thought in some underground. It is a thinking with words, with thoughts that escape your vigilance."[41] Lacan thus shifts the locus of the unconscious from within the self to beyond it. Language unfolds the connection between self and the unconscious, since it can be used "to say something quite other than what it says."[42]

For Lacan, the structure of language resides in Saussure's binary opposition of signifier/signified. However, he criticizes Saussure's concept of the unity of signifier and signified in the sign; instead, within the sign the signifier dominates over the signified. There is a chain of signifiers, with each signifier being what it is only in differential relations with the other signifiers of the chain. Therefore, the sign is never constant. "Only the correlations between signifier and signifier supply the standard for all research into meaning. . . . For the signifier, by its very nature, anticipates on meaning by unfolding its dimension before it."[43] Following the classic study of Jakobson,[44] Lacan delineates two axial movements of the signifier within the chain: one metaphoric, in terms of similarity; the other metonymic, in terms of contiguity. Or to put this in the language of Freud, condensation is the speech wherein a similar signifier is substituted for another; and displacement is when a contiguous signifier is substituted for the proximate one. Hence, instead of the constancy of the sign, there is "an incessant sliding of the signified under the signifier."[45]

The subject in discourse utilizes the chain of signifiers, with the signified sliding underneath. It is in relation to this chain of signifiers that the ego (*moi*) is constituted. However, "the subject has to emerge from the given of the signifiers which cover him in an Other which is their transcendental locus; through this he constitutes himself in an existence where [desire] is possible."[46] The subject in desiring the symbolic Other transcends its ego and the chain of signifiers. This Other is the fourth point in the quadrilateral relations consisting in addition of subject, signifiers, and ego. Desire is the axial movement from the subject toward the symbolic Other. In turn, "the condition of the subject depends on what is being unfolded in the Other. . . . What is being unfolded there is articulated like a discourse . . . whose syntax Freud first sought to define for those fragments of it which come to us in certain privileged moments, dreams, slips of the tongue or pen, flashes of wit."[47] It is in this sense that "the unconscious is the discourse of the Other."[48]

Roland Barthes, in *Elements of Semiology* (1964), criticized Saussure's idea that linguistics was part of a more general science of the signs, with the implication that nonlinguistic signs could constitute semiological systems in themselves. Instead, Barthes believed,

> [it is] difficult to conceive a system of images and objects whose signifieds can exist independently of language; to perceive what a substance signifies is inevitably to fall back on the individuation of a language: there is no meaning which is not designated, and the world of signifieds is none other than that of language.[49]

There is no nonlinguistic semiological system. Hence, Barthes would reverse the Saussurean order of classification, and say that semiology is a part of linguistics, and that the analysis of any semiological system must expose its linguistic components. Thus, the semiological analysis of garments, food, furniture, and architecture as systems of communication must deal with the metaphoric and metonymic axes of those languages which systematize garments, food, furniture, and architecture.[50] For example, in *Système de la mode,* a semiological analysis of fashion, Barthes studied not fashion per se, but the language of fashion.

In addition to a system of communication, there can be, according to Barthes, staggered systems of signification, when one system is imbricated with another. Each system comprises signifiers and signifieds, uniting to form its signs. But, in *connotation,* the signs of one system become the signifiers of the next staggered system, so that the signifieds of the connotative system become ideologically diffused and global. On the other hand, in *metalanguage,* the signs of one system operate as the signifieds of the next, as, for example, in scientific language.[51]

In "Myth Today" (1957), Barthes characterized the system of communication in bourgeois society as a staggered system of connotation, although at the time he called it a metalanguage. Myth, a type of speech, is "a second-order semiological system. That which is a sign in the first system, becomes a mere signifier in the second."[52] Thus, the meaning imbedded in the sign of one system becomes the form of mythic communication in the next. For example, according to Barthes, a young black African in French uniform saluting is a signifier for the myth that France is a great empire. It does not matter that one can see through this, because the aim of myth is to cause an immediate impression. Myth, in effect, is stolen language, using the signs of other languages for its own purpose. Bourgeois society "is the privileged field for mythical significations."[53] Bourgeois ideology, in spreading itself anonymously over everything, transforms history into universal nature, thus hiding itself behind its communication of myth.

The structural analysis of the signifier is a distinctly twentieth-century methodology, emerging out of the perceptual revolution of 1905–15. With the collapse of the objective spatio-temporal framework, the sign was exposed as the new focus for analytic knowledge, displacing the positive fact. Structure as an immanent, self-contained, atemporal system became the sign's grid, displacing the event-in-time. Structural analysis is a new positivism, caring neither for causality nor for dynamics, referring neither to a speaking, acting subject, nor to the world of intersubjectivity or things.[54] This is the price paid for the abstract, logical system of the signs. But can it not also be attacked as a solipsist reflection of the scientific mentality? Lévi-Strauss admitted as much, when he said that his "book of myths is itself a kind of myth."[55] Nevertheless, the application of structuralist method to certain previously nonlinguistic topics can be fruitful, as, for example, in Lévi-Strauss's study of the social exchange of the signifiers; Lacan's extension of the language model to the Freudian unconscious; and Barthes's ideas concerning the second-order semiological system.

Michel Foucault repeatedly insists he is not a structuralist. But his works are appropriate to mention here, because they are an explicit critique of structuralism. In opposition to the synchronic structure of the sign, Foucault studies the internal economy of discourse, namely, its *epistemes,* i.e., the underlying a priori in discursive formations. Though as unconscious as structures, the epistemes are not universal but historical, changing from period to period. In his inaugural lecture at the Collège de France in 1970, Foucault pointed out that every society has certain procedures to control, select, organize, and redistribute the productions of discourse. These procedures are Foucault's subject matter, for his basic purpose is "to restore to discourse its character as an event; to abolish the sovereignty of the signifier."[56] Foucault rejects the structural analysis of *langue,* in favor of the historical study of discursive events. These events, however, are located in discontinuous series. His history of discourse is the exact opposite of Lévi-Strauss's structural anthropology.

The Spatio-Temporality of Film

While semiology has been analyzing the system of linguistic signs, cinematography has created a new, different reality out of visual image and sound.[57] This reality is a three-level perceptual structure, consisting of the basic ingredients of image and sound; the immanent perspective of camera and editing; and the spatio-temporality peculiar to film.

The new spatio-temporality created by cinematography is a substitute for the lived space-time of the audience. Sitting passively in a darkened cinema, the audience is transported into the illuminated space-time of the silver screen. This is not a lived space-time, yet it is inherently more compelling than that experienced in viewing a framed painting or reading a novel. The action on the screen pulls the audience along inexorably, with its own tempo. The spatio-temporality of a film transports the audience beyond itself. Thus it is a vicarious substitute for the embodied, lived space-time of the everyday world. First only image; then sound and color; eventually cinemascope and stereophonic sound—there is projected on the screen an extrapolated, expanded visual-auditory reality lacking the smell, taste, and touch of everyday reality. Yet precisely because of its visual-auditory intensity, filmic reality can be more gripping than everyday reality.

Camera shots and editing cuts constitute the immanent perspective of a film. Each scene in a film is the result of a calculated camera shot, whether angled or straightforward; mise-en-scène or close-up; stationary, tracking, or pan; lighted or dimmed; focused or diffused. In addition, the cutting and editing of these scenes, whether in sequence or in juxtaposition, whether mere editing or montage, again offer innumerable possibilities. Together, camera and editing constitute the multi-perspectivity of a film, being much more dynamic than the visual perspective of a painting or the narrator in the novel. Camera and editing define the unique spatio-temporality of each film.

Image and sound are the basic ingredients of film. The filmic image is already an analog, a visual trace of the world. As such it is concrete, vivid, and immediately cognizable. The image is an iconic sign, as distinct from a linguistic sign.[58] As Christian Metz admitted, the film's "raw material is the image—that is to say, the photographic duplication of a real spectacle, which always and already has a meaning. . . . The cinema [communicates] *with no codes other than that of perception.*" However, any perception of image is always within certain codes of language. When we recognize an image, we are reading it. Therefore, the image not only possesses an inherent iconicity, but acquires linguistic codes. This combination of iconicity and linguistic signification makes the image a much more powerful means of communication than the linguistic sign. Precisely because of its inherent iconicity, the cinematographic reality constituted by filmic image can be profoundly evocative. Pier Paolo Pasolini recognized this quality of the film, and likened it to the world of dream and memory.[59] The visual, oneiric power of film is unique, unmatched by any other medium. Maya Deren has said:

> Inasmuch as the other art forms are not constituted of reality itself, they create metaphors of reality. But photography being itself the reality or the equivalent thereof, can use its own reality as a metaphor for ideas and abstractions. . . .
> This image, with its unique ability to engage us simultaneously on several levels . . . is the building block for the creative use of the [film] medium.[60]

Filmic sound includes human speech, natural sounds, music, and dissonance. Sound can be used to support and reinforce image; or, in juxtaposition with image, it can become a study in contrast. Together, image and sound are the basic ingredients within the dynamic, multi-perspectival spatio-temporality of the film.

Film, as a self-contained visual-auditory reality, is an autonomous *presentation* of image and sound, which does not necessarily have to be a *representation* of anything beyond itself, although it can be used for that purpose. However, the representational expection of the bourgeois audience overlies the unique, presentational quality of the film. In other words, film is not inherently realistic and narrative; but in its expectation the audience imposes the ideology of realism onto the visual, oneiric potential inherently in the film. Therefore, filmic image often is not presented on its own term, but as a realistic representation of the world, and filmic sound is often presented as a vehicle for narrative discourse. From this conflict between the direct visual-auditory potential of film and the representational expectation of the audience, there emerged three types of film: (1) fictional film, which imitated first the language of the theater, then that of the novel, in the fictive representation of the world; (2) factual film, which seeks the nonfictional representation of the world; and (3) experimental film, variously known as avant-garde, poetic, underground, visionary, or abstract-formal, which directly explores the visual, auditory qualities of image and sound (or substitutes graphics for image), rather than undertaking any realistic representation. Each type of film has a different perceptual prospect.

Fictional Film

The cinematographic potential of the film combined with the representational expectation of the audience to produce the fictional film, which soon became the dominant type of film, overshadowing the other two types. In the course of its growth, fictional film had to solve such problems as narrative technique, visual representation, visual-audio synchronization, and the critique of filmic reality.

Fictional film tells a story. It has a plot, with a beginning, a conflict, and a denouement. In this, it followed the pre-1905 bourgeois novel. However, film had to discover its own technique of narrative, so that prose description and action could be translated into a sequence of framed images. Quite appropriately, it was during the crucial decade of perceptual revolution that the technique of film narrative was worked out.[61] In 1903, Edwin S. Porter, in *The Life of an American Fireman*, crosscut scenes to tell a story; then in *The Great Train Robbery*, he sequenced scenes from different places and different times. From 1908 to 1914, D. W. Griffith broke the staged scene into separate shots, ranging from close-up to panorama, and edited them with rhythmic tempo and parallel and intercutting. Utilizing both camera and editing to tell a story, Griffith reached the height of his career in *The Birth of a Nation* (1915), and launched fictional film on its long, profitable career.

Beyond the narrative technique of camera and editing, there was the problem of visual representation. The filmic image is already a visual reality; but within the context of fictional film, the image assumes a representational function. The esthetic problem was how best to fulfill this representational function. The expressionist style of *The Cabinet of Dr. Caligari* (1919) was one solution which was an interesting failure. The style of that film, as Panofsky pointed out, was designed into the stage setting, rather than being the result of camera or editing. Hence it was theatrical and ornamental, rather than cinematographic, and remained merely interesting from the standpoint of "art."[62] The lesson learned from this failure is that the representational connection between filmic image and fictional narrative must be direct, explicit. Film, according to Béla Balázs, is a new visual culture. "This is not a language

of signs . . . it is the visual means of communication, without intermediary, of souls clothed in flesh.''[63] If the expressionist ornamentalism
of *The Cabinet of Dr. Caligari* was abortive, then the comedy of Chap-
lin's gesture, the drama of cowboy and gangster chase, the romance
of Garbo's face became successful genres of the silent films of the
twenties, because these were based on the specific potential of visual
representation in film.

After 1928, sound supplemented the visual image of fictional film
with voice, music, noise, and even the newly significant silence, to
structure a visual-auditory reality. There emerged the problem of the
synchronization of image and sound, because inevitably sound modified the visualization of gesture, movement, and facial expression.
Sound could supplement visual representation in comedy, western, and
romance; in addition, it produced a new genre, the musicals of the
thirties. However, the potential for the counterpoint between image
and sound remained largely unexplored in the thirties. By the end of
that decade, the technical achievement of the fictional film was more
or less complete. The most notable examples of that era were *La Règle
du jeu* (1939) by Renoir, and *Citizen Kane* (1941) by Welles and Toland.

Fictional film resulted from the concourse of the cinematographic
potential of the film and the realist expectation of the audience; and
it was determined by the economics of the Hollywood studio system.
That system promoted glamour and personality, in order to maintain
its hold on the audience. It was a subsystem of controlled consumption
in corporate capitalism. And any criticism of that filmic reality had to
come from outside Hollywoood.

In the period before World War II, it was Eisenstein who undertook the most thorough critique of camera and editing in fictional film.
According to him, the shot was the basic ingredient in film, with each
shot composed of formal, analyzable elements, such as lighting, line,
movement, volume. In addition, the shot was not simply a discrete
unit, to be linked with other shots; rather, each shot was a montage
cell, which could be organically constructed in collision with other
shots. In the conflict of shots a new synthesis was achieved. Montage
therefore was conflict, as opposed to mere editing. Eisenstein mentioned such diverse possibilities as rhythmic montage, metric montage,
tonal montage, overtonal montage, and ultimately even intellectual
montage. In addition, montage could also include the counterpoint of
image and sound, of image and color. On the basis of the montage of
image, color, and sound, a new synesthesia could be achieved. Instead
of editing shots mechanically in terms of a plot, montage organically
constructed shots around a theme; and the totality of the montages in

a film was its form. Film, according to Eisenstein, could be dialectical expression, rather than mere surface reality.[64]

In the forties, the critique of the reality of fictional film took new turns, first with the Italian neorealists, then with the French New Wave. Neorealism began with Visconti's *Ossessione* (1942), then achieved acclaim with Rossellini's *Rome, Open City* (1945) and de Sica's *Bicycle Thief* (1948), the latter scripted by Cesare Zavattini, the leading theoretician of Italian neorealism. Neorealism criticized the supposed reality of the Hollywood fictional film from the standpoint of the reality of concrete, everyday life. That life, according to Zavattini, was rich, and should be looked at directly. "The cinema's overwhelming desire to see, to analyze, its hunger for reality, is an act of concrete homage towards . . . what is happening and existing in the world. And, incidentally, it is what distinguishes 'neo-realism" from the American cinema.''[65] Film therefore should project the reality of everyday life, without glamour. On the other hand, the New Wave of Truffaut, Godard, Chabrol, Rohmer, and Rivette, beginning in 1958, approached the critique of filmic reality from the opposite end, i.e., concern with its visual, auditory language. Nurtured by the Cinémathèque Française and *Cahiers du Cinéma,* the New Wave filmmakers were interested in bringing out the technique and mannerism which underlay the Hollywood fictional film, to show that its concept of filmic reality was in effect an idiosyncratic style. Out of the consciousness of film history, each New Wave director then went on to make highly personal, stylized films of his own.[66]

More recently, three filmmakers have contributed most to the perceptual critique of fictional film, namely, Resnais, Antonioni, and Godard. Resnais, especially in *Last Year at Marienbad* (1961), is concerned with the visual representation of time-consciousness, without the convention of chronological sequence: As he said: "The interior monologue is never in the sound track; it is almost always in the visuals, which, even when they show events in the past, correspond to the *present* thoughts in the mind of the character. So what is presented as the present or the past is simply a reality which exists while the character is speaking.''[67] No more, and no less. The visual, auditory reality of Resnais's films seeks to approximate the complex fluidity of thought. Antonioni, in his own words, "set out to do a montage that would be absolutely free . . . through a juxtaposition of separate isolated shots and sequences that had no immediate connection with one another.''[68] By means of this juxtaposition, he created his peculiar filmic reality. In *L'Avventura* (1960), *La Notte* (1961), and *Red Desert* (1964), he succeeded in expressing the symptoms and behavior of restlessness in contemporary bourgeois life, through the counterpoint of image, sound, and eventually color. Godard in his films of the sixties went beyond Resnais and Antonioni. Filmmaking was for him a form of semiological criticism. From a critique of the narrative technique of fictional film, he advanced to a critique of the "bourgeois concept of representation."[69] Within his films Godard questioned the perceptual relation between image and reality, between filmmaker and film, and between film and audience. In effect, he was out to destroy the autonomy of representational reality in the fictional film. Thus, after *One Plus One* (1968), his works transcended the boundary between fiction and documentary. He put more of himself into his films than other filmmakers, and demanded more intellectually from his audience.

Factual Film

In both fictional and factual films, image and sound assume a representational function, and are not presented on their own terms. However, fictional image and sound represent the world within the story, whereas factual image and sound represent the world outside. In the former, the representation is dictated by the story; but in the latter, the representation opens up the question of the relation of sound and image to the outside world. In addition, because it refers to the world outside the film, the factual film reveals much more explicitly the filmmaker's underlying attitude or ideology.

There are many types of factual film—ethnographic record, instructional film, travelogue, newsreel, documentary. Here, I shall restrict myself to the documentary, and in particular to the works of Robert Flaherty; Alberto Cavalcanti and Walter Ruttmann; J. Grierson and associates; Leni Riefenstahl; Dziga Vertov; and *cinéma vérité* or direct cinema. Depending on the filmmakers' attitudes, their works reveal different representational relations between the documentary and the world.

In filming his *Nanook of the North* (1922), Flaherty lived among the Eskimos and got them involved in his film production. He was able to achieve a rapport with them; yet his film ignored that aspect of reality, to represent the world of Nanook as solely a conflict between man and nature. The reality of this film was predicated on Flaherty's romantic ideology of the noble savage. And that ideology intervened between the naive realism of the film and the real world of the Eskimos.

On the other hand, Cavalcanti, in *Rien qu les heures* (1926), depicted the lives of a number of people in different parts of Paris, at intervals throughout the day. And Ruttmann, in *Berlin: Symphony of a City* (1927), orchestrated scenes to convey the multivarious ways and tempos of a city. With these two films began the collage representation of urban scenes. But the collage depended on the underlying attitude of the filmmaker. Cavalcanti was the more socially conscious and critical of the two, and showed the contrast between the rich and the poor in the city.[70]

In Britain during the 1930s, the works of John Grierson and as-. sociates accepted the challenge of defining the documentary's relation to the world. Grierson believed that the camera's capacity for getting around, for observing and selecting from life could be exploited in a new, vital art form, because the original person and actual scene were always better guides to the representation of the modern world, and materials and stories taken from the raw could be finer than fiction. However, the documentary that resulted was no longer art for art's sake, but a social democratic inquiry into the workings of our modern world. It was therefore "a creative treatment of actuality."[71] In spite of the fact that he had to depend upon the state or industry for financial support, Grierson produced such outstanding works as *Night Mail* (1936) and *Fires Were Started* (1943). His documentaries became a model for others elsewhere.

Leni Riefenstahl's *The Triumph of the Will* (1936) undertook quite a different definition of the relation between the documentary and the world. That film was about a Nazi rally in Nuremberg; but the rally was staged with the filming in mind.[72] Therefore, instead of film representing reality, here the event was accentuated and glamorized in the film, so that film as pseudoevent loomed larger than the original event. If Grierson's documentary was a liberal inquiry into the world, then Riefenstahl's was a Nazi transfiguration of the world.

Each of the documentary styles mentioned was founded upon an explicit nonfilmic ideology, whether romantic, impressionist, liberal, or Nazi. The particular ideology defined that film's representation of the world. But, already in the twenties, Dziga Vertov had realized this perceptual connection. The camera eye was for him mobile, unlike the human eye, and much more powerful. It could perceive and record quite differently than the human eye. A documentary taking full advantage of the mobile camera would be quite different also from theater or literature. It would consist of "a dashing survey of visual events deciphered by the movie camera, with their intervals condensed into a cumulative whole by the great mastery of an editing technique."[73] Such, in effect, was his own *The Man with a Movie Camera* (1928).

Dziga Vertov had provided the theoretical argument for direct cinema. Or to put it the other way around, direct cinema was the technical realization of Vertov's kino eye. That realization had to wait for the invention of light, portable camera, and sound equipment, so that a two-person team could synchronize the visual and audio recording of events. In the sixties, the direct cinema or *cinéma vérité* of Richard Leacock in the U.S., of Pierre Perrault in Canada, and of Jean Rouch in France took advantage of the new equipment.[74] The result was a more intimate encounter between film and the world. As Leacock explained it:

> What's happening, the action, has no limitations, neither the significance of what's happening. The filmmaker's problem is more a problem of how to convey it. . . . When you watch the action through the camera, you always see it as it never happened before. . . .
> I am always aware of the fact that our concept of what's going to happen is wildly wrong. . . . Because, usually, what's happening is more intriguing.[75]

Direct cinema provided a new possibility for the documentary representation of the world, revealing much more the dynamics of that world.

Experimental Film

Instead of representing a fictional or factual world, image and sound can be freed from that constraint and presented for the sake of their own cinematographic potential. Furthermore, abstract graphics can be substituted for visual images. Experimental film is not one particular genre or style, but leads to different innovative, hitherto undreamed of, directions. Basically, it is nonrepresentational, in exploring the cinematographic potential of image, sound, and/or graphics themselves.

In the 1920s, the two major trends in experimental film were the avant-garde and surrealism. Under the influence of cubism and abstract art, avant-garde film dealt with plastic forms and rhythmic movement. Both Viking Eggeling's *Diagonal Symphony* (1921) and Hans Richter's *Rhythm 21* (1921) orchestrated abstract forms; and Fernand Léger's *Ballet mécanique* (1924) subordinated image and graphics to rhythmic movement.[76] Nevertheless, these experiments can be accused of being mere abstract forms put into motion, rather than taking advantage of the intrinsic potential of cinematography. On the other hand, Bunuel and Dali in *Un Chien andalou* (1929) utilized visual image in an entirely unexpected manner. Nominally, the film was the story of a man and a woman; but the images in the film were often dislodged from their representational function, to assume a surreality of their own. As Bunuel said of this film:

> Its aim is to provoke in the spectator instinctive reactions of

attraction and of repulsion. . . . The motivation of the images was, or meant to be, purely irrational! They are as mysterious and inexplicable to the two collaborators as to the spectator. NOTHING, in the film, SYMBOLIZES ANYTHING.[77]

The controversy between abstract graphics and surrealist image defined the range of nonrepresentational experiments in the 1920s. Formalism replaced the image with abstraction, whereas surrealism liberated the image from its ordinary perceptual framework. Against this background, Cocteau's *Le Sang d'un poète* (1930), though containing some interesting scenes, was a failure which did not profit from the lessons of the twenties. That film was an allegory of the poet's pilgrimage, told in terms of personal and literary symbols. Cocteau did not explore fully the nonrepresentational potential of film. Instead, he considered film "a powerful weapon for the projection of thought."[78] Thus, the images in *Le Sang d'un poète* were burdened with excessive representational references.

In contrast, Maya Deren's *Meshes of the Afternoon* (1943), with camera work by Alexander Hammid and music by Teiji Ito, was an outstanding achievement that explored imaginatively the potential of the filmic image and sound. Deren took advantage of the ability of film to manipulate space and time, by vertically exploring in depth and quality all the ramifications of a moment.[79] Her own observation is still worth quoting:

> [*Meshes of the Afternoon*] is concerned with the relationship between the imaginative and the objective reality. The film begins in actuality and, eventually, ends there. But in the meantime the imagination . . . intervenes. It seizes upon a casual incident and, elaborating it into critical proportions, thrusts back into reality the production of its convolutions. . . .
> Such a development is, obviously, not a function of some "realistic" logic; it is a necessity, a destiny established as a logic of the film itself. . . . It is a whole creation out of the elements of reality . . . but these are so combined as to form a new reality, a new context which defines them according to their function within it. Consequently, *they are not symbols in the sense of referring to some meaning or value outside the film . . . they are images whose values and meaning are defined and confined by their actual function in the context of the film as a whole.*[80]

If Deren vertically restructured an event out of its realistic temporal framework, then Stan Brakhage in *Dog Star Man* (1960–64) restored to visual image its instantaneous purity, unhindered by any remembrance or anticipation, and unrestrained by reason. As he said in "Metaphors of Vision":

> Imagine an eye unruled by man-made laws of perspective, an eye unprejudiced by compositional logic. . . . Imagine a world alive with incomprehensible objects and shimmering with an endless variety of movement and innumerable gradations of color. . . .
> [This is] perception in the original and deepest sense of the word. . . .
> [The result is] transforming optic abstract impressions into *non-representational* language.

The images of Brakhage, liberated from representational constraint, revealed a Blakean vision of "birth, sex, death, and the search for God."[81]

More recently, experimental film, as Malcolm Le Grice pointed out, has gone beyond mere image and sound to explore the formal, cinematographic properties of the medium. First, it takes into account the actual material and process of film itself, to get away from representation of any reality. Second, within the film, it is concerned with the relationship between filmmaker, medium, and audience. And, third, it seeks to counteract the emotional manipulation of representational films, by developing conscious, reflexive modes of perception.[82]

Film is a projection of image and sound, within the context of a dynamic, multi-perspectival spatio-temporality. The filmic image is more concrete and immediate than linguistic sign. It is a visual trace, lacking the double articulation of the sign. And it can be used for many different purposes. The spatio-temporality of a particular film provides the context for the signification of its image and sound. In this sense, every film defines its own context. Nevertheless, the signifying level of image and sound depends upon whether that particular film is fictional, factual, or experimental. The image and sound in fictional film represent a fictive world, whereas those in factual film represent the real world. In contrast, experimental film detaches image and sound from their representational function, in order to explore other possibilities. Fictional, factual, and experimental films have taught us that in the post-1905 world of multi-perspectivity image and sound have acquired new versatility to communicate at different levels of signification.

Six

The Meta-Communication of Image

The content of communication presupposes a stable, unquestioned communicatonal framework which is acceptable to all its addressees. However, with the transformation from one culture of communications media to another, the explicit content of communication in one culture assumes extra-dimensional signification in the new culture. In other words, the new culture of communications media can *meta-communicate* the content of the old.[83] The perceptual revolution of 1905–15 marked the transformation from the old bourgeois field of perception to a new, twentieth-century perceptual field. The transformation from visual, objective linearity to multi-perspectivity resulted from the submersion of typographic culture with its mentality and personality makeup beneath a sediment of electronic culture with its new, different mentality and personality makeup still in formation. This cultural transformation is the background for the meta-communication of image.

Image rather than linguistic sign is the appropriate means for twentieth-century meta-communication. A sign is a unit within a self-contained language system. It does not refer directly to anything, except differentially in relation to all the other signs in that system of double articulation. This is what semiology has taught us. On the other hand, an image at once oneiric and signifying is already motivated and refers directly to an intended object, whether real or illusory. It is a trace in the perceptual field and can be used for many different purposes. Cinematography has shown us its prospects, in different filmic spatio-temporalities. The linguistic sign is a unit in a closed language system; but the image as an iconic sign is open-ended. Hence the latter can be the most effective means for meta-communication. Language presupposes synchronic structure; but every image has a sedimented past which can be used for other purposes in the future. We therefore need to clarify the image on its own terms, rather than "read" it as a linguistic sign.

Image originally referred to a physical likeness or figure; it was a copy or imitation of something. However, since the sixteenth century, image has increasingly become an interior, mental concept; and it is usually with the latter meaning that we associate the word.[84] The new, subjective meaning was related to the advent of typographic culture, which shifted the sensing hierarchy from hearing and touching to the primacy of sight. Perception therefore became more visual; with the result that the person began to possess an interior at variance with the outside.[85] Image results from the perceptual connection of the person in the world. Thus, the typographic image was at once more visual and more subjective than earlier ones.

However, beginning in the mid-nineteenth century, the typographic image increasingly and successively came under the impact of photography, film, surrealism, and advertising via the new audio-visual media. Together, these have brought about a fundamental turnover in the meaning and efficacy of the image. Thus, currently, "vivid image [has come] to overshadow pale reality."[86]

During the second half of the nineteenth century, the photographic image came to displace the typographic image as the criterion for exactitude. Typography made possible standardized visual communication in print. But the print still relied on certain syntactical rules of engraving and etching. Though more directly visual than the type, the print was still a syntactical generalization, not really an exact duplicate of anything. Photography on the other hand was able to capture an instantaneous trace of the world, seemingly without distortion. Its explicit trace soon made the photographic image the standard of truthfulness in reporting.[87] With the photographic image, seeing is believing.

Photography actually introduced us not to an absolutely faithful representation, but to an entirely different sense of reality. As Susan Sontag observed, "photographed images do not seem to be statements about the world so much as pieces of it."[88] Photography peels off an image from the world by capturing and preserving a unique, instantaneous aspect of it. Afterward, all the original connections fade away, while we hold on to the explicit image. The vividness of the photographic image compensates for the detachment of the image from its original context. We are in effect taught by the photographic image to see the world in fragmentation and dislocation. Already in the late nineteenth century, E. J. Marey and Eadweard Muybridge tried to capture motion with photography, i.e., to fragment motion into a series of successively different yet static images.[89] By the twentieth century, the photographic way of seeing was ingrained into us.

Although photography paved the way for a new conception of reality, the presuppostion of objective space and time in bourgeois society was still able to contain its implication. By itself, the photographic image did not displace the typographic image. However, in the new perceptual field defined by the revolution of 1905–15, the photographic sense of reality led to the filmic image, surrealist image, and publicity image.

The filmic image is more autonomous and dynamic than the photographic image. The static, uni-perspectival image of photography became the dynamic, multi-perspectival image of film. As discussed in the previous section, the specific value of the filmic image depends on the spatio-temporality of a particular film. Within that film, images can tell a story, document an aspect of the world, or experiment with their own oneiric potential. The filmic image, though an extrapolation of sight and sound, is more vivid than everyday life; and the filmic reality is at the expense of everyday reality.

Unlike the photographic and filmic images, the surrealist image was an explicit attack on reason and common sense. In his 1924 manifesto, André Breton criticized the realist attitude which has dulled our imagination. Analysis and classification by visual, objective reason have even triumphed over the search for truth. Instead, Breton advocated the resolution of dream and everyday reality into an absolute surreality. The surrealist image was the springboard that would reveal to us the marvelous, the beautiful. It would come to us spontaneously, almost despotically, beyond consciousness and the control of reason:

> It is, as it were, from the fortuitous juxtaposition of the two [unrelated] terms that a particular light has sprung, *the light of the image*. . . . The value of the image depends upon the beauty of the spark obtained; it is, consequently, a function of the difference of potential between the two conductors. . . . The two terms of the image . . . are the simultaneous product of the activity I call Surrealist.[90]

Continued Breton: "For me, their greatest virtue . . . is the one that is arbitrary to the highest degree."[91]

Initially, the surrealist image was undertaken in poetry. Louis Aragon wrote in 1924: "It was as if the mind, having reached that turning point of the unconscious, had lost the power of recognizing what it was veering towards. . . . We felt all the forces of the images surging up before us. But we had lost the power of controlling them."[92] However, Breton in *Surrealism and Painting* (1928) extended the surrealist image to painting. The surrealist image in painting would penetrate beneath and beyond the surface of rationality. Magritte dislocated objects from their ordinary world, to present them as images without connection. And Dali would describe his images as the product of paranoiac-critical activity, "a spontaneous method of irrational knowledge based on interpretative critical association of delirious phenomena."[93]

At its best, the surrealist image transcends recognition, for every recognition is a re-cognition which returns us once more to the ordinary. Instead, it seeks to provoke an unexpected shock of cognition; and that shock is a spark of energy which will lift us beyond the mundane. Therefore, the surrealist image can have neither temporal nor spatial connection. That is, it cannot depend upon any recall of memory, or hope of anticipation, or familiarity or resemblance of space. Instead, it emphasizes the scintillating, the oneiric, the absurd—everything that is not rational or expected. Hence, the surrealist image is momentary, unstable. The very strength of the surrealist image is its effervescence and vulnerability.

Perhaps these qualities are also its weakness, for what has triumphed in the twentieth century is not the surrealist image, but its packaging by corporate capitalism as the publicity image. As John Berger said:

> In the cities in which we live, all of us see hundreds of publicity images every day of our lives. No other kind of images confronts us so frequently. In no other form of society in history has there been such a concentration of images.[94]

The publicity image works upon our anxiety, to stimulate appetite and consumption. As the production of the assembly line became more efficient, there was need to develop a more responsive consumer market. In the twenties, advertising agencies worked on that by means of publicity image.[95] Publicity for industrial design, brand names, slogans and jingles, testimonials, macho sexuality, and feminine seduction began to bombard us via the press and magazines, but also via the newly discovered radio broadcasting. As a result, the image, not just visual but now also audio, has become more public and less subjective. However, it was not until after World War II that the meta-communication of publicity image became ubiquitous. This accomplishment can be attributed to the "new advertising" across the new media of sight and sound.

The new advertising began in 1949, when David Ogilvy and William Bernbach each organized his own agency, and produced a number of new publicity images.[96] Ogilvy of Hathaway and Schweppes fame saw the basic importance of image:

> Every advertising must be considered as a contribution to the complex symbol which is the brand image. . . . The manufacturers who dedicate their advertising to building the most favorable image, the most sharply defined personality for their brands are the ones who will get the largest shares of these markets at the highest profit—in the long run.[97]

And Bernbach in his Levy's rye bread and Volkswagen campaigns succeeded in making image the crucial attribute of a product. The publicity image of the new advertising is no longer uni-perspectival. Instead, the most current fashionable signs and images are taken from their original contexts to create an image for the product. The explicit meanings of the original signs and images, which the public recognizes, are used in the publicity image to refer to the product.[98] This is meta-communication of image. The publicity image with its borrowed values is therefore more than the product itself. A product might be obsolescent and its use quite limited; but its image can be made to appear dynamic, thus inducing us to consume more of it. The result is a consumption of image value, rather than of the product itself. For instance, some wear clothes designed by Yves Saint-Laurent, not because they are clothing, but because they are Yves Saint-Laurents, with all the aura surrounding that label.

Technologically, the meta-communication of publicity images is made possible by the extrapolated, extended sight and sound of radio, television, hi-fi, and audio/video tapes and discs. Instead of lodging signs in a visually objective, typographic space, or images in a filmic spatio-temporality, the new electrical, electonic media do not provide self-contained, autonomous spatio-temporal contexts, but extend and extrapolate visual and audio images into our everyday reality, so that the images and their accompanying messages become a part of our environment. This ubiquitous property of the new media makes them appropriate means for the meta-communication of publicity images, since publicity images take advantage of the current communication of sight and sound.

Take, for example, television as a medium, which since the 1950s has overtaken newspapers, magazines, and radio broadcasting in importance. Television intrudes into and redefines our perceptual reality. In contrast to the self-contained spatio-temporality of a particular film which we observe in a darkened cinema, the series of necessary close-ups and details on the small TV screen requires our participation to integrate.[99] The forms and genres in television are not as autonomous and important as in film. In film, each form or genre provides a specific spatio-temporal context, within which the filmic images are edited into a whole. But television is a part of our living space; and its time is a flow or sequencing of programs, in which the various forms or genres lose their autonomy.[100] It is this open-ended flow or programming in television which dislodges audio-visual images from their specific contexts, and enables them to meta-communicate more effectively within our perceptual reality. Too often, by criticizing a particular program, we lose sight of the forest for the trees, failing to realize the fundamental imortance of programming, which facilitates the meta-communication of publicity images of all kinds, whether in a program, a newscast, or a commercial.

The meta-communication of publicity images via the new electrical, electronic media has succeeded in reversing the relation we perceive between image and reality. Previously, the image was dependent on the referent. One's image always referred to something more real, whether Platonic or immanent. However, currently, the image refers to itself as the value. Publicity is able to repackage a product, so that we consume its attached image value rather than its use value. And electronic media have the capacity to create a new pseudoevent out of the raw material of an actual event.[101] In fact, media can transform publicity itself into an event, and we experience it as an important event. This is how political communication is undertaken nowadays. Our reality is infiltrated through and through by publicity image. Meta-communication of image has taken over the definition of reality in the bureaucratic society of controlled consumption.

Transformations of the Image

from
etching

1

Piranesi, "View of the Bridge and Mausoleum Built by the Emperor Hadrian" (1756). H. Levit, *Views of Rome, Then and Now* (New York, 1976), plate 18.

to

photography

2
Herschel Levit, "View of the Bridge and Mausoleum Built by the Emperor Hadrian." H. Levit, *Views of Rome, Then and Now* (New York, 1976), plate 18.

Seven

from
the nude

3
Cabanel, "Naissance de Vénus" (1862). Museé du Louvre, Paris.

to

the naked

4
Manet, "Le Déjeuner sur l'herbe" (1863). Museé du Louvre (Jeu de
Paume), Paris.

Seven

from
perspectival painting

5

Cézanne, "The Large Bathers" (1898–1905). Philadelphia Museum of Art:
The W. P. Wilstach Collection.

144

to

cubism

6

Picasso, "Les Demoiselles d'Avignon" (1907). Oil on canvas, 8′ x 7′8″.
Collection, The Museum of Modern Art, New York. Acquired through the Lillie
P. Bliss Bequest.

Seven

from
cubism

7
Braque, "Man with a Guitar" (1911). Oil on canvas,
45¾ x 31⅞". Collection, The Museum of Modern Art, New York.
Acquired through the Lillie P. Bliss Bequest.

146

to
surrealism

8

Cadavre Exquis, "Figure" (1928?). Collage of pasted
paper. Sheet: 11⅜ x 9″. Composition: 7¾ x 3½″.
Collection, The Museum of Modern Art, New York.
Van Gogh Purchase Fund.

Seven

from
painting

9

Cézanne, "The Basket of Apples" (ca. 1895). The Art Institute of Chicago.
Helen Birch Bartlett Memorial Collection.

to

collage

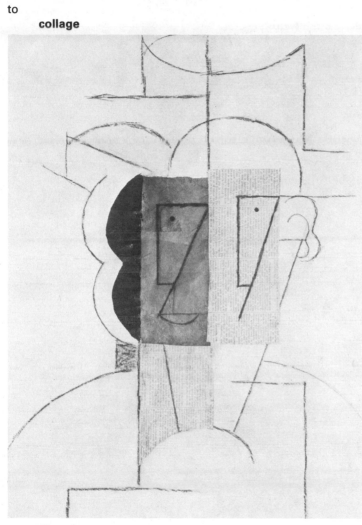

10
Picasso, "Man with a Hat" (December 1912). Charcoal and ink with collage (pasted paper) on buff paper. Sheet: 24½ x 18⅝″. Collection, The Museum of Modern Art, New York.

Seven

from

perspectival photography

11
The author at the age of five (1933)

to

photo image

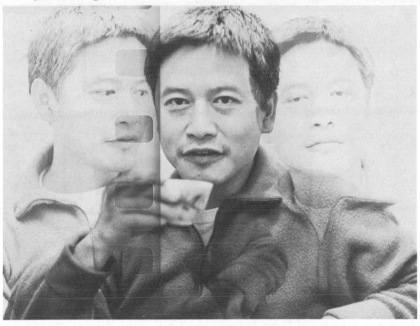

12
The author at the age of forty-four (1972) by David Ming-li Lowe

Seven

from
film screen

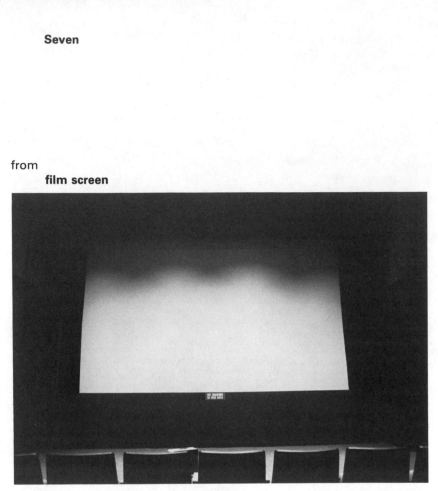

13
Photograph by David Ming-li Lowe

Transformations of the Image

to

television screen

14
Photograph by David Ming-li Lowe

from
advertising sign

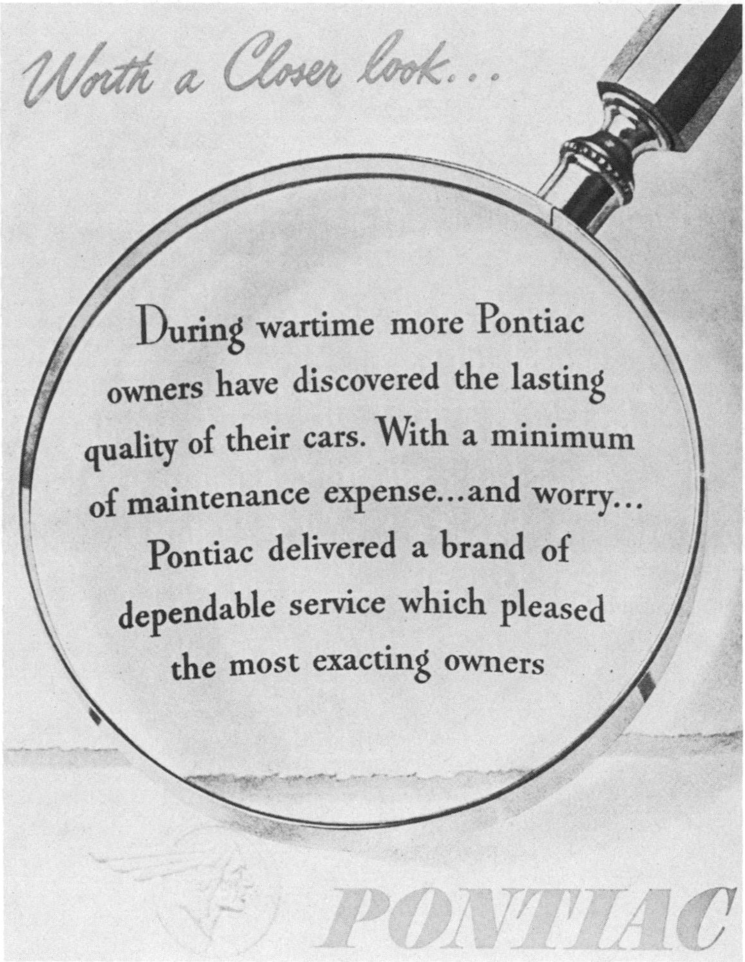

15
1945 Pontiac advertisement

to

advertising image

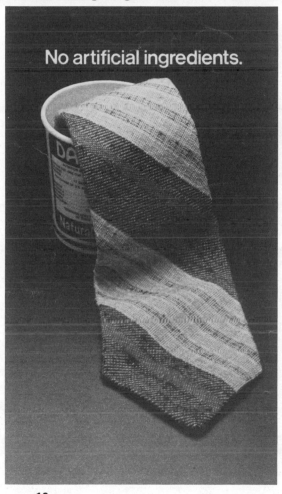

16
1980 Jones New York necktie advertisement

Seven

from
surrealist painting

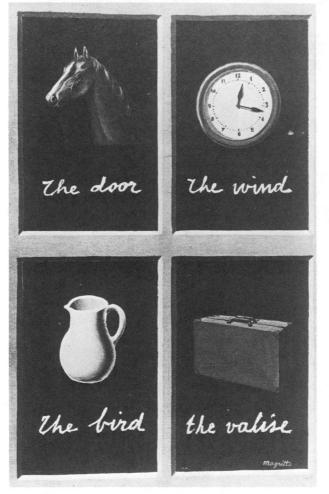

17
Magritte, ''The Key of Dreams'' (1932)
Collection of Jasper Johns. © by ADAGP, Paris 1981

to

surrealist advertisement

18
1980 Selig dream-piece sofa advertisement

from
use value

19
1939 Oldsmobile advertisement

to

image value

20
1980 Oldsmobile advertisement

Eight

A Retrospect

Freedom is an intentionality within the perceptual field; but that field is determined by the multi-level structure in transformation. Looking back from the present vantage point across periods of time, we are able to discern the following historical transformation:

The horizonal field of perception in bourgeois society was constituted by a culture of typographic media; a sensing hierarchy which emphasized visuality; and an epistemic order of development-in-time. Within this perceptual field emerged new concepts such as "function," "structure," "dynamics," "organism," and "evolution," to refract the new forces generated by industrial capitalism. The ideological limit of that perception was its beliefs in objective space-time, and individual personality. These beliefs were ideological because they deflected the alienation and estrangement of bourgeois society into various compartmentalized activities.

In the transformation from bourgeois society to the bureaucratic society of controlled consumption, the perceptual revolution of 1905–15 introduced a new perceptual field, constituted by a culture of electronic media; a sensing hierarchy of extended and extrapolated hearing and seeing; as well as an epistemic order of synchronic system. Within the new field, space and time are relativized by physics, intentionalized by phenomenology, perspectivized by film. Space and time are no longer the framework of our perception. There is no continuity from one period to another, from Newton to Einstein, from realism to cubism, from *Middlemarch* to *Ulysses,* from hypotaxis to parataxis,[1] from neurosis to schizophrenia.[2] The transformation is from a communication of signs to the meta-communication of image. Under the assault of that meta-communication, the human being now possesses less of an interior than formerly. We have ideological limits to our own perception. But that is difficult to discern, from within the ongoing reality.

Yet so long as we continue to view our world with concepts derived from bourgeois society, we shall miss the new tendencies in the bureaucratic society of controlled consumption. We need to examine our world on its own terms. Only then can we begin to confront the real gaps in our lives.

Time is certain: already the man that I will be has the man that I am by the throat, but the man that I have been leaves me in peace. This is called my mystery, but I do not believe in (I do not prize) the impenetrability of this mystery, and no one wholly believes in it for himself. The great veil that falls over my childhood only half conceals the strange years that will precede my death. And I shall one day speak of my death. Inside myself I am several hours ahead of myself, the proof is that what happened to me surprises me only to the exact degree that I need not be surprised *any more.* I want to know everything. . . .

André Breton
"A Letter to Seers"

Methodology

There is no knowledge without method; and a method necessarily depends upon a set of presuppositions. The examination of the relationship between method and presuppositions is methodology. The following is the methodology for this work.

The Knower and the Known

I shall begin with the connection between the knower and the known.[1] There is no knowledge without a knower. And the knower, before anything else, is already a living human being. Both the knower and the content of knowledge belong to a specific historical world. They change together with the world. The human being is not an opaque object, but a reflexive subject. By reflexive, I mean conscious of the interacting, interdependent relation between the subject and the world. It is not possible to know oneself without knowing one's place in the world. Furthermore, the world is not an objective structure in itself, but a structured, dynamic interaction of human beings organized into groups, strata, and classes. Life as social interaction presupposes knowledge of self and the world. It is impossible to speak of knowledge without implying the knower, and vice versa.

On the other hand, it is possible to conceive of knowledge as being objective, that is, not connected to any knower. This disconnection of the known from the knower is what Hannah Arendt called the myth of Archimedes.[2] The myth assumes that the knower does not occupy any place within the known world; rather, from a null point outside of space and time, the knower is able to know the world and its inhabitants objectively. Nevertheless, objective knowledge, by denying the spatio-temporal location of the knower in the world, reveals in a subtle way that intimate connection between the knower and the known. The discounting of human subjectivity by objective knowledge results in the estrangement of human beings from an objectified world.

It was in the seventeenth century that Descartes posited knowledge should be empirical, mathematical, and indubitable. That ideal of objective knowledge, since then, has succeeded in exploiting the forces of nature and transforming the landscape of the world. Because of objective knowledge, we now live in a human-made, artificial environment. In addition, objective knowledge has fostered a behaviorial science to manipulate human beings, as if they were mirror images of objects.

However, from the New Science of Vico in the early eighteenth century to present-day Marxism and phenomenology, there is an opposing, anti-Cartesian tradition of knowledge.[3] This tradition focuses on the important distinction between scientific study of objects and holistic study of subjects. Human beings are more than objects. By studying them as objects, one ignores that level of reality unique to human subjects. It is from this anti-Cartesian tradition that I posit the necessary connection between the knower and the known.

Since the knower and the known are connected, it would be a distortion to study the social world and knowledge in that social world separately. There is no world-in-itself, without reference to the type of knowledge available to its inhabitants. Together, the world and its available knowledge constitute a whole. The human beings in a world undertake their living on the basis of the knowledge available in that world. However, that world is not a random collection of human beings and their knowledge. It is an intersubjective structure, in the sense that the inhabitants of a world are already organized into a structure of hopes and expectations. They then maintain and transform that structure by their action and counteraction. As Marx observed: "Men make their own history, but they do not make it just as they please; they do not make it under circumstances chosen by themselves, but under circumstances directly encountered, given and transmitted from the past."[4] Knowledge is the means by which social action is undertaken; in turn, social action transforms knowledge. Such knowledge, not objective but instrumental, is at the center of the world and provides it with possibilities. The interaction has been aptly called the social construction of reality[5]

Knowledge in the world consists of what Alfred Schutz, the phenomenological social theorist, called first-degree constructs of reality. "Social reality," according to him, "has a special meaning and relevance structure for the human beings living, acting and thinking within it. . . . It is these thought objects of theirs which determine their behavior by motivating it." The first-degree constructs of social reality are an inherent part of the world. They are different from the thought objects of the social scientists, which "are, so to speak, constructs of the second degree, that is constructs of the constructs made by the actors on the social scene, whose behavior the social scientist has to observe and explain."[6] What the social scientist or historian knows about the world is ex post facto, outside of its spatio-temporal confine, and unable to alter it, whereas what the inhabitants knew of their world constituted its reality.

The central question in the methodology of the human sciences is the relation between the first-degree construction of reality and the second-degree explanation by the social scientist or historian of that reality. Will the second-degree explanation be able to elucidate rather than reduce the meaning of the first-degree reality in that world? That is the crux. The concept of a first-degree construction of reality presupposes the necessary connection between the knower and the known. But the ideal of objective knowledge denies the relevance of that connection. Therefore, any second-degree explanation premised on objective knowledge will reduce the first-degree reality in that world. (Of course, the second-degree knowledge of the social scientist becomes a part of the first-degree reality, when it is incorporated into the discourse and institutionalization of the scientist's world.)

Herein lies the importance of phenomenology for the social sciences, because it provides us with second-degree constructs which can hermeneutically describe the meaning of the first-degree reality in the world.

Phenomenology of Perception

Phenomenology as a way of thinking is at once direct yet difficult. Unlike the Cartesian *cogito* which objectifies the world or the Platonic idea that judges the world in reference to a transcendent concept, phenomenology seeks knowledge of the world from within the world. Maurice Merleau-Ponty has said, "the only pre-existent Logos is the world itself." There is no other rationality behind the appearance or beyond the world, upon which the world is founded. Instead, "true philosophy consists in relearning to look at the world" on its own terms, without the mediation of any other rationality.[7] Here lies the difficulty of the phenomenological language, for we are so accustomed to philosophizing from an extrinsic standpoint, whether Cartesian or Platonic, that we can no longer comprehend the phenomenological standpoint within the world.

We need to discard the language of objective analysis, which has placed a screen between ourselves and the world. Only then can we begin to explore the intersubjective connections which are an inherent part of our world. The body, cause and effect, time, the world, and perception are familiar concepts. They have been studied and objectified by behavioral science. However, when approached in phenomenological terms as embodiment, intentionality, temporality, life-world, and the phenomenology of perception, they reveal the ground of intersubjective experience which previously was suppressed by objective science. These key concepts, when phenomenologically clarified, can be the hermeneutic second-degree constructs for the history of perception. Here in this section, I shall briefly summarize what phenomenologists mean by these concepts:

Embodiment

For too long we have likened the human body to a machine. Let us abandon that objectifying standpoint and begin with the experience we already have as bodily subjects.[8] I am not an object, although others may objectify me, and I in turn can approach them as objects. Then I would lead a disembodied life. My body is not other than me, as though a pre-bodily "I" inhabits "it." My body is not a mere instrument. I feel myself in an entirely different way than I feel others. I am this embodied subject. And it is from the standpoint of my embodied subjectivity located in the world that I reach out to others. The fundamental fact of my embodiment has many implications which can be phenomenologically drawn out, if I do not approach it objectively.

As an embodied subject, the point of departure for me is the upright posture. Unlike other animals, I belong to that species which orients itself in the world from an upright, standing, moving position. The human being is what it is because of the upright posture. From this stance we see, grasp, and handle things differently than other animals. Humanity is the ability to exercise these potentials at a level of existence unlike those of the other species.

From my upright posture, I reach out into the world, and the world accordingly opens horizons for my living. There is a reflexive engagement between the bodily me located here and now, and the horizons which unfold into the distance, there and then. The extension from here to there is a spatial distance, whereas that from now to then is a temporal distance, both starting from my embodied location in the world. These distances constitute the real-life framework, within which I recollect, calculate, act, and anticipate. Other animals also have their spatio-temporal horizons. However, the upright posture has enlarged for me immensely the spatio-temporal horizons of the world, thus providing me with distinctly human possibilities.

Within these spatio-temporal horizons, I engage other subjects through an ascending order of sensing, feeling, emotion and expression. Each level in the order of embodied engagement is already a reflexive consciousness of myself and what is beyond. Together, they constitute my specific bodily engagement in the world. I am my engagement in the world.

Methodology

My senses of hearing, touching, smelling, tasting, and seeing open me to the world. Sensing is the primordial engagement between the self and the world. Hearing, touching, smelling, and tasting are intensive and enwombing; whereas seeing is distancing and extensive. Seeing is much more discriminating, enabling us to locate objects against broad backgrounds. For each person, there is a specific hierarchy of sensing. For some, hearing and touching prevail over seeing; whereas for others, smelling may be the most acute sense. In addition, different historical periods with different communications media provide for different hierarchical organizations of the five senses. For instance, in the Middle Ages, hearing and touching were more assured than seeing; whereas in the modern West, seeing has predominated.

If sensing is the primordial level at which I begin to engage and be conscious of the world, then feeling, emotion, and expression are the ascending levels of that conscious, embodied engagement. It is through feeling, emotion, and expression that I increasingly engage the world and correlatively realize myself. Feeling is a more self-revealing consciousness than sensing. Each feeling is unique and signifies a particular mood in which the self responds to the world. On the other hand, emotion is that sustained state when the subject in reaction to the world is wrapped up in his or her own feeling. Unlike feeling, which links the self to the world, emotion is more focused upon the self apart from the world. Emotion can be restrained as sensitivity, or expressed as sensibility. Expression finds the conscious subject creatively engaging the world. Gesture, speech, and act are progressive forms of self-conscious expression, wherein the sensing, feeling, emotional subject realizes himself or herself in the world.

From sensing through feeling, to emotion, culminating in expression—these are the ascending levels of the conscious, embodied subject engaging the world. They are ascending, because from one level to the next the subject becomes more self-conscious, as he or she engages the world more actively. Freedom is the progressive engagement of the embodied subject in the world through these levels of consciousness, as one reaches out into the spatio-temporal horizons. This is the intentional structure of the embodied subject.

Intentionality

I have been using the term engagement to characterize the reciprocal, interacting relation between the subject and the world. It is a more realistic term than cause and effect. Cause and effect are a linear, sequential correlation of observable facts, derived from supposedly discrete, independent objects. But the concepts of cause and effect, of discrete objects are second-degree constructs undertaken from an objective standpoint. Before the imposition of these objective constructs, there already exist conscious, reflexive relations among embodied subjects in the world. Here, we are not concerned with the logic of objective science, but the lived experience of intersubjective relations in the world. A hermeneutic description of these relations must begin with the phenomenological concept of intentionality.

Intentionality is the "intendedness" of a subject toward other subjects and objects in the world. The subject has the ability to direct its attention toward them, but also to disengage and shift attention to something else. This intendedness is an embodied consciousness, which enables the subject to know the world through the ascending levels of sensing, feeling, emotion, and expression. Because intentionality is embodied consciousness, relations among subjects and between subject and object are never invariable. Each time, the relation is a different reflexive engagement between the subject and beyond, with different sensing, feeling, emotional, and/or expressive connection. Objects do not have intentionality. Other animals, with more constricted spatio-temporal horizons, have at least quite different, if not less, intentionality than the human being. I am not denying that a dog has a better sense of smell, or that other animals have more acute senses or reflexes than I. But upright posture and a sustained intentionality in an enlarged spatio-temporal world constitute the perspective of the human being. This intentionality of the upright, embodied consciousness distinguishes the human person from other animals, in the engagement with other subjects and objects in the world.

Temporality

Since birth, I have grown and aged in the world. Intentionality is my embodied potential to recollect and anticipate, and on that basis to live beyond the present. Therefore both embodiment and intentionality presuppose temporality as lived time. Temporality is not mechanical, chronological time. We need to explore phenomenologically its many dimensions.[10]

The human body, from the standpoint of its nonconscious workings, is an organic unity of phylogenetic and ontogenetic growth. Born with a nervous system, the infant slowly acquires patterns of waking and sleeping, eating and playing. Later, it begins to distinguish day and night, the twenty-four-hour cycle, and the seasons. Thus, the lived body is organized into a rhythmic pattern, which biologists have observed as diurnal physiological oscillations. This human physiological clock precedes consciousness. It is a preconscious synchronization of the lived body and the world. Most of the time, we are unaware of its workings. Nevertheless, it does show up as time zone dyschronization or jet lag, when the lived body is still accustomed to one time zone, while consciousness had already advanced to a new time zone.

Life is the embodiment of needs and desire. At the nonconscious level, life is mere physiological rhythm. But at the level of intentional consciousness, it becomes the reflexivity of the self. That reflexivity attenuates the physiological rhythm by enlarging the subject's awareness of the world, both retrospectively and prospectively, so that within embodied consciousness new dimensions of learning, habituation, and innovation become possible. Reflexive consciousness thus modifies the physiological rhythm.

Beyond the subject's physiological rhythm and reflexive consciousness, there is the world with its varying paces of life. We experience them in different ways. There is the pace of the seasonal cycle, which provides us with an intimation of the rhythm of nature. This natural pace is more evident in the countryside than in the urban centers. There is the pace of the cultural world, with its symbolizations of time. For example, the pace of a religious, liturgical world is less mechanical and constricted than the pace of the secular, rational world. There is the pace of the mechanical measurement of time, with its regularity and monotony. Mechanical time became important with the use of clocks and watches in early modern Europe, and was further accentuated by the time-and-motion approach to industrial labor in the nineteenth and twentieth centuries.

We experience the paces in the world as an irreversible, onward rush of events, pulling us along toward an as yet undisclosed future. We age and grow old, constantly surprised by our encounter with and discovery of the new. The future is unknowable. Yet living is to face that future with both hope and anxiety.

Our internal time-consciousness seeks to comprehend the paces of the world. This time-consciousness is not an irreversible arrow in flight. It is filled with remembrance and anticipation. It opens us to the past as well as to the future, within the lived, ongoing present. Because of it, we can retrospect and prospect in the world. We prospect on the basis of our recollection, and retrospect for the sake of our living into the future. There is no anticipation without recollection of the past; nor recollection without anticipation. Though the paces of the world are irreversible, the time of our consciousness is reflexive. To live in the world is to synchronize the reflexivity of our internal time-consciousness with the diverse paces in the world. This conscious synchronization is the lived time of the everyday world.

Appendix

Temporality as the endurance of change is a synchronization of the rhythm and reflexivity of the subject and the various paces in the world. We experience synchronization in sex and music, in mythic ritual, or we repress it through the objective language of quantitative, mechanical measurement. The rhythm of the subject varies from person to person; and the paces of the world are a cultural, historical growth, which varies from period to period. Thus we experience temporal synchronization within a broad spectrum of fluidity and constriction, duration and tension, continuity and fragmentation.

Life-World

The world that I live in is not an objective, centerless world.[11] Before anything else, it is for me a real, pretheoretical world, wherein I undertake everyday living. This is my primary reality. I may study and analyze the world as an objective structure. But the scientific study of the world is secondary, when compared with the reality of everyday life. I approach the everyday world from my embodied location, here and now, prospecting into the distant horizons, there and then. These spatio-temporal horizons form a framework of meaning for me. They shift, contract and enlarge with my changing interests and motives. This world is for me a perspectival, horizonal field.

There are subjects in the world other than myself. The world is therefore intersubjective. The world unfolds different spatio-temporal horizons for diverse subjects, depending on their perspectival centers. Each subject approaches the world with a different, as well as changing, set of interests and motives. Action, communication, and interaction among subjects maintain and transform the world. This intersubjective world is stratified into groups, strata, and classes, as a structure of hopes and expectations.

The world is infiltrated through and through with knowledge. There is no world-in-itself, just as there is no knowledge without a knower. The subject approaches the world from within the framework of his or her knowledge. Knowledge in turn is revised by action, communication, and interaction. It consists of a necessary stock of useful, typical expectations in dealing with others, extending from the personal and intimate to the anonymous and remote. Typical expectations are first-degree constructs of reality. The subject acquires them for the sake of living; in the process they are revised. Social structure is therefore a stratification of knowledge.

The life-world consist of multiple realities. Besides the reality of the everyday world, there are others such as the world of children, the world of science, the world of art, the world of the occult, the world of the insane, and so on. Each reality is a symbolic order with its internal coherence and meaning. However, in relation to the primary reality of the everyday world, these others are subordinate, and always refer to the primary reality of everyday living. Nevertheless, different periods present different ways of ordering multiple realities. The world of the occult which previously pervaded everyday life has by now diminished in validity. Besides, the very criterion defining the reality of a world may change, or even disappear. For example, the world of the insane, which is now institutionally segregated, was in the Middle Ages a part of the everyday world, lacking a separate identity.

Perception

There is no act of perception without a perceiver and a content of the perceived.[12] The perceiver is a subject in the world, who undertakes an act of perception. That world from the standpoint of the perceiver is a horizonal field, extending from the close and intimate to the remote and anonymous. Perception is the conscious, reflexive connection between the subject and the world.

The subject's act of perception is embodied, perspectival, and projective. It is embodied, in that the subject approaches the world not as a Cartesian *cogito,* but through the ascending levels of sensing, feeling, emotion, and expression, with each level a *Gestalt* between the self and the world. It is perspectival, in that the subject's approach is never 360 degrees wide, but necessarily aspectal, determined by a particular set of interests and motives. It is projective because the subject does not perceive with a blank Lockean mind, but rather anticipates with the stock of first-degree constructs available.

From the standpoint of the perceiver, the world unfolds different spatio-temporal horizons of familiarity and anonymity. However, the world is a cultural, historical growth and sedimentation. There are in it different epistemic orders (such as anagogy, similitude, representation-in-space, development-in-time, and synchronic system), different communications media (such as oral, chirographic, typographic, and electronic), different forms of expression (such as the novel, fictional film, the television commercial, etc.). Perception is always by means of these cultural, historical legacies.

To recapitulate, perception is a reflexive connection between the embodied perceiver and the life-world. It is organized by the sensing, feeling, emotion, and expression of the subject, as well as realized by means of the cultural, historical legacies available in the world; for no perception is an instantaneous communion, but rather is always perspectival and projective. A phenomenological description of perception therefore connects the intentionality of the perceiver with the cultural, historical legacies in that world, as lived horizonal fields.

Intentionality and Dialectic

Both phenomenology and Marxism are antipositivist; both derive their concepts of reason from the world. However, each proposes a different "reason" for a different world configuration. What the life-world, as described above, is to phenomenology, totality is to Marxism. Phenomenologists use the concept of intentionality to describe the life-world, whereas Marxists use the concept of dialectic to analyze totality.

The concept of intentionality is concerned with the lived, perceptual connections in the world. It is fundamentally descriptive. On the other hand, dialectic introduces a concept of reason which proposes the unity of theory and practice, within an ongoing totality. Dialectical knowledge aims at *praxis* and is revised by *praxis*. Knowledge in the Marxist sense can comprehend the world as totality, because it is tested and revised through intervention in the world.[13] Unlike phenomenological description, Marxist analysis is activist.

Intentionality describes the life-world as intersubjective, perspectival, and horizonal. From the embodied perspective of the subject, that world is a horizon for living. The life-world is therefore a prospective reality. In contrast, dialectic analyzes totality as a multi-level structure:

> In the social production of their existence, men inevitably enter into definite relations, which are independent of their will, namely relations of production appropriate to a given stage in the development of their material forces of production. The totality of these relations of production constitutes the economic structure of society, the real foundation, on which arises a legal and political superstructure, and to which correspond definite forms of social consciousness. The mode of production of material life conditions the general process of social, political and intellectual life.[14]

Instead of a horizonal field, dialectic reveals the world as a multi-level structure. The legal, political superstructure and the corresponding forms of social consciousness are autonomous levels; yet each is conditioned by the substructure of the social relations of production. "It is not the consciousness of men that determines their existence, but their social existence that determines their consciousness."[15] The stress and strain generated by the development in time of these different levels are ultimately seismic, leading to a revolutionary transformation.

Methodology

For phenomenology, the intentionality of consciousness is the starting point to unravel the world. It reveals a perceptual field as the framework of meaning. But Marxism considers this consciousness to be superstructural, i.e., conditioned by the economic substructure. The underside of consciousness, Marxism argues, is alienation, the key to being-in-the-world. Consciousness, according to Marxism, is eccentric in refracting the multi-level structure from the top down; superstructural consciousness is always at variance with economic substructure. Alienation is the fate of the human being stretched across the multi-level structure of totality. Only the unity of Marxist theoretical consciousness and revolutionary *praxis* can overcome alienation.

Marxism is correct, in that there is always more than consciousness; and totality determines that consciousness. However, phenomenology is able to clarify the perceptual connections in the world, connections which Marxism is unable to perceive. The weakest link in the historical materialist analysis of totality is its concept of ideology. It is able to locate ideology as the top level of a structured totality. But it does not provide a hermeneutic context to clarify the perceptual content of ideology or consciousness. Thus, the first-degree constructs within an ideology are reduced by the second-degree constructs of Marxist explanation.

Yet, the very strength of phenomenology in being able to clarify real perceptual connections in the world is also its limitation. The life-world as an intentional reality is a horizontal field which lacks structure in depth. It is, when compared with the Marxist totality, partial and incomplete. On the other hand, Marxism cannot clarify consciousness, but instead reduces it to ideology. There is a necessary grid between intentionality and life-world, just as there is a grid between dialectic and totality. Using different, though equally antipositivist, concepts of reason, each reveals a different world configuration. Hence, intentionality cannot account for totality, nor dialectic clarify perceptual consciousness. The two approaches have different assumptions, prescribing different knowledge of the world.

Nevertheless, the world is the common ground to which both phenomenology and Marxism refer. Each, from a different methodological standpoint within the world, reveals a different order of the world. If dialectic is the structure of totality in transformation, intentionality is the subjectivization of that dialectic structure. Intentionality clarifies the first-degree perception of totality as an ongoing reality; dialectic is the second-degree explanation of the life-world, from the standpoint of a structure beneath and beyond consciousness. Since knowledge is a totalization within totality,[16] it can never entirely capture that totality. Hence, it is possible to supplement phenomenology's concept of intentionality with the structure of totality. The life-world is the limit of phenomenological description, whereas dialectic reveals the multi-level structure of totality which is more than the life-world. In other words, Marxist structure explains the phenomenological life-world, whereas phenomenological perception clarifies Marxist ideology.

History and the Past

We experience past and present as different modes of time-consciousness. We live in the ongoing present, which is a prospective reality with its future as yet undisclosed. In the present, there is always the open dimension of the unknown. On the other hand, there is no past. That past was, once upon a time, an ongoing present; but now it is foreclosed by a subsequent present. We experience our present as an ongoing reality; but we cannot directly experience a past. Instead, we behold in the present vestiges, monuments, and legacies from the past. On the basis of these, we then can have a history of that past. History therefore is not the past; it is a representation of the past. Every past was once an ongoing present; but history can never recapture all its dimensions. It can re-present only those aspects of a past for which we have evidence. There can be no history without evidence, for history is neither memory nor fiction. The vestiges, monuments, and legacies from a past necessarily prescribe the boundary of its representation.

In addition, the relation between the knower and the known obtains in history, as in any other form of knowledge. There is no history without a historian. History as a form of knowledge stems from a specific present. From his or her present vantage point, a historian writes about a past which is now no more. Since history is the present representation of a past, necessarily the perspective of the historian, the horizon, the structure of his or her world all affect that representation. Over a span of time, some of the evidences from a past may get lost, while other new ones are discovered. In addition, successive historians will write about that past from different present vantage points. With changing evidence and changing historical perspective, the representation of that past will also change. There is no fixity in history. Nor can we know the past-in-itself. Instead, there is always a necessary connection between past evidence and present representation. Historiography is the history of that changing connection, in the successive attempts to represent a past.

The reality of an ongoing present is prospective. Living into the unknown future is a type of prospecting in the ongoing present. On the other hand, historical representation is a retrospection of the past. When we look back upon a past, we known what the consequences were for its inhabitants, a future they could have no knowledge of, just as we cannot know about the consequences of our own present. From our present vantage point, the past is now foreclosed. But that past too, once upon a time, had a prospective reality. How is it possible to represent a past without losing sight of its unique prospective reality? This I believe is the crucial problem in historical method.[17] History ought to be the present *re-presentation* of the prospective reality of a past, within the historian's retrospection. Every retrospection is already a representation. But historical representation is that retrospection which seeks to re-present the prospective reality of a past, within the context of a subsequent present. This unique quality should distinguish historical study of past human societies from social scientific study of contemporary societies.

Prospectivity within retrospection is the reflexivity of historical consciousness. Beyond the mere ascertaining of "facts" and "events," the historian will have to apprehend the prospective reality of a past, as well as locate it within an explanatory context undertaken from the vantage of the present. Not merely do we see the French Revolution from our present vantage point, but we need to show how the various groups of French people in 1789 saw their unfolding revolution, and in our explanation of it we should not reduce the significance of their experience. Narrative history with its emphasis on chronological time tends to present events as a process. On the other hand, behavioral analysis with its objective models would explain 1789 not in its own terms, but in our terms. I am pointing to a new problem in historical method, namely, that of reflexivity in historical consciousness, which can lead to a new prospect in history.

The historian deals with the past in terms of his or her present-day concern. Retrospection is a second-degree construction. It is therefore a context of explanation. I believe Marxism is the most comprehensive form of explanation available to us. It explains the past as a totality of multi-level structure. On the other hand, the inhabitants of that past prospected their world through their first-degree constructs. Phenomenological description enables us to apprehend the first-degree construction of the past. Hence the complementary relation between phenomenology and Marxism that I mentioned at the end of the previous section is really a reflexive one. Beyond the intentional description of the first-degree construction of a past reality, we locate that reality in a Marxist context of explanation. Within the reflexive consciousness of history, phenomenology is to prospectivity as Marxism is to retrospection.

Appendix

In addition, Marxism teaches us the importance of periodization. Each period is a structured totality. There are changes within a period, as well as changes between periods. The changes within a period are always alluvial, and do not fundamentally transform its structure; changes between periods are seismic, involving transformation from one structure to another. We need to emphasize the discontinuity from one period to another, for otherwise we see all changes as continuous, i.e., alluvial, and miss the really seismic transformations in the past. In this I agree with Michel Foucault, who said: "Discontinuity was the stigma of temporal dislocation that it was the historian's task to remove from history. It has now become one of the basic elements of historical analysis." [18]

A Procedure for the History of Perception

Phenomenology describes thought as prospective reality; whereas Marxism explains society as multi-level structure. *The history of perception* is the intermediary link between the content of thought and the structure of society. Its procedure is to

1. periodize a society, in terms of its multi-level structure;

2. within the context of the period, constitute the ongoing field of perception, in terms of its culture of communications media, its hierarchy of sensing, and its epistemic order of discourse;

3. within that perceptual field, describe the lived experience of time, space, and bodily life.

Notes

One

1. For a general introduction to the distinction between the objective-behaviorial study of perception and the phenomenology of perception, see P. Tibbetts, ed., *Perception* (Chicago, 1969).

2. M. Merleau-Ponty, *Phenomenology of Perception,* tr. C. Smith (London, 1962), esp. "Preface."

3. W. Ong, *The Presence of the Word* (New Haven, 1967). Ong speaks of three stages in communications media, (1) oral, (2) script and print, (3) electronic. I shall divide script and print into two separate stages, chirographic and typographic.

4. J. Vansina, *Oral Tradition,* tr. H. M. Wright (London, 1965); and F. Yates, *The Art of Memory* (London, 1966).

5. E. Havelock, *Preface to Plato* (Cambridge, Mass., 1963).

6. M. T. Clanchy, *From Memory to Written Record* (Cambridge, Mass., 1979).

7. E. Eisenstein, *The Printing Press as an Agent of Change* (Cambridge, 1979), chap. 2.

8. J. R. Pierce, *Symbols, Signals and Noise* (New York, 1961).

9. M. Bloch, *Les Rois thaumaturges* (Paris, 1924); L. Febvre, *Le Problème de l'incroyance au XVIe siècle* (Paris, 1942); and R. Mandrou, *Introduction à la France moderne* (Paris, 1961).

10. D. Ihde, *Sense and Significance* (Pittsburgh, 1973).

11. W. Ivins, Jr., *Prints and Visual Communication* (Cambridge, Mass., 1953).

12. Ong, *The Presence of the Word,* pp. 301–2.

13. S. Sontag, *On Photography* (New York, 1977), pp. 155–56.

14. M. Foucault, *The Order of Things* (New York, 1970), "Preface."

15. M.-D. Chenu, *Nature, Man, and Society in the Twelfth Century,* ed. J. Taylor and L. K. Little (Chicago, 1968), chap. 3; M. L. Colish, *The Mirror of Language* (New Haven, 1968), "Introduction"; C. Erickson, *The Medieval Vision* (New York, 1976).

16. Foucault, *The Order of Things,* p. 29.

17. Ibid., p. 60.

18. E. Le Roy Ladurie, *Montaillou,* tr. B. Bry (New York, 1978), chap. 17.

19. D. W. Robertson, Jr., *Chaucer's London* (New York, 1968), p. 5.

20. E. Panofsky, "Die Perspektive als 'Symbolische Form,'" *Vorträge der Bibliothek Warburg* (1924–25); W. M. Ivins, Jr., *Art and Geometry* (Cambridge, Mass., 1946), chap. 6.

21. W. von Leyden, "Antiquity and Authority: A Paradox in Renaissance Theory of History," *Journal of the History of Ideas* 19 (1958).

22. N. Elias, *The Civilizing Process,* tr. E. Jephcott (New York, 1978), p. 55.

23. A. Koyré, *From the Closed World to the Infinite Universe* (Baltimore, 1957), p. vi.

24. H. Arendt, *The Human Condition* (Chicago, 1958), chap. 6, sec. 36.

25. Foucault, *The Order of Things*, p. 207, also the chart on p. 201.
26. *Oxford English Dictionary.*

Two

1. E. J. Hobsbawm, *The Age of Revolution, 1789–1848* (London, 1962), "Preface." "The original process always takes place in England; she is the demiurge of the bourgeois cosmos. On the continent, the different phases of the cycle through which bourgeois society is ever speeding anew, occur in secondary and tertiary form." K. Marx, *The Class Struggles in France* (New York, 1964), p. 134.
2. H. Lefebvre, *Everyday Life in the Modern World*, tr. S. Rabinovitch (New York, 1971), p. 60.
3. K. Marx, *A Contribution to the Critique of Political Economy*, ed. M. Dobb (New York, 1970), "Preface."
4. P. L. Berger and T. Luckmann, *The Social Construction of Reality* (Garden City, 1966), chap. 1.
5. Merleau-Ponty, *Phenomenology of Perception*, p. xi.
6. Arendt, *The Human Condition*, chap. 3.
7. P. Mantoux, *The Industrial Revolution in the Eighteenth Century*, tr. M. Vernon, rev. ed. (New York, 1961), pt. 2, chap. 2; S. Giedion, *Mechanization Takes Command* (New York, 1948), pp. 77–127.
8. A. Briggs, "Middle-Class Consciousness in English Politics, 1780–1846," *Past and Present* 9 (1956), and "The Language of 'Class' in Early Nineteenth-Century England," in *Essays in Labour History*, ed. A. Briggs and J. Saville (London, 1960).
9. R. Meek and A. Skinner, "The Development of Adam Smith's Ideas on the Division of Labor," *Economic Journal* 83 (1973), quoted by G. Wills in *New York Review of Books* (February 9, 1978), pp. 40–41.
10. *Oxford English Dictionary.*
11. Ibid.
12. R. Williams, *Keywords* (Oxford, 1976), pp. 270–73.
13. L. Rauhala, *Intentionality and the Problem of the Unconscious* (Turku, 1969), pp. 208–11.
14. H. F. Ellenberger, *The Discovery of the Unconscious* (New York, 1970), chaps. 2 and 3; J. H. van den Berg, *The Changing Nature of Man*, tr. H. F. Croes (New York, 1961), chap. 3.
15. H. F. Ellenberger, *The Discovery of the Unconscious*, p. 800.
16. F. Heer, *The Medieval World*, tr. J. Sondheimer (Cleveland, 1962), chap. 1.
17. D. Matthew, *The Medieval European Community* (London, 1977), p. 119.
18. Ibid., p. 123.
19. E. Panofsky, *Gothic Architecture and Scholasticism* (New York, 1957), pp. 14–15.
20. E. Panofsky, *Renaissance and Renascences in Western Art* (Stockholm, 1960), p. 120.
21. G. Duby, *Foundations of a New Humanism, 1280–1440*, tr. P. Price (Geneva, 1966), pp. 11–12; M. Becker, "An Essay on the Quest for Identity in the Early Italian Renaissance," in *Florilegium Historiale: Essays Presented to Wallace K. Ferguson*, ed. J. G. Rowe and W. H. Stockdale (Toronto, 1971).
22. Mandrou, *Introduction à la France moderne*; J. H. Elliott, "Revolution and Continuity in Early Modern Europe," *Past and Present* 42 (1969); P. Burke, *Tradition and Innovation in Renaissance Italy* (London, 1972), p. 221.

23. Foucault, *The Order of Things,* pp. 168–74.

24. J. A. Schumpeter, *History of Economic Analysis* (New York, 1954), p. 97.

25. L. Febvre, *Life in Renaissance France,* ed. M. Rothstein (Cambridge, Mass., 1977), chap. 5.

26. P. Jeannin, *Merchants of the Sixteenth Century,* tr. P. Fittinoff (New York, 1972), pp. 108–13.

27. R. Mousnier, "French Institutions and Society, 1610–61," *New Cambridge Modern History,* vol. 4, ed. J. P. Cooper (Cambridge, 1970); D. Marshall, "La Structure sociale de l'Angleterre du XVIIIe siècle"; *Problème de stratification sociale,* ed. R. Mousnier (Paris, 1968).

28. R. Mandrou, *Magistrats et sorciers en France au XVIIe siècle* (Paris, 1968); K. Thomas, *Religion and the Decline of Magic* (New York, 1971); P. Burke, *Popular Culture in Early Modern Europe* (New York, 1978).

29. M. Foucault, *Madness and Civilization,* tr. R. Howard (New York, 1965), chap. 2.

30. Foucault, *The Order of Things,* chap. 6.

31. B. Groethuysen, *The Bourgeois,* tr. M. Ilford (New York, 1968); E. Barber, *The Bourgeoisie in Eighteenth Century France* (Princeton, 1955); P. Goubert, *L'Ancien Régime,* 2d ed. (Paris, 1969).

32. D. Marshall, *English People in the Eighteenth Century* (London, 1956); R. Grassby, "English Merchant Capitalism in the Late 17th Century," *Past and Present* 46 (1970).

33. P. Zumthor, *Daily Life in Rembrandt's Holland,* tr. S. W. Taylor (New York, 1963).

34. Briggs, "Middle-Class Consciousness in English Politics, 1780–1846," *Past and Present* 9, and "The Language of 'Class' in Early Nineteenth-Century England"; H. Perkin, *The Origins of Modern English Society, 1780–1880* (London, 1969), pp. 26, 177.

35. J. Lhomme, *La Grande Bourgeoisie au pouvoir* (Paris, 1960), pp. 1–17; Hobsbawm, *The Age of Revolution,* pp. 220–21; L. O'Boyle, "The Middle Class in Western Europe, 1815–1848," *American Historical Review* 71 (1966), 836–37.

36. F. M. L. Thompson, *English Landed Society in the Nineteenth Century* (London, 1963), p. 158.

37. A. Cobban, "The 'Middle Class' in France, 1815–48," in *France since the Revolution* (New York, 1970), pp. 19–20.

38. K. Marx, *The Eighteenth Brumaire of Louis Bonaparte* (New York, 1963), p. 48.

39. Thompson, *English Landed Society in the Nineteenth Century,* p. 12.

40. K. Mannheim, *Ideology and Utopia,* tr. L. Wirth and E. Shils, Harvest ed. (New York, n.d.), pp. 229–39.

41. G. Wright, *Rural Revolution in France* (Stanford, 1964), p. 10.

42. *Cambridge Economic History of Europe,* vol. 6, ed. H. J. Habakkuk and M. Postan (Cambridge, 1965), pp. 603, 628.

43. L. Chevalier, *Classes laborieuses et classes dangereuses à Paris pendant la première moitié du XIXe siècle* (Paris, 1958), pp. 497–518.

44. M. Halbwachs, *The Psychology of Social Class,* tr. C. Delavenay (Glencoe, 1958). chap. 5; E. J. Hobsbawm, *Primitive Rebels* (Manchester, 1959), pp. 162–74, and *The Age of Revolution,* chap. 11; E. P. Thompson, *The Making of the English Working Class* (New York, 1963), pp. 418–29, 711–12, 807–32; G. Rudé, *The Crowd in History* (New York, 1964), pp. 164–91.

45. Thomas, *Religion and the Decline of Magic;* D. P. Walker, *The Decline of Hell* (London, 1964); Mandrou, *Magistrats et sorciers en France au XVIIe siècle;* R. Mandrou, *De la culture populaire aux XVIIe et XVIIIe siècles* (Paris, 1964).

46. F. Yates, *The Rosicrucian Enlightenment* (London, 1972), p. 218; N. MacKenzie, ed., *Secret Societies* (New York, 1967), chaps. 6 and 7.

47. J. Caro Baroja, *The World of the Witches,* tr. O. N. Glendinning (London, 1964), pp. xi, 214, 238–41.

48. A. Viatte, *Les Sources occultes du romantisme* (Paris, 1928).

49. See A. L. Constant's *Dogme et rituel de la haute magie* (1854–56), *Histoire de la magie* (1860), *La Clef des grands mystères* (1861), *La Science des esprits* (1865).

50. See H. Blavatsky's *Isis Unveiled* (1877), *The Secret Doctrine* (1888).

51. E. Howe, *The Magicians of the Golden Dawn* (London, 1972).

52. E. Howe, *Astrology* (New York, 1968), pp. 21, 72.

53. J. Webb, *The Flight from Reason* (London, 1971); F. King, *Rites of Modern Occult Magic* (New York, 1971).

Three

1. J. Le Goff, "Au Moyen Age: Temps de l'église et temps du marchand," *Annales, E.S.C.,* 15 (1960); C. Cipolla, *Clocks and Culture, 1300–1700* (London, 1967), chap. 1; L. Mumford, *Technics and Civilization* (New York, 1934), pp. 17, 134, 197–98; E. P. Thompson, "Time, Work-Discipline, and Industrial Capitalism," *Past and Present* 38 (1967).

2. A. F. Weber, *The Growth of Cities in the Nineteenth Century* (New York, 1899); P. Lavedan, *Histoire de l'urbanisme,* 3 vols. (Paris, 1926–52); L. Mumford, *The Cities in History* (New York, 1961); E. A. Wrigley, *Population and History* (New York, 1969); G. Dupeux, *La Société française, 1789–1960,* 3d ed. (Paris, 1964); E. Lampard, "The Urbanizing World," and L. Lees, "Metropolitan Types," in H. J. Dyos and M. Wolff, eds., *The Victorian City* (London, 1973).

3. D. Landes, "Technological Change and Development in Western Europe, 1750–1914," *Cambridge Economic History of Europe,* vol. 6, pp. 521–53: Giedion, *Mechanization Takes Command,* pp. 173–78; S. Pollard, "Factory Discipline in the Industrial Revolution," *Economic History Review,* 2d ser., vol. 16 (1963); R. Bendix, *Work and Authority in Industry* (New York, 1956), chap. 2; Thompson, *The Making of the English Working Class,* pp. 199–204, 365, 401–2, 409–10.

4. E. Ashby, "Education for an Age of Technology," and C. Wilson, "Technology and Industrial Organization," in C. Singer, et al., *A History of Technology,* vol. 5 (Oxford, 1958); J. B. Rae, "The Invention of Technology," in M. Kranzberg and C. W. Purcell, Jr., eds., *Technology in Western Civilization,* vol. 1 (New York, 1967); S. Pollard, *The Genesis of Modern Management* (Cambridge, Mass., 1965); L. Urwick and E. Brech, *The Making of Scientific Management,* 3 vols. (London, 1948–51); S. Kakar, *Frederick Taylor* (Cambridge, Mass., 1970).

5. L. Girard, "Transport," *Cambridge Economic History of Europe,* vol. 6; C. I. Savage, *An Economic History of Transport* (London, 1959); P. Rousseau, *Histoire des transports* (Paris, 1961); H. J. Dyos and D. H. Aldcroft, *British Transport* (Leicester, 1969); S. Margetson, *Journey by Stages* (London, 1967); J. R. Kellett, *The Impact of Railways on Victorian Cities* (London, 1969); W. T. Jackman, *The Development of Transportation in Modern England,* 2d rev. ed. (London, 1962).

6. H. A. Innis, *Empire and Communications* (Oxford, 1950), pp. 7, 199–208; M. McLuhan, *The Gutenberg Galaxy* (Toronto, 1962); E. Carpenter and M. McLuhan, eds., *Explorations in Communication* (Boston, 1960); R. D. Altick, *The English Common*

Reader (Chicago, 1957); R. K. Webb, *The British Working Class Reader* (Chicago, 1955); R. Williams, *The Long Revolution* (London, 1961), pp. 156–213; C. Ledré, *Histoire de la presse* (Paris, 1958).

7. Ivins, *Prints and Visual Communication*, chaps. 5–7; H. and A. Gernsheim, *The History of Photography* (Oxford, 1955), chaps. 30 and 31; Giedion, *Mechanization Takes Command*, pp. 17–30, 100–107; M. McLuhan, *Understanding Media* (New York, 1964), chaps. 15 and 20; Sontag, *On Photography*.

8. F. Gilbert, "Revolution," *Dictionary of the History of Ideas*, ed P. P. Wiener (New York, 1973); Williams, *Keywords*.

9. K. Mannheim, "Conservative Thought," in *Essays on Sociology and Social Psychology* (New York, 1953); S. Coleman, "Is There Reason in Tradition?" in P. King and B. Parekh, eds., *Politics and Experience* (London, 1968). See also J. R. Levenson, *Confucian China and Its Modern Fate* (Berkeley, 1968), vol. 1, pp. xxvii–xxxiii.

10. *Oxford English Dictionary.*

11. E. Klein, *A Comprehensive Etymological Dictionary of the English Language* (Amsterdam, 1967).

12. W. E. Houghton, *The Victorian Frame of Mind* (New Haven, 1957), pp. 77–89; H. G. Schenk, *The Mind of the European Romantic* (London, 1966), chap. 3; J. H. Buckley, *The Triumph of Time* (Cambridge, Mass., 1966), chap. 6; F. Haskell, "The Manufacture of the Past in Nineteenth-Century Painting," *Past and Present* 53 (1971).

13. G. Bazin, *The Museum Age*, tr. J. van Nuis Cahil (New York, 1967), chaps. 9 and 10; G. Daniel, *The Idea of Prehistory* (Harmondsworth, 1962), chaps. 2 and 3; B. Feldman, "Myth in the Eighteenth and Early Nineteenth Centuries," *Dictionary of the History of Ideas*.

14. [W. Scott], *Waverley; or 'Tis Sixty Years Since* (Edinburgh, 1814), chaps. 1 and 72.

15. G. Lukács, *The Historical Novel*, tr. H. and S. Mitchell (Boston, 1963); L. Maigron, *Le Roman historique a l'époque romantique* (Paris, 1912); A. Fleishman, *The English Historical Novel* (Baltimore, 1971).

16. W. K. Ferguson, *The Renaissance in Historical Thought* (Boston, 1948), pp. 119–26; R. G. Collingwood, *The Idea of History* (Oxford, 1946), pp. 86–88; K. Clark, *The Gothic Revival* (London, 1928); G. Germann, *Gothic Revival in Europe and Britain*, tr. G. Onn (Cambridge, Mass., 1973).

17. S. Toulmin and J. Goodfield, *The Discovery of Time* (New York, 1965), chap. 7.

18. Daniel, *The Idea of Prehistory*, chap. 2.

19. H. V. White, "The Irrational and the Problem of Historical Knowledge in the Enlightenment," in H. E. Pagliaro, ed., *Irrationalism in the Enlightenment* (Cleveland, 1972).

20. R. H. Shryock, "Medicine and Public Health," in G. Métraux and F. Crouzet, eds., *The Nineteenth-Century World* (New York, 1963); Kranzberg and Pursell, eds., *Technology in Western Civilization*, vol. 1; Giedion, *Mechanization Takes Command;* D. Davis, *Fairs, Shops, and Supermarkets* (Toronto, 1966); D. and G. Hindley, *Advertising in Victorian England* (London, 1972); M. Lochhead, *The Victorian Household* (London, 1964); J. Gloag, *Victorian Comfort* (New York, 1961); J. A. Banks, *Prosperity and Parenthood* (London, 1954); M. Perrot, *La Mode de vie des familles bourgeoises* (Paris, 1961); P. Beaver, *The Crystal Palace* (London, 1970); R. D. Mandell, *Paris, 1900* (Toronto, 1967).

21. Mannheim, *Ideology and Utopia*, chap. 4; S. L. Thrupp, ed., *Millennial Dreams in Action* (The Hague, 1962); Thomas, *Religion and the Decline of Magic*, R. Knox, *Enthusiasm* (New York, 1950); E. L. Tuveson, *Millennium and Utopia* (Berkeley,

1949); R. V. Sampson, *Progress in the Age of Reason* (Cambridge, Mass., 1956); W. W. Wagar, *Good Tidings* (Bloomington, 1972); Hobsbawm, *Primitive Rebels*.

22. F. E. Manuel, "Toward a Psychological History of Utopias," in *Utopias and Utopian Thought,* ed. F. E. Manuel (Boston, 1966), p. 79. See also L. Mumford, *The Story of Utopias* (New York, 1923); M. Buber, *Paths in Utopia,* tr. R. F. C. Hull (London, 1949); R. Ruyer, *L'Utopie et les utopies* (Paris, 1950); F. E. Manuel, *The Prophets of Paris* (Cambridge, Mass., 1962).

23. W. H. G. Armytage, *Yesterday's Tomorrows* (London, 1968); S. Moskowitz, *Explorers of the Infinite* (Cleveland, 1963); H. L. Sussman, *Victorians and the Machine* (Cambridge, Mass., 1968); K. Amis, *New Maps of Hell* (New York, 1960); C. Walsh, *From Utopia to Nightmare* (New York, 1962); I. Raknem, *H. G. Wells and His Critics* (Oslo, 1962).

24. J. Morley, *Death, Heaven, and the Victorians* (Pittsburgh, 1971); J. S. Curl, *The Victorian Celebration of Death* (Devon, 1972); P. Ariès, *Western Attitudes toward Death,* tr. P. M. Ranum (Baltimore, 1974), chap. 3; R. Darnton, "Death's Checkered Past," *New York Review of Books* (June 13, 1974), and "Giving New Life to Death," ibid. (June 27, 1974).

25. *Oxford English Dictionary.*

26. Foucault, *The Order of Things,* pp. 126–62, 226–32, 263–79. See also Toulmin and Goodfield, *The Discovery of Time,* chaps. 7–9; J. Rostand, "The Development of Biology," in Métraux and Crouzet, eds., *The Nineteenth-Century World;* L. Eiseley, *Darwin's Century* (New York, 1958); G. Himmelfarb, *Darwin and the Darwinian Revolution* (New York, 1962); M. Grene, *The Knower and the Known* (New York, 1966), chap. 7; B. Glass, et al., eds., *Forerunners of Darwin* (Baltimore, 1959).

27. Grene, *The Knower and the Known,* p. 190.

28. P. Laslett, *The World We Have Lost* (New York, 1965); Banks, *Prosperity and Parenthood;* P. Ariès, *Centuries of Childhood,* tr. R. Baldick (New York, 1962); I. Pinchbeck and M. Hewitt, *Children in English Society,* 2 vols. (London, 1969–73); P. Coveney, *The Image of Childhood* (Harmondsworth, 1967); J. R. Gillis, *Youth in History* (New York, 1974); P. Abrams, "Rites de Passage: The Conflict of Generations in Industrial Society," *Journal of Contemporary History* 5 (1970).

29. Van den Berg, *The Changing Nature of Man,* chap. 2.

30. Laslett, *The World We Have Lost,* chap. 2; Perkin, *The Origins of Modern English Society,* chap. 2.

31. Briggs, "The Language of 'Class' in Early Nineteenth-Century England"; Williams, *Keywords.*

32. Chevalier, *Classes laborieuses et classes dangereuses,* book 3, pt. 1. G. S. Jones, *Outcast London* (Oxford, 1971), pt. 3.

33. G. Bryson, *Man and Society: The Scottish Inquiry of the Eighteenth Century* (Princeton, 1945); D. G. MacRae, *Ideology and Society* (New York, 1961), chaps. 2, 11; J. W. Burrow, *Evolution and Society* (London, 1966); Manuel, *The Prophets of Paris;* T. Parsons, *The Structure of Social Action* (Glencoe, 1949); A. W. Gouldner, *The Coming Crisis of Western Sociology* (New York, 1970), chap. 4; R. A. Nisbet, *Social Change and History* (New York, 1969), chap. 4; M. Mandelbaum, *History, Man and Reason* (Baltimore, 1971).

34. For critiques of objective reason, in addition to Hegel and Marx, see E. Husserl, *The Crisis of European Sciences and Transcendental Philosophy,* tr. D. Carr (Evanston, 1970); H. Jonas, *The Phenomenon of Life* (New York, 1966); L. Kolakowski, *The Alienation of Reason,* tr. N. Guterman (New York, 1968); M. Horkheimer and T. Adorno, *Dialectic of Enlightenment,* tr. J. Cumming (New York, 1972); J. Habermas, *Knowledge and Human Interests,* tr. J. J. Shapiro (Boston, 1971).

35. M. H. Abrams, *Natural Supernaturalism* (New York, 1971), p. 65. Quote from Wordsworth is from *The Prelude* (III 194: X 726ff.).

36. G. Poulet, "Timelessness and Romanticism," *Journal of the History of Ideas* 15 (1954); Buckley, *The Triumph of Time*, chaps. 7–8; W. A. Madden, "The Victorian Sensibility," *Victorian Studies* 7 (1963).

37. G. A. Kelly, *Idealism, Politics and History* (London, 1969), pt. 5; S. D. Crites, "Fate and Historical Existence," *The Monist* 53 (1969); M. N. Friedrich, "The Role of Time in Hegel's Philosophy" (unpublished manuscript, 1973).

38. "The worker is related to the product of his labor as to an alien object. For on this premise it is clear that the more the worker spends [i.e., externalizes] himself, the more powerful becomes the alien world of objects which he creates over and against himself, the poorer he himself—his inner world—becomes, the less belongs to him as his own." K. Marx, *The Economic and Philosophic Manuscripts of 1844*, ed. D. J. Struik, tr. M. Milligan (New York, 1964), p. 108.

39. Marx, *A Contribution to the Critique of Political Economy*, p. 21.

40. F. Nietzsche, *On the Genealogy of Morals and Ecce Homo*, ed. W. Kaufmann (New York, 1969), p. 254.

41 F. Nietzsche, *The Will to Power*, tr. W. Kaufmann and R. J. Hollingdale (New York, 1968), p. 265.

42. F. Nietzsche, *Twilight of the Idols and The Anti-Christ*, tr. R. J. Hollingdale (Harmondsworth, 1968),, pp. 47–54.

43. F. Nietzsche, *The Portable Nietzsche*, ed. W. Kaufmann (New York, 1967), p. 227.

44. Nietzsche, *The Will to Power*, p. 361.

45. Ibid., p. 500.

Four

1. Foucault, *The Order of Things*; Schumpeter, *History of Economic Analysis*; W. Stark, *The History of Economics in Its Relation to Social Development* (London, 1944); R. V. Eagly, ed., *Events, Ideology and Economic Theory* (Detroit, 1968); M. Dobb, *Theories of Value and Distribution since Adam Smith* (Cambridge, 1973).

2. Marx, *The Economic and Philosophic Manuscripts of 1844*, p. 108.

3. G. Rudé, ed., *Robespierre* (Englewood Cliffs, 1967), pt. 1.

4. E. Burke, *The Works of Edmund Burke* (Oxford, 1907), vol. 4, p. 106.

5. In his 1840 review of de Tocqueville's *Democracy in America*, Mill agreed: "The ascendancy of the commercial class in modern society and politics is inevitable, and, under due limitations, ought not to be regarded as evil. That class is the most powerful; but it need not therefore be all-powerful. Now, as ever, the great problem of government is to prevent the strongest from becoming the only power; and repress the natural tendency of the instincts and passions of the ruling body, to sweep away all barriers which are capable of resisting, even for a moment, their own tendencies. Any counterbalancing power can henceforth exist only by sufferance of the commercial class; but that it should tolerate some such limitation, we deem as important as that it should not itself be held in vassalage." J. S. Mill, *Collected Works*, vol. 18, ed. J. M. Robson, introd. A. Bray (Toronto, 1977), p. 200.

6. See de Tocqueville's *Democracy in America*, pt. 1 (1835) and pt. 2 (1840), *Recollections* (1850–51), and *The Old Régime and the French Revolution* (1856).

7. F. Choay, *The Modern City: Planning in the Nineteenth Century*, tr. M. Hugo and G. R. Collins (New York, 1969). See also Lavedan, *Histoire de l'urbanisme*, vol. 3; Mumford, *The City in History*; S. Giedion, *Space, Time and Architecture*, 5th ed.

(Cambridge, Mass., 1967); L. Benevolo, *The Origins of Modern Town Planning,* tr. J. Landry (London, 1967); W. Ashworth, *The Genesis of Modern British Town Planning* (London, 1954); D. Olsen, *Town Planning in London* (New Haven, 1964); W. L. Creese, *The Search for Environment* (New Haven, 1966).

8. D. H. Pinkney, *Napoleon III and the Rebuilding of Paris* (Princeton, 1958); H. Saalman, *Haussmann: Paris Transformed* (New York, 1971); G. F. Chadwick, *The Works of Sir John Paxton* (London, 1961).

9. D. Wiebenson, *Tony Garnier: The Cité Industrielle* (New York, 1969).

10. W. J. Goode, *World Revolution and the Family Patterns* (New York, 1963), chap. 1; I. J. Goody, "The Evolution of the Family," P. Laslett with R. Wall, *Household and Family in Past Time* (Cambridge, 1972); R. Wheaton, "Family and Kinship in Western Europe," and L. K. Berkner, "The Use and Misuse of Census Data for the Historical Analysis of Family Structure," in *The Journal of Interdisciplinary History* 5 (1975); M. Poster, *Critical History of the Family* (New York, 1978).

11. D. V. Glass and D. E. C. Eversley, eds., *Population in History* (Chicago, 1965); Ariès, *Centuries of Childhood;* Laslett, *The World We Have Lost;* O. and P. Ranum, eds., *Popular Attitudes towards Birth Control in Pre-Industrial France and England* (New York, 1972).

12. L. Davidoff, "Mastered for Life," *Journal of Social History* 7 (1974).

13. Marx, *The Economic and Philosophic Manuscripts of 1844,* pp. 147–48, 165–69.

14. Banks, *Prosperity and Parenthood;* J. A. and O. Banks, *Feminism and Family Planning in Victorian England* (New York, 1964); T. Zeldin, *France: 1848–1945,* vol. 1 (Oxford, 1973), pt. 2; Lochhead, *The Victorian Household.*

15. Giedion, *Mechanization Takes Command,* pp. 329ff.; W. Benjamin, "Louis-Philippe oder der Interieur," *Schriften,* vol. 1 (Frankfurt, 1955); M. Praz, "The Victorian Mood; A Reappraisal," Métraux and Crouzet, eds., *The Nineteenth-Century World.*

16. Banks, *Feminism and Family Planning in Victorian England,* pp. 21–23, 135ff.; Zeldin, *France: 1848–1945,* vol. 1, pp. 297–301; M. Vicinus, ed., *Suffer and Be Still* (Bloomington, 1972).

17. J. Ruskin, *Sesame and Lilies* (New York, 1916), lecture II. See also Houghton, *The Victorian Frame of Mind,* pp. 341–48.

18. Banks, *Feminism and Family Planning in Victorian England;* Zeldin, *France: 1848–1945,* vol. 1, pp. 346–50.

19. M. Poster, ed., *Harmonian Man: Selected Writings of Charles Fourier,* tr. S. Hanson (Garden City, 1971), pp. 202–37; J. Beecher and R. Bienvenu, eds., *The Utopian Vision of Charles Fourier* (Boston, 1971), pp. 169–88.

20. E. Goldman, *Anarchism and Other Essays,* 3d rev. ed. (New York, 1917).

21. G. Lukács, *The Theory of the Novel,* tr. A. Bostock (Cambridge, Mass., 1971), and *Studies in European Realism,* tr. E. Bone (London, 1950); F. Jameson, *Marxism and Form* (Princeton, 1971); E. Auerbach, *Mimesis,* tr. W. Trask (Princeton, 1953); W. Ong, *Rhetoric, Romance, and Technology* (Ithaca, N.Y., 1971); N. Friedman, "Point of View in Fiction," *PMLA* 70 (1955); W. C. Booth, *The Rhetoric of Fiction* (Chicago, 1961); P. de Man, "The Rhetoric of Temporality," in C. S. Singleton, ed., *Interpretation: Theory and Practice* (Baltimore, 1969); G. Poulet, *Studies in Human Time,* tr. E. Coleman (Baltimore, 1956); A. A. Mendilow, *Time and the Novel* (London, 1952); E. Kahler, *The Inward Turn of the Narrative,* tr. R. and G. Winston (Princeton, 1973); I. Watt, *The Rise of the Novel* (London, 1957); D. Van Ghent, *The English Novel* (New York, 1953); J. H. Miller, *The Form of Victorian Fiction* (Notre Dame, 1968); R. Williams, *The English Novel from Dickens to Lawrence* (London, 1970); V. Mylne, *The Eighteenth-Century*

French Novel (Manchester, 1965); P. Brooks, *The Novel of Worldliness* (Princeton, 1969); M. Raimond, *Le Roman depuis la Révolution* (Paris, 1967).

22. J.-J. Mayoux, "Variations on the Time-Sense in Tristram Shandy," in A. H. Cash and J. M. Stedmond, eds., *The Winged Skull* ([Kent, Ohio], 1971).

23. See below, pp. 115–16; on the structure of modern novel, see S. Spencer, *Space, Time and Structure in the Modern Novel* (New York, 1971).

24. E. H. Gombrich, *Art and Illusion* (Princeton, 1960); P. Francastel, *Peinture et société* (Lyon, 1951); J. Clay, *L'Impressionisme* (Paris, 1971), and *Modern Art, 1890–1918* (New York, 1978); H. Read, *A Concise History of Modern Painting* (New York, 1959); J. Berger, *Ways of Seeing* (New York, 1973); J. Argüelles, *The Transformative Vision* (Berkeley, 1975).

25. J. T. Goden, "From Spatial to Aesthetic Distance in the Eighteenth Century," *Journal of the History of Ideas* 35 (1974): 64.

26. E. G. Holt, ed., *A Documentary History of Art*, vol. 3: *From the Classicists to the Impressionists* (Garden City, 1966), p. 12.

27. Ibid., p. 166.

28. Ibid., p. 171.

29. W. Blake, *The Marriage of Heaven and Hell*, ed. G. Keynes (London, 1975), plate 4. See also N. Frye, *Fearful Symmetry* (Princeton, 1947); K. J. Raine, *Blake and Tradition*, 2 vols. (Princeton, 1969); J. H. Hagstrum, *William Blake, Poet and Painter* (Chicago, 1964); T. R. Frosch, *The Awakening of Albion* (Ithaca, N.Y., 1974).

30. Holt, ed., *A Documentary History of Art*, vol. 3, p. 352.

31. J. Rewald, *The History of Impressionism*, 4th rev. ed. (New York, 1973), p. 210.

32. Ibid., p. 150.

33. Rewald, *The History of Impressionism*, p. 456.

34. P. Cézanne, *Letters*, tr. M. Kay, ed. J. Rewald (London, 1941), p. 234; M. Merleau-Ponty, "Le Doute de Cézanne," in *Sens et non-sens* (Paris, 1948); L. Brion-Guerry, *Cézanne et l'expression de l'espace* (Paris, 1966).

Five

1. Foucault, *The Order of Things*; G. Gusdorf, *Introduction aux sciences humaines* (Paris, 1960); P. Lain-Entralgo, *Mind and Body*, tr. A. M. Espinosa, Jr. (New York, n.d.); Thomas, *Religion and the Decline of Magic;* T. S. Hall, *Ideas of Life and Matter*, 2 vols. (Chicago, 1969); G. Zilboorg, *A History of Medical Psychology* (New York, 1941); L. S. King, *The Growth of Medical Thought* (Chicago, 1963); D. W. Hamlyn, *Sensation and Perception* (London, 1961); R. M. Young, *Mind, Brain and Adaptation in the Nineteenth Century* (Oxford, 1970); W. Coleman, *Biology in the Nineteenth Century* (New York, 1971); G. J. Goodfield, *The Growth of Scientific Physiology* (London, 1960); W. M. O'Neil, *The Beginnings of Modern Psychology* (Harmondsworth, 1968); Ellenberger, *The Discovery of the Unconscious;* H. Jonas, *The Phenomenon of Life*.

2. J. H. van den Berg, *Divided Existence and Complex Society* (Pittsburgh, 1974).

3. A. Comte, *Cours de philosophie positive*, 6 vols. (Paris, 1830–42) *Système de politique positive*, 4 vols. (Paris, 1851–54), *Testament d'Auguste Comte avec les documents qui s'y rapportent* (Paris, 1884); P. Ducassé, *Essai sur les origines intuitives du positivisme* (Paris, 1939); Manuel, *The Prophets of Paris*, chap. 6.

4. J. S. Mill, *Collected Works*, ed. F. Priestley and J. Robson (Toronto, 1963ff.); F. A. Hayek, ed., *John Stuart Mill and Harriet Taylor* (Chicago, 1951); J. S. Mill and H. Taylor Mill, *Essays on Sex Equality*, ed. A. Rossi (Chicago, 1970); M. St. J. Packe,

The Life of John Stuart Mill (London, 1954); B. Mazlish, *James and John Stuart Mill* (New York, 1975).

5. G. S. Haight, ed., *The George Eliot Letters,* 7 vols. (New Haven, 1954–55); T. Pinney, ed., *The Essays of George Eliot* (London, 1963); G. S. Haight, *George Eliot* (Oxford, 1968); R. V. Redinger, *George Eliot* (New York, 1975); B. Hardy, *The Novels of George Eliot* (London, 1959); J. Thale, *The Novels of George Eliot* (New York, 1959); W. J. Harvey, *The Art of George Eliot* (New York, 1961); B. J. Paris, *Experiments in Life* (Detroit, 1965); U. C. Knoepflmacher, *George Eliot's Early Novels* (Berkeley, 1968).

6. F. Steegmuller, ed., *Selected Letters of Gustave Flaubert* (New York, 1953); B. F. Bart, *Flaubert* (Syracuse, N.Y., 1967); M. Nadeau, *The Greatness of Flaubert,* tr. B. Bray (New York, 1972); E. Starkie, *Flaubert: The Making of the Master* (London, 1967), and *Flaubert: The Master* (New York, 1971); J.-P. Sartre, *L'Idiot de la famille,* 3 vols. (Paris, 1971ff.); A. Thorlby, *Gustave Flaubert and the Art of Realism* (New York, 1957).

7. E. Panofsky, "The History of the Theory of Human Proportion as a Reflection of the History of Styles," in *Meaning in the Visual Arts* (Garden City, 1955), p. 91. See also G. B. Ladner, *Ad Imaginem Dei* (Latrobe, Pa., 1965); L. Barkan, *Nature's Work of Art* (New Haven, 1975).

8. E.g., Leonardo da Vinci claimed that he would rather be deaf than blind, since seeing was a more fundamental motivation for him: "To lose one's sight means to be deprived of the beauty of the universe. . . . Do you not see that the eye embraces the beauties of the whole world?" *Leonardo da Vinci on Art and the Artists,* ed. A. Chastel, tr. E. Callman (New York, 1961), p. 37. Yet the beauty that he saw was the physical image of cosmic proportion, not yet an Archimedean visualization.

9. Elias, *The Civilizing Process,* pp. 53–55; Mandrou, *Introduction à la France moderne;* Ong, *The Presence of the Word.*

10. M. Foucault, *The Birth of the Clinic,* tr. A. M. S. Smith (New York, 1973), pp. xii–xiv, 107–22, 153–72.

11. Giedion, *Mechanization Takes Command,* pp. 324–25, 628–29, 653–92; Elias, *The Civilizing Process;* L. Wright, *Clean and Decent* (London, 1960).

12. Giedion, *Mechanization Takes Command,* pp. 655–58; P. C. McIntosh, *Physical Education in England since 1800* (London, 1952); E. Weber, "Gymnastics and Sports in *Fin-de-Siècle* France," *American Historical Review* 76 (1971).

13. Giedion, *Mechanization Takes Command,* pp. 309–19, 321–22, 377, 396; C. W. and P. Cunnington, *Handbook of English Costume in the Nineteenth Century* (London, 1959), pp. 24–29, 347–52; Gloag, *Victorian Comfort;* E. Fox-Genovese, "Yves Saint Laurent's Peasant Revolution," *Marxist Perspective* 1, no. 2 (1978).

14. Berger, *Ways of Seeing,* chap. 3; G. Pelles, *Arts, Artists and Society* (Englewood Cliffs, 1963), pp. 137–46; T. B. Hess and L. Nochlin, eds., *Women as Sex Object* (New York, 1972).

15. Frosch, *The Awakening of Albion.*

16. F. Buytendijk, "The Phenomenological Approach to the Problem of Feelings and Emotions," in M. L. Reymert, ed., *Feelings and Emotions* (New York, 1950); J.-P. Sartre, *The Emotions, Outline of a Theory,* tr. B. Frechtman (New York, 1948).

17. Van den Berg, *Divided Existence and Complex Society,* chap. 10.

18. Zeldin, *France, 1848–1945,* vol. 1, pp. 285–91; Banks, *Prosperity and Parenthood,* p. 33; Houghton, *The Victorian Frame of Mind,* pp. 341–48.

19. P. Ariès, "An Interpretation to Be Used for a History of Mentalities," in Ranum, ed., *Popular Attitudes toward Birth Control in Pre-Industrial France and England.*

20. Abrams, *Natural Supernaturalism,* pp. 292–99.

21. T. Zeldin, *France, 1848–1945*, vol. 2 (Oxford, 1977), pp. 832–33, 1040.

22. Translated and cited in G. Gorer, *The Life and Ideas of the Marquis de Sade* (New York, 1962), p. 189, requoted in P. Robinson, *The Modernization of Sex* (New York, 1976), p. 194.

23. G. Bataille, *Death and Sensuality* (New York, 1962).

24. Berger, *Ways of Seeing*, chaps. 2 and 3 (the quote is from p. 47); Pelles, *Art, Artists and Society*, pp. 137–46; L. Nochlin, "Eroticism and Female Imagery in Nineteenth-Century Art," J. L. Connolly, Jr., "Ingres and the Erotic Intellect," R. Rosenblum, "Caritas Romana after 1760," G. Needham, "Manet, 'Olympia' and Pornographic Photography," and B. E. White, "Renoir's Sensuous Women," in Hess and Nochlin, eds., *Woman as Sex Object*.

25. M. Bakhtin, *Rabelais and His World*, tr. H. Iswolsky (Cambridge, Mass., 1968), pp. 18–24; D. Foxon, "Libertine Literature in England, 1600–1745," *The Book Collector* 12 (1963); W. H. Epstein, *John Cleland: Images of a Life* (New York, 1974), chap. 6; N. St. John-Stevas, *Obscenity and the Law* (London, 1956); H. M. Hyde, *A History of Pornography* (London, 1964); S. Marcus, *The Other Victorians* (New York, 1966); B. Harrison, "Underneath the Victorians," *Victorian Studies* 10 (1967).

26. G. Lely, "Le Marquis de Sade et Rétif de la Bretonne," *Mercure de France*, no. 1130 (1957); M. Blanchot, "Sade," in *The Marquis de Sade: The Complete Justine, Philosophy in the Bedroom and Other Writings*, ed. R. Seaver and A. Wainhouse (New York, 1965); M. Poster, *The Utopian Thought of Restif de la Bretonne* (New York, 1971).

27. S. Kern, *Anatomy and Destiny* (Indianapolis, 1975), chap. 5.

28. Houghton, *The Victorian Frame of Mind*, pp. 341–53; P. T. Cominos, "Late-Victorian Sexual Respectability and the Social System," *International Review of Social History* 8 (1963); K. Millett, "The Debate over Women: Ruskin vs. Mill," and P. T. Cominos, "Innocent Femina Sensualis in Unconscious Conflict," in Vicinus, ed., *Suffer and Be Still;* P. Branca, "Image and Reality: The Myth of the Idle Victorian Woman," in M. Hartman and L. W. Banner, eds., *Clio's Consciousness Raised* (New York, 1974); S. de Beauvoir, *The Second Sex*, tr. H. M. Parshley (New York, 1952), pt. 3; Zeldin, *France, 1848–1945*, vol. 1, chap. 11; Kern, *Anatomy and Destiny*, chap. 9.

29. Banks, *Prosperity and Parenthood;* Banks, *Feminism and Family Planning in Victorian England;* K. Thomas, "The Double Standard," *Journal of the History of Ideas* 20 (1959); C. N. Degler, "What Ought to Be and What Was: Women's Sexuality in the Nineteenth Century," *American Historical Review* 79 (1974); F. Henriques, *Prostitution and Society*, vol. 3; *Modern Sexuality* (London, 1968); E. Trudgill, "Prostitution and Paterfamilias," in Dyos and Wolff, eds., *The Victorian City*.

30. Kern, *Anatomy and Destiny*, chaps. 10 and 11; P. Grosskurth, *John Addington Symonds* (London, 1964), chap. 11; Robinson, *The Modernization of Sex*, chap. 1.

31. M. Foucault, *The History of Sexuality*, vol. 1: *An Introduction*, tr. R. Hurley (New York, 1978), p. 23.

32. H. Ey, *La Conscience*, 2d ed. (Paris, 1968); A. Gurwitsch, *The Field of Consciousness* (Pittsburgh, 1964); Tauhala, *Intentionality and the Problem of the Unconscious*.

33. Ellenberger, *The Discovery of the Unconscious*, pp. 126–41; van den Berg, *Divided Existence and Complex Society*.

34. Ellenberger, *The Discovery of the Unconscious*, chap. 2.

35. Ibid., chap. 3.

36. Ibid., pp. 83–85, 120–21, 311–18.

37. Ibid., chap. 6.

38. Ibid., pp. 480–500, esp. pp. 496–99.

39. S. Freud, "The Interpretation of Dreams," in *The Standard Edition of the Complete Psychological Works,* ed. J. Strachey (London, 1953ff.), vol. 5, pp. 577–78.
40. Ellenberger, *The Discovery of the Unconscious,* p. 800.
41. L. Kubie, "Fallacious Use of Quantitative Concepts in Dynamic Psychology," *Psychoanalytic Quarterly* 16 (1947).

Six

1. R. Shattuck, *The Banquet Years* (New York, 1958), p. 332.
2. See R. Shattuck, *The Banquet Years;* H. S. Hughes, *Consciousness and Society* (New York, 1958); J. Romein, *The Watershed of Two Eras* (Middletown, 1978); Lefebvre, *Everyday Life in the Modern World,* p. 112.
3. M. Heidegger's "Editor's Foreword" to E. Husserl, *The Phenomenology of Internal Time-Consciousness,* tr. J. S. Churchill, introd. C. O. Schrag (Bloomington, 1964), pp. 15–16.
4. Quoted in H. A. Lorentz, et al., *The Principles of Relativity,* tr. W. Perrett and G. B. Jeffery (London, 1923), p. 75.
5. P. G. Bergman, "Relativity," *Encyclopaedia Britannica,* 15th ed. (1974): *Macropaedia,* vol. 15, p. 586.
6. W. Heisenberg, *Physics and Philosophy* (New York, 1962), pp. 198–99. See also M. Merleau-Ponty, "Einstein and the Crisis of Reason," in *Signs,* tr. R. C. McCleary (Evanston, 1964).
7. S. C. Kline, "Mathematics, Foundations of," *Encyclopaedia Britannica,* 15th ed.: *Macropaedia,* vol. 11, pp. 632ff.
8. E. Panofsky, *Early Netherlandish Painting* (Cambridge, Mass., 1953), p. 5; Francastel, *Peinture et société,* pp. 10–11; R. Rosenblum, *Cubism and Twentieth-Century Art* (New York, 1960), p. 9; J. Golding, *Cubism,* 2d ed. (London, 1968), pp. 15, 185; D. Cooper, *The Cubist Epoch* (New York, 1971), p. 11.
9. H. B. Chipp, *Theories of Modern Art* (Berkeley, 1968), p. 196.
10. Rosenblum, *Cubism and Twentieth-Century Art,* chaps. 7–11; Cooper, *The Cubist Epoch,* chap. 3.
11. Chipp, *Theories of Modern Art,* p. 157.
12. Giedion, *Space, Time and Architecture,* p. lvi.
13. C. Rosen, *Arnold Schoenberg* (New York, 1975), p. 63.
14. Quoted in W. Reich, *Schoenberg, A Critical Biography,* tr. L. Black (London, 1971), p. 49.
15. Henry James, *The Art of the Novel,* introd. R. P. Blackmur (New York, 1934), p. 327.
16. Spencer, *Space, Time and Structure in the Modern Novel,* pp. 117—19.
17. Ibid., pp. 36–39.
18. M. Friedman, *Stream of Consciousness: A Study in Literary Method* (New Haven, 1955), pp. 178–87.
19. R. Vigneron, "Creative Agony," in R. Girard, ed., *Proust* (Englewood Cliffs, 1962), p. 26.
20. R. Shattuck, *Marcel Proust* (New York, 1974), appendix.
21. R. Shattuck, *Proust's Binoculars* (New York, 1963).
22. H. Kenner, *Flaubert, Joyce and Beckett* (Boston, 1962), p. 35, quoted in Spencer, *Space, Time and Structure in the Modern Novel,* p. 164.
23. H. S. Hughes, *Oswald Spengler* (New York, 1962), pp. 6–7.
24. V. Woolf, *The Captain's Death Bed, and Other Essays* (New York, 1950), pp. 96–97.

25. F. de Saussure, *Course in General Linguistics,* ed. C. Bally, A. Sechehaye, A. Riedlinger, tr. W. Baskin (New York, 1959).

26. Ibid., p. 120.

27. Ibid., p. 114.

28. Priority should be given to C. S. Peirce's "Logic as Semiotic: The Theory of Signs" (1897). However, semiotics lacked an audience until after World War I. U. Eco, "A Logic of Culture," in T. Seboek, ed., *The Tell-Tale Sign* (Lisse, 1975), p. 10.

29. Saussure, *Course in General Linguistics,* p. 68.

30. E. F. K. Koerner, in *Ferdinand de Saussure* (Braunschweig, 1973), pp. 290–91, questioned whether the editors of *Cours de linguistique générale* might not have stressed the synchrony/diachrony opposition much more than Saussure had originally intended, even if Saussure did emphasize synchronic linguistics against the background of historical phonology. It was Jakobson, in the 1920s, who pointed out the difference between synchrony/diachrony and static/dynamic, so that synchrony was not equivalent to static. See E. Holenstein, *Roman Jakobson's Approach to Language,* tr. C. and T. Schelbert (Bloomington, 1976), pp. 26ff. Nevertheless, "what is important is the subordination, not the opposition of diachrony to synchrony; it is this subordination which is questioned in hermeneutic comprehension, that diachrony is meaningful only through its relation to synchrony and not the inverse." P. Ricoeur, *The Conflict of Interpretations,* ed. D. Ihde (Evanston, 1974), p. 33.

31. R. Jakobson, *Selected Writings,* vol. 2 (The Hague, 1971), p. 711, quoted in Holenstein, *Roman Jakobson's Approach to Language,* p. 1.

32. C. Lévi-Strauss, *Structural Anthropology,* tr. C. Jacobson and B. G. Schoepf (New York, 1963), p. 276.

33. C. Lévi-Strauss, *Totemism,* tr. R. Needham (Boston, 1963), p. 16.

34. C. Lévi-Strauss, *The Raw and the Cooked,* tr. J. and D. Weightman (New York, 1969), pp. 1–3; Lévi-Strauss, *Structural Anthropology,* pp. 88–89.

35. Lévi-Strauss, *Totemism,* p. v.

36. Lévi-Strauss, *The Raw and the Cooked,* p. 10.

37. Lévi-Strauss, *Structural Anthropology,* p. 275.

38. Ibid., p. 82.

39. C. Lévi-Strauss, *The Savage Mind* (Chicago, 1966), p. 197.

40. J. Lacan, "The Insistence of the Letter in the Unconscious," *Yale French Studies,* nos. 36/37 (1966), p. 136.

41. J. Lacan, "Of Structure as an Inmixing of an Otherness Prerequisite to Any Subject Whatever," in R. Macksey and E. Donato, eds., *The Structuralist Controversy* (Baltimore, 1972), p. 189.

42. Lacan, "The Insistence of the Letter in the Unconscious," *Yale French Studies,* nos. 36/37, p. 123.

43. Ibid., p. 121.

44. "Two Aspects of Language and Two Types of Aphasic Disturbances," in R. Jakobson and M. Halle, eds., *Fundamentals of Language* (The Hague, 1956).

45. Lacan, "The Insistence of the Letter in the Unconscious," *Yale French Studies,* nos. 36/37, p. 121.

46. J. Lacan, "Remarque sur le rapport de Daniel Lagache" (1961), quoted in J. Lacan, *The Language of the Self,* tr. A. Wilden (New York, 1975), p. 106.

47. J. Lacan, "Traitment possible de la psychose" (1958), quoted in Lacan, *The Language of the Self,* p. 107.

48. Lacan, *The Language of the Self,* p. 27, also p. 110, n. 59.

49. R. Barthes, *Elements of Semiology,* tr. A. Lavers and C. Smith (Boston, 1970), p. 10.

50. Ibid., pp. 61, 63.

51. Ibid., pp. 89–93.

52. R. Barthes, *Mythologies,* tr. A. Lavers (New York, 1972), p. 114.

53. Ibid., p. 137.

54. See the criticisms of J. Derrida, *Of Grammatology,* tr. G. C. Spivak (Baltimore, 1976); J. Kristeva, "The System and the Speaking Subject," in Sebeok, ed., *The Tell-Tale Sign*; Ricoeur, *The Conflict of Interpretations*; F. Jameson, *The Prison-House of Language* (Princeton, 1972); A. Wilden, *System and Structure* (London, 1972).

55. Lévi-Strauss, *The Raw and the Cooked,* p. 6.

56. M. Foucault, *The Archaeology of Knowledge,* tr. A. M. S. Smith (New York, 1976), appendix: "The Discourse of Language," p. 229.

57. My concept of perceptual reality is different from S. Kracauer's concept of physical reality in *Theory of Film* (New York, 1960), and A. Bazin's concept of realism in *What Is Cinema?,* tr. H. Gray, 2 vols. (Berkeley, 1967–71). It is closer to R. Jakobson's model of communication in "Linguistics and Poetics," in T. A. Sebeok, ed., *Style in Language* (Cambridge, Mass., 1960), p. 353.

58. See *Film Language,* tr. M. Taylor (New York, 1974), pp. 212–13. See also R. Barthes, "Rhetoric of the Image," *Image - Music - Text,* tr. S. Heath (New York, 1977).

59. P. P. Pasolini, "The Cinema as Poetry," in B. Nichols, ed., *Movies and Methods* (Berkeley, 1976), p. 544.

60. M. Deren, "Cinematography: The Creative Use of Reality," in G. Kepes, ed., *The Visual Arts Today* (Middletown, 1960), pp. 160–61, 163.

61. J. Mitry, *Esthétque et psychologie du cinéma,* vol. 1 (Paris, 1963), pp. 158–60; L. Jacobs, *The Rise of the American Film* (New York, 1939).

62. E. Panofsky, "Style and Medium in the Motion Pictures," in G. Mast and M. Cohen, eds. *Film Theory and Criticism* (New York, 1974), p. 169.

63. B. Balazs, "Theory of Film," in D. Talbot, ed., *Film: An Anthology* (Berkeley, 1966), p. 205.

64. S. Eisenstein, *Film Form and The Film Sense,* ed. J. Leyda (Cleveland, 1957), and *Film Essays and A Lecture,* ed. J. Leyda (New York, 1970). See also J. D. Andrew, *The Major Film Theories* (New York, 1976), chap. 3.

65. C. Zavattini, "Some Ideas on the Cinema," in R. D. MacCann, ed., *Film: A Montage of Theories* (New York, 1966), p. 218.

66. J. Monaco, *The New Wave* (New York, 1976), p. 9.

67. A. Resnais, "Trying to Understand My Own Film," in H. M. Geduld, ed., *Film Makers on Film Making* (Bloomington, 1969), p. 157.

68. M. Antonioni, "Two Statements," ibid., p. 200.

69. Quoted in J. R. MacBean, "*Vent d'Est* or Godard and Rocha at the Crossroad," in Nichols, ed., *Movies and Methods,* p. 96. See also J.-L. Godard, *Godard on Godard,* ed. J. Narboni and T. Milne, introd. R. Roud (New York, 1972), p. 171.

70. J. Chapman, "Two Aspects of the City: Cavalcanti and Ruttmann," in L. Jacobs, ed., *The Documentary Tradition* (New York, 1972), p. 39.

71. Greierson, quoted in R. M. Barsam, *Nonfiction Film* (New York, 1973), p. 2. See also J. Grierson, "First Principles of Documentary," in MacCann, ed., *Film: A Montage of Theories,* pp. 209–10.

72. S. Kracauer, *From Caligari to Hitler* (Princeton, 1947), p. 301.

73. D. Vertov, "Kinoks-Revolution," in Geduld, ed., *Film Makers on Film Making,* p. 88.

74. L. Marcorelles, *Living Cinema,* tr. L. Quigly (New York, 1973), pp. 49–92.

75. G. Bachmann, et al., "The Frontiers of Realist Cinema," in MacCann, ed., *Film: A Montage of Theories,* pp. 292–93, 298.
76. H. Richter, "A History of the Avantgarde," in F. Stauffacher, ed., *Art in Cinema* (San Francisco, 1947), pp. 11–13.
77. L. Bunuel, "Notes on the Making of 'Un Chien andalou,' " in Stauffacher, ed., *Art in Cinema,* pp. 29, 30.
78. A. Fraigneau, "Dialogue with Cocteau," in Geduld, ed., *Film Makers on Film Making,* p. 142.
79. M. Deren, in "Poetry and the Film: A Symposium," *Film Culture,* no. 29 (1963).
80. Quoted in Stauffacher, ed., *Art in Cinema,* p. 58, italics added.
81. *Film Culture,* no. 30 (1963), no pagination, italics added.
82. M. Le Grice, *Abstract Film and Beyond* (London, 1977), pp. 152–53.
83. G. Bateson, in *Steps to an Ecology of Mind* (New York, 1972), proposed the concept of communication about communication as logically belonging to a higher class than communication itself. In the words of his colleagues, P. Watzlawick, J. H. Beavin, and D. D. Jackson, in *Pragmatics of Human Communication* (New York, 1967), "every communication has a content and a relationship aspect such that the latter classifies the former and is therefore a metacommunication" (p. 54).
84. Williams, *Keywords.*
85. Ong, *The Presence of the Word,* pp. 49–50; McLuhan, *The Gutenberg Galaxy,* pp. 27ff.
86. D. J. Boorstin, *The Image* (New York, 1961), p. 13.
87. Ivins, *Prints and Visual Communication,* chaps. 3 and 4.
88. Sontag, *On Photography,* p. 4.
89. Giedion, *Mechanization Takes Command,* pp. 21–23.
90. A. Breton, *Manifestoes of Surrealism,* tr. R. Seaver and H. R. Lane (Ann Arbor, 1969), p. 37.
91. Ibid., p. 38.
92. L. Aragon, *Une vague de rêves,* quoted in G. Picon, *Surrealists and Surrealism, 1919–1939,* tr. J. Emmons (New York, 1977), p. 23.
93. J. Pierre, *Surrealism,* tr. P. Eve (London, 1970), pp. 112–13, 107.
94. Berger, *Ways of Seeing,* p. 129.
95. S. Ewen, *Captains of Consciousness* (New York, 1976), pts. 1 and 2.
96. R. Glatzer, *The New Advertising* (New York, 1970), p. 10.
97. Quoted in M. Mayer, *Madison Avenue, U.S.A.* (New York, 1958), p. 36.
98. Barthes, "Myth Today," in *Mythologies;* J. Williamson, *Decoding Advertisements* (London, 1978).
99. H. Zettl, *Sight, Sound, Motion* (Belmont, Cal., 1973), p. 113.
100. R. Williams, *Television* (London, 1974), p. 86; G. Klavan, *Turn That Damned Thing Off* (Indianapolis, 1972), p. 59.
101. Zettl, *Sight, Sound, Motion,* p. 226; Klavan, *Turn That Damned Thing Off,* p. 59; J. Mander, *Four Arguments for the Elimination of Television* (New York, 1978).

Eight

1. This is the thesis of Anne Janowitz at Stanford University.
2. G. Deleuze and F. Guattari, *Anti-Oedipus,* tr. R. Hurley, M. Seem, and H. R. Lane (New York, 1977).

Appendix

1. I have borrowed the title of this section from Marjorie Grene's book of that name.

2. Arendt, *The Human Condition,* chap. 6, sec. 36.

3. See the suggestive article by E. Paci, "Vico, Structuralism, and the Phenomenological Encyclopaedia of the Sciences," in G. Tagliacozzo and H. V. White, eds., *Giambattista Vico: An International Symposium* (Baltimore, 1969).

4. Marx, *The Eighteenth Brumaire of Louis Bonaparte,* p. 15.

5. This is the title of the work by Berger and Luckmann.

6. A. Schutz, "Concept and Theory Formation in the Social Sciences," in *Collected Papers,* vol. 1: *The Problem of Social Reality,* ed. M. Natanson (The Hague, 1962), pp. 58–59.

7. Merleau-Ponty, *Phenomenology of Perception,* p. xx.

8. My understanding of embodiment is derived in part from G. Marcel, "Incarnate Being as the Central Datum of Metaphysical Reflection," in *Creative Fidelity,* ed. R. Rosthal (New York, 1964); Merleau-Ponty, *Phenomenology of Perception,* pt. 1; E. W. Strauss, "The Upright Posture," in *Phenomenological Psychology* (New York, 1966); E. W. Strauss, *The Primary World of the Senses,* tr. J. Needleman (New York, 1963); Jonas, "The Nobility of Sight," in *The Phenomenon of Life;* Ihde, *Sense and Significance;* Buytendijk, "The Phenomenological Approach to the Problem of Feelings and Emotions," in Reymert, ed., *Feelings and Emotions.*

9. In accordance with Merleau-Ponty's "Preface" to *Phenomenology of Perception,* I have grounded Husserl's concept of intentionality in the concept of embodiment. In other words, I approach intentionality from the standpoint of existential phenomenology, rather than transcendental phenomenology. For Husserl's concept of intentionality, in addition to his own writings, see A. Gurwitsch, "On the Intentionality of Consciousness," in *Studies in Phenomenology and Psychology* (Evanston, 1966), and "Husserl's Theory of the Intentionality of Consciousness in Historical Perspective," in E. N. Lee and M. Mandelbaum, eds., *Phenomenology and Existentialism* (Baltimore, 1967).

10. See E. Bünning, *The Physiological Clock,* 2d ed. (Berlin, 1964); J. A. Meerloo, *Along the Fourth Dimension* (New York, 1970); D. Schon, "Rationality in Retrospective and Prospective Deliberation," *Philosophy and Phenomenological Research* 20 (1960); H. F. Ellenberger, "A Clinical Introduction to Psychiatric Phenomenology and Existential Analysis," in R. May, et al., eds., *Existence* (New York, 1958); C. O. Schrag, "Existence and History," *Review of Metaphysics* 13 (1959); Schutz, "Choosing among Projects of Action," in *Collected Papers,* vol. 1; also Husserl, *The Phenomenology of Internal Time-Consciousness.*

11. See E. Husserl, *Cartesian Meditations,* tr. D. Cairns (The Hague, 1960); A. Schutz, *The Phenomenology of the Social World,* tr. G. Walsh and F. Lehnert (Evanston, 1967); Schutz, *Collected Papers,* vol. 1; A. Schutz, *Collected Papers,* vol. 2: *Studies in Social Theory,* ed. A. Brodersen (The Hague, 1964); Berger and Luckmann, *The Social Construction of Reality.*

12. See J. C. Bouman, *The Figure-Ground Phenomenon in Experimental and Phenomenological Psychology* (Stockholm, 1968); Grene, *The Knower and the Known;* Merleau-Ponty, *Phenomenology of Perception;* M. Merleau-Ponty, *The Primacy of Perception,* ed. J. Edie (Evanston, 1964); Schutz, "On Multiple Realities," and "Symbol, Reality and Society," in *Collected Papers,* vol. 1; Ong, *The Presence of the Word;* Foucault, *The Order of Things.*

13. K. Marx, "Theses on Feuerbach" (1845).

14. Marx, *A Contribution to the Critique of Political Economy,* 1859 "Preface."

15. Ibid.

16. J.-P. Sartre, *Search for a Method,* tr. H. E. Barnes (New York, 1963), chap. 1.

17. D. M. Lowe, "Intentionality and the Method of History," in M. Natanson, ed., *Phenomenology and the Social Sciences* (Evanston, 1973).

18. Foucault, *The Archaeology of Knowledge,* p. 8.

Index

Index

Index

Index

Economic action, the rationality of, 19–20, 24, 25–26, 27, 29, 32, 36–37, 52, 55, 62, 81, 100

Economic man, 20, 61, 62, 63, 102, 103, 104

Economic space. *See* Circulation and exchange; Production and consumption; Production and exchange; Supply and demand

Economic structure, 17, 18, 20, 57, 63, 66, 74, 109, 172–73

Economy. *See* Marginal utility; Marxism; Political economy; Wealth, analysis of

Education, 52, 70, 72, 96, 102

Eggeling, V., 131

Einstein, A., 112, 161

Eisenstein, E., 4

Eisenstein, S., 127–28

Electronic culture, 2, 4–5, 7, 8–9, 11, 14, 15, 75, 111, 134, 137, 138, 139

Elements, the four, 85

Eliot, George. *See* Evans, Mary Anne

Ellis, H., 104

Embodiment, 17, 19, 23, 55, 81, 85–108, 111, 166–67, 169, 192

Emotion, 41, 46, 47, 52, 81, 85, 88, 89, 91, 98–100, 102, 104, 105, 108, 133, 166–67

Empiricism, 54, 87

Encyclopaedia Britannica (1842 edition), 103

Energy, 57, 81, 85–86, 97, 98, 136

Engels, F., 74

Engineers, 37

England, 26, 27, 28, 29, 31, 35, 36, 37, 41, 54, 71, 81, 96, 178

Engraving. *See* Prints

Enlightenment, the, 42

Epistemic order, 2, 9–12, 15, 16, 18, 19, 21, 24, 25, 26, 28, 49, 53, 54, 55, 59, 64, 111, 119, 171. *See also* Anagogy; Development-in-time; Representation-in-space; Similitude; Synchronic system

Erasmus, D., 95

Eschatology, 45, 48, 49

Estate society (seventeenth–eighteenth century), 4, 8, 10–11, 13, 15, 18, 21, 26–28, 32, 42, 45, 48, 51, 53, 59, 63, 67, 70, 80, 86, 95, 99, 101, 109

Estrangement (*Entfremdung*), 21, 22, 29, 32, 39, 40, 56, 57, 63, 75, 77, 79, 80, 100, 161, 163

Etching. *See* Prints

Eternity, 56, 58, 65, 79, 81

Ethnography, 120

Etty, W., 97

Evans, Mary Anne, 78, 79, 92–95, 108, 161

Evolution, 21, 49–51, 53–55, 87, 109, 111–12

Exoticism, 22

Explanation, 11, 22, 23, 38, 54, 55, 87, 88, 121, 165, 175

Expression, 30, 48, 88, 93, 95, 108, 114, 166–67; forms of, 171

Eye, the. *See* Seeing

F

Family, 20, 25, 51–52, 59, 63, 66, 70–74, 78, 89–94, 100

Fashion, 96, 97, 98, 122, 138

Feeling, 76, 77, 98, 99, 166–67

Feminism and feminists, 71, 72–74

Fetishism, olfactory, 103

Feuerbach, L., 92

Figure, 10, 134

Film, 2, 9, 111, 117, 124, 135, 138, 152; experimental, 131–33; factual, 129–31, 133; fictional, 126–29, 133

Flaherty, R., 129

Flaubert, G., 78, 89, 93–95, 108

Flournay, T., 106

Ford, H., 19

Form/content, 4, 114, 115

Foucault, M., 9, 9n, 10, 14, 104, 123–24, 176

Fourier, C., 46, 68, 73

Fragonard, J.-H., 101

France, 26, 27–28, 29, 31, 36, 37, 54, 66, 70, 71, 81, 96, 110

Franciscans, 24

Freud, S., 14, 23, 107–8, 121, 122, 123

Frye, N., 81

Function, 21, 51, 54, 55, 82, 87, 88, 109, 117

Future, the, 14, 18, 43–49, 56, 64, 69, 74, 87, 109, 169, 174, 175

Futurism, 114

Index

G

Galilei, G., 13
Garbo, G., 127
Garden city, 69
Garden and landscape, 26, 67, 68–69
Garnier, T., 68–69, 70
Gauguin, P., 82
Geddes, P., 68, 69, 70
Gentry, 20, 27, 28–29, 32, 76
Geology, 42, 50
Gessner, J. J., 22
Giedion, S., 114
Gilman, C. P., 73
Giotto, 25
Gleizes, A., 113
Glory, 27
God, 9–10, 29, 45, 50, 63, 86, 93
Godard, J.-L., 128, 129
Goldman, E., 74
Grammar, general, 14
Gramsci, A., concept of cultural hege-
mony, 14, 28
Great chain of being, 50, 65, 85
Greenwich Mean Time, 38
Grene, M., 51, 192
Grierson, J., 129, 130
Griffith, D. W., 117, 126
Gropius, W., 114

H

Hardy, T., 78–79
Harvey, W., 59
Haussman, G.-E., 68, 70
Hearing, 6, 7, 8, 12, 13, 15, 24, 25, 31,
95, 101, 102, 134
Heart, the, 64, 76, 89, 90
Hegel, G., 55, 56, 58, 67, 102
Heisenberg, W., 113
Hempstead Garden, 69
Héricourt, J., 106
Hermeneutics. See Phenomenology
Hermes Trismegistus, 13, 32, 33, 86
Hermetic Order of the Golden Dawn, 33
Hi-fi stereo, 9, 138
Hilbert, D., 113
Historical discontinuity, 2, 9, 12, 17, 24,
27–28, 32, 64, 70, 80, 85, 95, 98,
100, 109, 161, 176. See also Trans-
formation
Historical materialism. See Marxism

Historicism, 43
History, vii, 11, 13, 41–43, 64, 65, 77, 78,
91, 101, 105, 116–17, 120, 174–76.
See also Past
Hobbes, T., 63, 87
Hobsbawm, E. J., 17
Hollywood studio system, 127
Home, the, 44, 70, 71, 96, 103, 104
Homosexuality, 104
Honor, 27, 63
Housework, 70, 73, 74
Howard, E., 68, 69, 70
Hudson, W. II., 47
Hughes, H. S., 110
Hume, D., 42, 87
Humors, the four, 85–86, 99
Husserl, E., 111, 192
Hutton, J., 42, 50
Huysmans, J.-K., 102
Hygiene, 96, 98. See also Cleanliness
and sanitation
Hypnosis and hypnotism, 22, 88, 99, 100,
106, 107, 108
Hypotaxis, 93, 161, 183
Hysteria, 22, 105, 106, 107

I

Iconography, 80–83, 97, 101
Idealism, 1, 56, 87
Identity and difference, logic of, 10, 11,
13, 42, 49, 86, 87, 88
Ideology, 14, 17, 18, 29, 45, 57, 61, 62,
71, 99, 103, 109, 122, 125, 161, 173
Illuminism, 32
Image, 2, 31, 101, 139, 186; advertising,
135, 137–39, 154–55, 157–59;
filmic, 124–33, 135–36, 152; history
of 134–35; photographic, 8, 9, 135,
136, 141, 150–51; pictorial, 79–83,
97, 98, 142–48, 156; surrealist,
135–37, 156, 157; televized, 153;
transformations of, 140–59; typographic, 8, 135, 140, 154. See also
Image/sign; Meta-communication
of image
Image/sign, 2, 124–25, 133, 134, 156
Imagination, 80–81, 82, 83, 93, 98, 110,
132, 133, 136
Immaculate Conception See Mary,
mother of God

Index

Index

Index

N

Naked, the, 143
Napoleon III, 68
Narrative, historical, vii, 116–17; fictional, 75–79, 93, 115–16; filmic, 125–26
Natural history, 14, 49, 50, 51, 87
Natural law, 53, 61, 62, 63, 64
Natural supernaturalism, 56
Naturalism, 78, 79, 82
Nature, 13, 20, 30, 42, 50, 53, 56, 63, 72, 81, 82, 83, 163; human, 42, 43, 73, 74
Nature/culture, 120
Nature/society, 64
Neoclassicism, 40, 67, 80, 81
Neorealism, Italian, 128
Netherlands, 26, 27–28
Neurosis, 23, 161
Newman, J. H., 30
Newspaper, 38, 44, 137, 138
Newton, I., 13, 112, 163
Newtonianism, social, 54
New Wave (film), 128
Nietzsche, F., 55, 57–58, 110
Noble savage, 42–43, 129
Non-representation. *See* Presentation
Nostalgia, 40, 41, 43, 78, 102
Novel, 2, 52, 59, 63, 93, 102, 110, 117, 124; bourgeois, 74–79; epistolary, 75–76, 80; historical, 41, 43, 100; modern, 79, 115–16
Nude, the, 86, 97, 101, 142

O

Object, 6, 7, 11, 18, 63, 101, 134
Object/subject, 22, 23, 29, 37, 55, 57, 101, 163
Objective knowledge and objectification, vii, 4, 5, 13, 18, 22, 23, 29, 30, 32, 55, 75, 80, 86, 108, 163–64
Objective process, 21, 22, 52, 54, 55, 56, 57, 58, 109
Objectivity, 7, 18, 21, 22
Occult, the, 26, 28, 32–33, 171
Ockham, William of, 25
Ogilvy, D., 137
Oldsmobile advertisement, 158, 159
Ong, W., 2, 5, 8, 177

Oral culture, 2, 3, 4, 7, 8, 9–10, 12, 15, 24, 25, 26, 31, 75
Organism, 21, 50, 51, 87, 95, 109
Orientalism, 40
Other, the anonymous, typified. *See* Exoticism; Madness; Noble savage; Orientalism; Primitivism; Subconscious; Unconscious; Wise mandarin
Other, the Lacanian, 122
Owen, R., 68, 73
Oxford Movement, 30

P

Pain, sensitivity to, 99–100
Painting, 42, 48, 59, 63, 86, 97, 98, 101, 102, 110, 117, 124; bourgeois, 79–83, 142–44, 148; modern, 80, 83, 113–14, 136, 145–47, 156
Paleontology, 51
Panofsky, E., 126
Paradigm/syntagm, 120
Parapraxis, 107
Parapsychology, 22, 106
Parataxis, 161
Paris, 36, 67, 68, 77
Parker and Unwin, 69
Pasolini, P. P., 125
Passion, 41, 73, 75, 77, 78, 79, 99
Past, the, 11, 14, 29, 39–43, 49, 55, 56, 64, 65, 69, 77, 87, 93, 94, 109, 174–76
Patmore, C., 103
Paxton, J., 68, 70
Peasantry, 20, 25, 28, 30–31, 32, 53, 66
Peirce, C. S., 189
Perception, field of, 1–2, 12, 15, 17–18, 161; in bourgeois society, 14, 18–19, 35, 49, 59, 85, 161; in the bureaucratic society of controlled consumption, 14, 110, 111, 134, 161; in estates society, 13, 26–27; in the Middle Ages, 12, 24; in the Renaissance, 12–13, 25–26
Perception: history of, 1–2, 7, 9n, 14–16, 176; phenomenology of, 1–2, 165–66, 171–72
Perceptual revolution of 1905–15, 14, 17, 109, 110, 111–17, 123, 134, 161
Perceptual stratification, 20, 23, 28–33. *See also* Multiple realities

Index

Index

Index

Index